When Women Offend

When Women Offend

Crime and the Female Perpetrator

Stephanie Scott-Snyder

cognella® | ACADEMIC PUBLISHING

Bassim Hamadeh, CEO and Publisher

Mary Jane Peluso, Senior Specialist Acquisitions Editor

Alisa Munoz, Project Editor

Laureen Gleason, Production Editor

Emely Villavicencio, Senior Graphic Designer

Danielle Gradisher, Licensing Associate

Jennifer Redding, Interior Designer

Natalie Piccotti, Director of Marketing

Kassie Graves, Vice President of Editorial

Jamie Giganti, Director of Academic Publishing

Cover image copyright © 2013 iStockphoto LP/Jewelee.

Printed in the United States of America.

Contents

Acknowledgments

Thank you to all of the women who so bravely and graciously shared their stories.

Special thanks to the Georgia Department of Corrections, the Indiana Department of Correction, the New Jersey Department of Corrections, the New York City Department of Correction, and the Pennsylvania Department of Corrections.

Much gratitude to Acquisitions Editor Mary Jane Peluso, who has been a true partner in this project from its inception, and to Project Editor Tim Pike, as well as Production Editor Laureen Gleason, who have been invaluable resources. Additional thanks to Melissa Eang and Christiana Rutkowski for their dedication and assistance.

Active Learning

For educators looking to complement the reading, this book has interactive activities available through Cognella Active Learning. To access the digital content, go to http://active.cognella.com or access through your home Learning Management System.

Interviews

Additionally, publicly accessible audio recordings of the offender interviews featured in this book are available through SoundCloud (https://soundcloud.com/user-798575661/sets/when-women-offend) or by visiting: https://active.cognella.com/courses/1846/modules.

Audio Interviews with Offenders

Publicly accessible audio recordings of the full interviews featured in this book are available by visiting https://soundcloud.com/user-798575661/sets/when-women-offend.

Part I

Chapter 1

Introduction

Hell's Belle

F lames swelled from the roof of the quaint farmhouse at the end of McClung Road in La Porte, Indiana. In a matter of minutes, the entire structure was devoured, and it seemed that the sweeping cinders had claimed multiple casualties. Amidst the smoldering ash lay the lifeless bodies of three young children and a woman; she was headless.

* * *

Long before the devastating fire, the fabled Midwestern farmhouse had been shrouded in mystery—plagued by unexplained deaths and disappearances. Belle Sorenson Gunness originally purchased the property in 1900 after the death of her first husband, Mads. He'd died of apparent strychnine poisoning, widowing Belle and leaving behind the couple's two biological daughters (Myrtle, age 3 and Lucy, age 2), as well as a foster child named Jennie.

The first physician who examined Mads suspected homicide, but a seemingly distraught Belle refused an autopsy. Wanting to protect Belle's ability to mourn privately, the family doctor stepped in and declared the cause of death to be heart failure. The case was officially closed before anyone grew suspicious of the fact that Mads had died on July 30, 1900, coincidentally the *only* day that his two life insurance policies overlapped, allowing his wife—and sole beneficiary—to collect a significantly larger sum.

Two years later, on April 1, 1902, Belle married Peter Gunness. Just after he and his two daughters moved into the La Porte farmhouse, Peter's infant daughter died of "unknown causes" while in Belle's care. Several months later, Peter was found dead, his skull smashed in. Under questioning, Belle claimed that a meat grinder had fallen on his head. Although her story was not impossible, it certainly was implausible. Peter had been a skilled butcher with extensive experience around such equipment. Upon examination of the corpse, the coroner suspected foul play and ordered an inquest. Shortly thereafter, it was rumored that Belle's foster daughter revealed to a classmate that she had actually seen her mother kill Peter. However, no concrete evidence was ever found, and with Belle continuing to play the grieving widow so convincingly, the case was closed. Belle was once again left to collect the insurance payout.

Twice widowed and many times richer, Belle placed the personal ad shown in Figure 1.1 in various Midwestern newspapers (Jones, 2009).

FIGURE 1.1

WANTED: A woman who owns a beautifully located and valuable farm in first class condition, wants a good and reliable man as partner in the same. Some little cash is required for which will be furnished first-class security.

Source: Adapted from Jones (2009).

Many men answered the ad. Among them was Andrew Helgelien, who soon began exchanging letters with Belle. In January of 1908 he received a passionate note from her inviting him to La Porte; the message concluded with the haunting line: "Come prepared to stay forever" (Bovsun, 2014). Convinced of his love for a woman whom he knew only through her writings, Andrew emptied his bank account and headed to Indiana; he was never seen or heard from again.

* * *

The bodies were draped with tarps and carried out of what was left of the farmhouse. Burnt trinkets lay scattered on the ground. Detectives sifted through the rubble, searching for clues as to the cause of the fire. However, their investigation took an abrupt turn when Asle Helgelien arrived in town. He announced that his brother had been murdered by the widow Gunness months before the farmhouse burned down. Asle's claim was initially met with skepticism and dread—no one wanted to complicate the already harrowing case at hand; Asle was promptly dismissed by the sheriff, but he refused to give up and thus launched a parallel probe into the happenings at the Gunness home.

In a distant corner of the property, Asle came across a hog pen enclosed by an unusually tall fence. The landscaping in the area was noticeably uneven, as though the earth had been disturbed; he began to dig. Soon he uncovered the nearly unrecognizable body of his brother. It had been chopped up and stuffed into multiple canvas sacks. But Andrew's mangled body wasn't Asle's only discovery. In total, he found what appeared to be 12 bodies—although the dismemberment and decomposition made it nearly impossible to know for sure.

As the official investigation moved forward, police determined that the fire had been caused by arson. They arrested Ray Lamphere, a farmhand previously in Belle's employ. In November of 1908 Lamphere was convicted of setting the fire, but the murders remained unsolved. It wasn't until January of 1910 that authorities learned the nature and scope of the macabre practices at the Gunness farm. In a deathbed confession, Lamphere reported that when prospective suitors answered her personal ad, Belle lured them to the farm and invited them to dine with her. During dinner, she either slipped poison into their food or bludgeoned them to death. She then cut up the bodies and the remains were fed to the hogs or buried. Lamphere admitted to having helped Belle dispose of multiple victims.

Fearing that her crimes would eventually be discovered, Belle enlisted Lamphere's help in one final plot—burning down the farm, faking her own death, and fleeing Indiana. He agreed, and the two traveled to Chicago days before the fire to find a body double for Belle. While there, Belle convinced a woman whose appearance was somewhat similar to her own to return with them to Indiana on the pretense that she would be hired as a housekeeper. Once back in La Porte, Belle drugged the woman before killing and ultimately decapitating her. She then tied weights to the severed head and dropped it in a nearby swamp. Lamphere claimed that Belle had dressed the victim in her old clothing before placing her own false teeth next to the body so that it would be assumed the corpse was hers.

Belle then chloroformed her children before smothering them to death and leaving their bodies to burn in the fire. According to Lamphere, Belle had slaughtered more than 40 people, thus accumulating nearly a quarter of a million dollars in insurance disbursements. Some sources, however, estimate that the fatalities could be as many as 180. As a result, the *Guinness Book of World Records* lists Belle Gunness as one of the most prolific serial killers in history (Bovsun, 2014).

But the story of Belle Gunness, or Hell's Belle as she is sometimes called, may not end there. For years after the fire, people reported "Gunness sightings," the last of which was in 1931, when a woman named Esther Carlson died while awaiting trial in Los Angeles for having poisoned a man for financial gain. Not only did Carlson bear a striking resemblance to Gunness, but she killed with the same MO. Perhaps even more curious is the fact that there was no record of Carlson's existence prior to 1908.

Overview of Female Offenders

Gendered stereotypes have historically shielded female offenders, preventing society from viewing them as capable of engaging in criminal activity, let alone as being violent. This perspective is, in part, what precluded early 20th-century authorities from labeling Belle Gunness a serial murderer. When Belle began killing, such antiquated philosophies were typical, and therefore her gender was one of the greatest tools at her disposal. She committed her criminal activity in a cultural milieu where women were considered incompetent and docile—not calculating or predatory.

Belle played on the stereotypes of her time brilliantly. She knew that cops and coroners alike would be loath to intrude upon her, as it was proper protocol to allow widows the respect to grieve privately. She also knew that as a member of the "weaker" or "fairer" sex, men would want to respond to her personal ad, as it would appeal to their sense of masculine pride. Belle was a woman, alone. In that time, that fact would carry certain connotations, such as her being seen as a "damsel in distress." Additionally, her suitors were also likely to be lured into a feeling of safety in traveling to meet a lone female, which allowed Belle to cast a wide net and expand her victim pool. As a woman, a widow, a mother, and the guardian of an orphaned child, Belle positioned herself as the quintessential female. In other words, she assumed caretaking and nonthreatening roles. Even the housekeeper whom she murdered and later beheaded likely felt comfortable moving to Indiana to work for such a seemingly kindhearted woman.

The fact that gender expectations caused law enforcement to underestimate Belle Gunness in the early 1900s may not come as a surprise. However, as recently as 1988, the Federal Bureau of Investigation (FBI) was hesitant to label a woman a serial killer—even after they unearthed the remains of seven bodies in the backyard of an unlicensed boarding house in Sacramento, California. The proprietor, Dorothea Puente, was thought to have killed her tenants, many of whom were older or disabled, in order to cash their Social Security checks. It was a clear case of serial murder for profit. However, when special agents discussed the case with criminal psychologist Eric Hickey, they said, "That's not serial killing." In an interview with *The New Yorker*'s Emily Anthes (2015), Hickey replied to these statements: "Of course, it was. They just didn't recognize it then. Women were not considered to be predators that way" (Anthes, 2015).

Dorothea Puente was convicted of three out of the nine murders for which she was tried. Like Belle Gunness, she didn't match society's vision of what a serial killer *should* look like. Dorothea's gender, grandmotherly appearance, status as a widow, and role as a rooming house caretaker put victims at ease while helping her to mislead the authorities.

Women and Crime: Myth vs. Fact

Similar to the misconceptions about Belle Gunness and Dorothea Puente, society continues to subscribe to various myths about women's involvement in and capacity for crime. For example, it is a commonly held belief that women are *not* violent and *cannot* exact the same type or intensity of violence as men. Similarly, it is assumed that women who commit crimes are often (and only) motivated by greed, jealousy, or love. They work alongside a (male) partner, or at the behest of a partner, but never mastermind a crime. As a seemingly small population, female offenders have long been ignored. After all, if so few women engage in criminal activity, it's more important to understand and rehabilitate male offenders, right? Wrong.

Population estimates indicate that slightly more than half of the general public is female, yet women have traditionally been excluded from discussions about crime and offending—especially when those dialogues have involved the etiology of violent crimes, such as those portrayed in the opening vignette. Because women have historically comprised only a small portion of arrestees and violent offenders, the argument has been made that criminological theory should focus on understanding male criminality, as males are more likely to engage in illegal activity. Therefore, research in this arena has largely focused on understanding male offending. This gender disparity has resulted in the widespread adoption of the notion that women are somehow incapable of extreme violence.

However, women are now entering the criminal justice system in record numbers. In 1970, there were fewer than 8,000 women in jails across the United States; by 2014, that number had increased to 110,000, making women the fastest growing population to be incarcerated (Jeltsen, 2016b). Some have explained this trend in terms of a convergence in male and female offending. However, the risk factors for female offending, as well as the types of crime in which women engage, including their expressions of aggression, differ from those of their male counterparts. Therefore, female perpetrators cannot simply be understood within the framework of male offending. For example, female offenders report a significantly greater prevalence of mental health difficulties as well as substance abuse and dependence. Women are also far more likely than men to be victims of certain types of crimes (e.g., sexual assault, domestic violence, stalking, etc.), and thus it is critical to explore the continuum that connects victimization and offending as well as the motivations and risk factors that influence female perpetrators.

> I never felt like I could be the kind of girl my friends were anyway, so I just decided to be myself. I realized that the best way to get out of the house was to act like a boy, which meant doing boy-like things . . . not listening, fighting, breaking rules in school. . . . Oh, I liked pretty dresses and to have my hair done, but I knew that would never get me anywhere. I just had to follow my own lead, even though it landed me in some bad places . . . like Rikers Island.
>
> —Letoya, 26-year-old female detained on a drug charges (Richie, 1996)

FIGURE 1.2

FAST FACTS

- Women comprise 18% of the total correctional population (U.S. jails, prisons, and community supervision).
- Women are most frequently charged with fraud (37%), forgery (34%), and theft (31%).
- Women are least commonly charged with weapons-related offenses (4%).
- Between 1991 and 2011, the number of females convicted of violent crimes increased by 83%.
- Women of color are disproportionately overrepresented in the prison population, with African American females aged 18 to 19 being three times more likely to be incarcerated than white women.
- Hispanic females ages 18 to 19 are twice as likely as same-aged white women to be imprisoned.
- Incarceration rates between Black and White women are closest among females in the age group spanning 25 to 39.

- In 2010, 25% of women in state prisons were incarcerated for drug offenses, with another 29% incarcerated for property crimes. That year, 17% of male inmates were serving time for drug charges and 18% for property crimes.

- In 2010, 37% of female state prison inmates (34,100) were convicted of violent offenses, compared with 54% (689,000) of male inmates.

- 73% of incarcerated women self-report mental health issues, compared to 55% of male prisoners.

- Nearly 80% of female inmates who suffer from mental illness *also* report having been subjected to physical or sexual abuse.

- Justice-involved women report higher rates of physical, sexual, or family violence than do justice-involved men.

- An estimated seven out of 10 female offenders are mothers with one or more minor children.

- Female offenders report higher drug usage (40%) than do males (32%).

Source: Adapted from Court Services and Offender Supervision Agency (CSOSA, 2014).

A Brief History of Feminism

The influence of feminism on Western society has transformed perspectives on topics ranging from psychology to criminology. Therefore, to fully understand female offenders, it is imperative to place their crimes within the social context and to examine them against a feminist backdrop.

Feminism has its political roots in 18th-century Europe. During the philosophical movement known as the Enlightenment, controversy over gender differences arose and gave way to a new intellectual discourse that regarded all people as rational beings entitled to the same basic rights. The subservient role of women continued to be an issue as the French Revolution broke out in 1789. At the outset of the war, the French estates drew up formal petitions, known as *cahiers*, through which they communicated their grievances to the Estates General. However, as only men and the widows of noblemen were given a voice in the creation of these documents, many women were forced to find other ways to ensure that their concerns were heard. Some published unofficial cahiers, whereas others saw the volatile political climate in France as an opportunity to assert militant action and engage in violent protests. Still others chose to write influential pieces on the importance of gender equality. Ultimately, not much came from this rush of feminist propaganda, as the French Constitution of 1792 banned women from public life and the Napoleonic Code of 1804 denied women access to divorce. Men were awarded control over their wives' property and income, thus confining women to subordinate and domestic status. Nonetheless, the boldness of women's activism continues to be considered significant to the feminist movement today.

The history of modern feminism is divided into three distinct time periods, or "waves," each with its own goals. First-wave feminism occurred during the 19th and early 20th centuries and focused on reversing legal inequities, specifically women's right to vote. The majority of women who joined the first-wave movement were more moderate and conservative in their actions. They were willing to work within the constructs of the political system to promote their agenda and understood the validity in working *with* men sympathetic to their cause. They gained ground by looking to get suffrage passed on a state-by-state basis first before attacking it on a federal level.

Many countries enacted women's suffrage following World War I. As a result of women's contributions to the war effort, it became more difficult to maintain the argument that women were physically and intellectually inferior to men and therefore should be kept out of the voting booths (Hume, 2016). The 19th Amendment was ratified in 1920, granting all American women the right to vote.

Second-wave feminism, which began in the early 1960s, sought to address cultural and social barriers that extended beyond basic political inequity. Such movements targeted sexuality, reproductive rights, family, the workplace, and miscellaneous legal standing. It was during this period that domestic violence and the marital rape exemption were brought to the fore as critical and discriminatory issues codified under the law to protect criminal men and abandon victimized women.

The third wave of feminist activity began in the early 1990s and can be viewed as both a continuation of second-wave feminism and a response to its shortcomings (Krolokke & Sorensen, 2005). In addition to continuing to work toward institutional gains, third-wave feminists have focused on changing the stereotypes, media portrayals, and verbiage used to describe and define women. They have celebrated diversity and have rejected the victim-feminist label in lieu of a poststructuralist view of sexuality and gender (Nicholson et al., 2010).

Exploitation of Women in the Media

Antiquated and sexist attitudes that objectify women and view them as less than rather than equal to men are mirrored in mainstream media ranging from print ads to TV to Hollywood blockbusters. It has been and continues to be common practice to sexualize women to promote products and boost ratings.

Studies on gender differences and sex in advertising reveal that men are portrayed as powerful and women as subordinate (Goffman, 1979). Even advertisements in women's magazines show stereotypes of nude or partially nude women. For example, in *Vogue*, posing women in positions depicting inferiority and low social power is common (Lindner, 2004). According to research by Hatton and Trautner (2011), *Rolling Stone* has increased its use of sexualized photos of men over the past four decades. On the surface, this may seem to even the playing field, so to speak. However, while such imagery of women is often representative of objectification, submissive standing in society, and victimization, it can alternatively denote confidence, attractiveness, and even power for men. Therefore, this is not the "feminist win" that it might appear to be.

In addition to advertising, movies, TV, music videos, and even video games often sexualize women, sending the sometimes blatant but often subtle message that women are not equal to men, thus devaluing them as human beings. For example, when heroines in superhero movies wear costumes that are clearly meant to highlight their sex appeal, girls became more aware of (and self-conscious of) their own bodies. Research has proven that exposure to such over-sexualization (as is popular throughout Hollywood) diminishes girls' self-esteem and promotes body image issues (Pennell & Behm-Morawitz, 2015).

The Women in This Book

Most theories of criminality were developed by men to explain crime perpetrated by other men. The relatively recent realization that the phenomenon of female offending does not fit neatly beneath the umbrella of male offending has given way to the notion that in order to explain female criminality, we must first acknowledge the gender-specific experiences of women and assess how they shape subsequent criminal behavior.

This book looks at those crimes and criminals that are most often misunderstood, politicized, and commercialized and analyzes the psychosocial dynamics at work. It examines actual cases in which real women have committed various offenses—many of which were atypically violent. Several of the case studies involve women who were convicted of non-stereotypically "female" crimes, like those perpetrated by Belle Gunness. Such cases involving callous brutality by women are not the norm, and are therefore not meant to be representative of female offending at large. In fact, extreme acts of violence by women are few and far between; more women are incarcerated for drug-related offenses, property crimes, simple assault, or white-collar crimes. However, the cases herein provide important information about women's capability to behave aggressively and to violate gender expectations, as well as about their pathways toward engaging in callous, violent, and deviant criminal activity.

In addition to the case studies, this book also includes original interviews with women incarcerated throughout the United States for various offenses ranging from trafficking to sexual assault to multiple-victim homicide. These women have experienced the victimization and gender barriers that are so common among justice-involved females. They have told their stories so that their voices will be heard and more people will begin to develop an understanding of how and why women come to offend.

Conclusion

As a convention of gender stereotyping, women have historically been viewed as incapable of engaging in criminal behavior, especially when said actions are of a violent or otherwise "masculine" nature (e.g., sexual assault, crimes against children, sex trafficking, etc.). This social paradigm has resulted in not only the underestimation of female-perpetrated crime by society, but also its under-detection by law enforcement.

As a result of these social constructs, females have largely been excluded from criminological discussions until recently. However, women are currently the fastest growing population to be incarcerated. Therefore, various theoretical perspectives have emerged to explain the phenomenon of female-perpetrated crime, all of which indicate that female offending cannot simply be understood within the context of male offending; women's pathways to crime are different, and this book explores these continuums and their intersection with victimization, mental health, feminism, and stigma.

Chapter 2

Criminological Theory Through the Feminist Lens

Theories of Crime

"What we look for most in the female is femininity, and when we find the opposite in her, we must conclude as a rule that there must be some anomaly."

—Cesare Lombroso (as cited in McLaughlin & Muncie, 2013, p. 201)

Experts agree that the gender gap in crime is universal: Women are less likely than men to engage in criminal activity. However, until recently gender-based experiences were largely ignored with regard to their impact on the development of female deviance (Belknap & Holzinger, 1998). Criminologists initially sought to develop a general theory of crime with which to explain all criminal behavior, but this line of thinking had significant shortcomings. This type of one-size-fits-all approach was based on an assessment of male-perpetrated crime and assumed that female offending was the same or similar. Thus, it essentially treated female crime as an offshoot of male crime. In other words, it overlooked the complex psychological, relational, and situational dynamics experienced by women as pertinent to the phenomenon of female offending (Mazerolle, 2008).

Gender figures prominently in discussions about female-perpetrated crime, both as a critical factor against which to assess existing theories about offending and with which to pursue new knowledge and research in an effort to expand the depth of data on gender-specific philosophies. Currently, generalist psychological, sociological, and biological theories of crime exist. While some of these have a masculine focus, others specifically address gender differences. The utility of other models does not differ based on gender, and those models are therefore considered gender neutral. In order to consider the relevance of various perspectives with regard to patterns of female offending, we must challenge our conceptualization of criminal behavior as a masculine activity and view crime committed by women through a feminist lens.

Feminist theory seeks to identify the impact of gender inequality through the application of related philosophies that hold that gender and its associated attitudes and behaviors (i.e., masculinity and femininity) are central to the organization of human interaction, including offending, victimization, and adjudicative processing. These beliefs recognize the marginalization of female offenders as a result of overarching patriarchal structures and compel the reshaping of generalist theories of crime to be inclusive of women (Renzetti, 2009). Following is an examination of several gender-neutral, gender-specific, and feminist models that seek to explain the causes of crime, as well as an analysis of their applicability to female offending.

Psychological Theories

As a group, psychological theories of offending encompass the motivational, decision-making, and learning processes that lead to criminal behavior (Farrington, 1993).

The Psychodynamic Approach

Psychodynamic theory was developed by Sigmund Freud and posits that personality is controlled by unconscious processes that have their roots in early childhood. Freud hypothesized that the human personality is composed of three elements: the id, the ego, and the superego, with the id being the most primitive structure and representing innate biological drives (e.g., food, sex, etc.). It is also known as the pleasure principle (Freud, 1933). According to psychodynamic ideology, offenders are often driven by the id—or the need for instant gratification.

Unlike the id, which is present at birth, the ego develops early in life and is responsible for restraining the demands of the id. The ego is known as the reality principle and intervenes when someone does not or cannot achieve what they want; the ego helps them to confine their behavior to the requirements of society (or the law).

The third element of personality is the superego, or moral compass, which develops as the individual acquires values. The ego mediates between the impulsive drive of the id and the strict morality imposed by the superego. It stands to reason that older children, teens, and adults know the difference between right and wrong. However, when it comes to criminal behavior, psychodynamic theory suggests that a person commits a crime because he or she has an underdeveloped (or nonexistent) superego. Alternatively, because the psychodynamic framework views the superego as an internalization of an individual's same-sex parent's values, an offender may develop a superego of normal strength, but with deviant or antisocial values (Sammons, n.d.). For example, a daughter raised by a mother who is a prostitute may not develop a superego that morally regulates (e.g., negatively responds to) prostitution-related offenses.

When it comes to gender differences, Freud hypothesized that men and women would differ in superego strength due to variations in development during the Oedipal period (the psychosexual stage during which a child resolves their feelings of desire toward the opposite-sex parent and jealousy toward the same-sex parent). He proposed that men would have a greater propensity for the "superego emotions" of shame and guilt than would women. According to a review by Tangney and Dearing (2002), evaluations of gender differences in moral emotions, moral reasoning, and moral behavior indicate that shame and guilt require the ability to differentiate one's self from others, in addition to the establishment of a behavioral code for oneself, and are therefore likely to be influenced by gender differences in socialization. According to their findings, shame is associated with maladjustment (e.g., minimal capacity for empathic concern, poor coping mechanisms for dealing with anger and interpersonal conflict). Guilt-proneness is correlated with better psychosocial adjustment (e.g., higher capacity for empathy, prosocial coping strategies for anger management). The authors state, "Compared to males, females of all ages report a greater propensity to shame and guilt. In this regard, girls and women are the beneficiaries of the best and the worst of superego emotions" (p. 258).

The Behavioral Approach

The behavioral approach stipulates that crime is a learned behavior or response to life's situations and that people alter their behavior depending on the reactions that their behavior elicits. Prominent social learning theorist Albert Bandura (1978) asserted that people do not have an inherent ability to act violently. Instead, aggression and violence are learned through observation and modeling. The three most common sources from which aggression is modeled are family interaction, media, and environment.

When considering modeling and a behavioral theory of crime, we must consider the fact that males and females are conditioned differently; masculinity and femininity are social constructs that are learned through observation, modeling, and reinforcement (rewards). Children develop gender identities as they begin to model behaviors and receive feedback. For example, if little Jenny is praised for acting in a sweet, polite, and dainty manner—all "feminine" behaviors—she will likely continue to follow a path of praise and social rewards and to shape her behavior accordingly (Shpancer, 2011).

Social norms dictate which behaviors are reinforced, and therefore they strongly influence gender identity. Males have traditionally been conditioned to be tough and sexually aggressive. Therefore, crimes such as assault, sexual assault, and even homicide have typically been thought of as masculine. However, over the years the scope of attitudes and behaviors associated with masculinity and femininity has become progressively more balanced. Women today can and do engage in what have conventionally been considered masculine behaviors such as running businesses, asking people out on dates, and initiating sex (including one-night stands). Although it may not be culturally expected, it has become more *accepted* for women to be outspoken, driven, and aggressive, rather than passive and assuming of the background "support your man" role. Could this convergence of gender roles through socialization somehow explain the rise in female offending or account for female-perpetrated violence?

Cognitive Theory of Crime

Cognitive theories of crime focus on cognition or the mental processes of offenders. In other words, they seek to understand how these individuals perceive the world around them (Knepper, 2001). Germane to cognitive theories is how offenders problem solve. Such perspectives also address information processing, specifically how offenders acquire, retain, and retrieve information as well as how they reason through moral dilemmas. Kohlberg (1984) hypothesized that, in general, offenders are significantly lower in their moral judgment development as compared with the rest of the population. While there appear to be no gender differences in moral reasoning level, men's sense of moral judgment tends to be guided by a principle of justice, whereas women are drawn to an ethic of care (Pincus, 2002).

Developmental Theories

Developmental theories of crime focus on offending as it relates to changes that occur across the life span and in individuals' life circumstances. This cluster of perspectives considers crime to be dynamic in that it is influenced by a confluence of biological, emotional, and cognitive processes and social interactions.

Adolescent Limited/Life-Course Persistent

Terri Moffitt (1993) created a developmental theory of crime to discern the various developmental processes that relate to the age–crime curve. The age–crime curve refers to the idea that the incidence of crime increases until an offender reaches between 16 and 20 years of age; criminal behavior then decreases in adulthood (Moffitt, 1993). This approach to criminology is concerned with the etiology and progression of antisocial behavior, risk variables as they occur at different ages, and the impact of life events on development (Farrington, 2003).

Moffitt's dual taxonomic theory proposes that offenders fall into two qualitatively distinct categories: adolescent limited (AL) and life-course persistent (LCP). These groups differ not only in the course of their offending, but also in the causes underlying their antisocial behavior. AL offenders engage in antisocial acts that are primarily nonaggressive in nature. These individuals do not exhibit neuropsychological impairments, and their criminal behavior is largely attributed to their struggles to cope with the gap between biological and social maturation (Moffitt, 1993). In other words, they want to be treated as adults but are children in the eyes of society. They therefore mirror the antisocial behavior of their LCP peers in a misguided attempt to gain status.

Individuals who fall into the LCP category, in contrast, exhibit high levels of aggression. Their antisocial behavior begins in child-hood, often taking the form of physical aggression toward other children (biting, kicking, etc.) and continues into adulthood with the commission of more serious offenses (child abuse, robbery, sexual assault, homicide, etc.). They are thought to have experienced childhood trauma and often present with neuropsychological impairment; LCP offending is considered a result of psychopathology (Fairchild et al., 2013). At the root of Moffitt's theory lies the concept of stability of criminality. AL offenders "grow out" of their antisocial behavior, whereas LCP offenders engage in stable and continuous antisocial behavior throughout their lives.

Although this theory is not designed to address the gender gap in crime, some experts suggest that its basic premise applies to both males and females, but that expansion is needed to differentiate how risk factors interact with gender (Farrington, 2003). For example, variables such as the need for excitement or the influence of peers may have less of an impact on females than males, whereas attachment and socialization processes may have more. Similarly, impulsivity may be lower in females than in males, making it less of a risk factor for female-perpetrated crime.

To that end, Kratzer and Hodgins (1999) tested Moffitt's theory by collecting data from both male and female offenders. The researchers identified four classifications among the offender-participants: stable early starters (ES), adolescence limited (AL), adult starters (AS), and discontinuous offenders (DO). They found that, in general, ES offenders committed more numerous and varied offenses than did the other groups. The ES subjects were additionally distinguished from the AL and AS offenders by a history of childhood difficulties and low intelligence. However, among female offenders, AS subjects (rather than ES subjects) were responsible for the most crimes. Additionally, childhood risk factors played a key role in AL offending among females. The researchers thus concluded that Moffitt's developmental typology fits male offenders better than it does female offenders (Kratzer & Hodgins, 1999).

Related research compares female offending patterns to those of AL and LCP males. According to Silverthorn and Frick (1999), both girls and boys are affected by similar risk variables during childhood, but onset of delinquency in girls occurs later due to the more stringent social controls imposed on them prior to adolescence. Therefore, it follows that adolescent-onset females are more similar to early-onset males than they are to adolescent-onset males in terms of their early exposure to risk (Silverthorn et al., 2001). Moreover, according to White and Piquero (2004), late-onset females present with constellations of risk, which most closely resemble those of early-onset males. However, there is evidence that some girls *do* begin to act antisocially in childhood. Despite this, it is important to note that some studies have identified groups of girls who exhibit high levels of antisocial behavior throughout childhood and early adolescence and are therefore at a higher risk for continued antisocial behavior (Schaeffer et al., 2006). In fact, 7.5% of girls between the ages of 7 and 15 display early-onset offending that continues into adolescence and that is similar to the offending of boys of the same age (Odgers et al., 2008). However, other studies indicate that although overtly aggressive behavior in girls younger than age 7 is rare, such behavioral difficulties are indicative of the potential for significant future problems (Hay, 2007; Odgers et al., 2008).

Taken as a whole, the findings suggest that chronic offending among females is perhaps more commonplace than had initially been thought, but because persistent offending in girls surfaces across a wider range of ages than it does in boys and may not begin until adolescence, it is more difficult to distinguish AL and LCP patterns in girls. Although opinions vary regarding the relative age at which boys and girls are most likely to begin offending, the span of female criminality tends to be shorter-lived than that of male offending, and crimes committed by females are often more harmful than those perpetrated by persistent male offenders (Cauffman, 2008).

The developmental or life-course model seeks to explain behavioral patterns in terms of social development across the life span. It examines developmental processes, including the impact of social controls, informal controls, and risk factors from childhood to adolescence and into adulthood (Belknap, 2015). Although the expanded research provides a broader picture of how this model applies to females, further work is needed for it to offer significant insight into female offending.

Attachment Theory

Attachment theory is a developmental concept that views psychopathology, juvenile delinquency, and offending as related to the impact of an insecure or disrupted parent–child bond during infancy or early childhood. By the same token, normal developmental outcomes are seen as the result of healthy secure attachments between parent and child (Sroufe et al., 1991).

Infants who are separated from their parents often cry and try to cling to their mothers; they experience extreme distress (Bowlby, 1973). This is a natural adaptive response to separation that serves an evolutionary purpose. If the parent–child relationship is disrupted during infancy, long-term negative consequences can result, such as the inability to show affection or empathic concern in addition to the development of delinquent and/or aggressive behavior (Bowlby, 1973). Several studies have found a link between disorganized attachment and aggressive and/or delinquent externalized behavior (Achenbach, 1991).

Experts disagree as to whether the link between attachment and delinquency is gender specific or gender neutral. The research is limited and the results are conflicting. For instance, some studies report a stronger impact of attachment on the development of antisocial behavior in females (e.g., Nye, 1958), while others indicate that the overall family bond, specifically strain within the family (Hay, 2003) and the quality of parenting (Rothbaum & Weisz, 1994), is more closely related to delinquency in boys.

Del Giudice (2009) hypothesized that gender influences the characteristics of attachment relationships, specifically that females are more likely to adopt a pattern of anxious-ambivalent attachment, whereas males are more prone to develop an avoidant attachment style. As a result, women tend to internalize problems, thus resulting in anxiety and depression, whereas men more frequently externalize their frustrations by employing aggression and ultimately engaging in delinquent behavior. Fearson and colleagues (2010) found that insecure attachment is a stronger predictor of externalized behavior in males than it is in females, whereas other researchers found very few between-sex differences (Hubbard & Pratt, 2002; Loeber & Stouthamer-Loeber, 1986). It is currently unknown whether the impact of insecure attachment changes over time and, if so, whether this potential developmental difference is also influenced by gender.

Sociological Perspectives
Sociological theories of deviance explain crime as a result of societal influence.

Strain Theory
Strain theories are perspectives that view negative emotionality (referred to as "strain") as a key predictor of criminal behavior. The most prevalent of these models identify the types of strains

most likely to result in criminal behavior, explain the relationship between strain and crime, and describe the factors that ultimately lead an individual to use antisocial behavior as a coping mechanism. All such theories acknowledge that only a small portion of strained persons resort to crime (Agnew & Scheuerman, 2015).

According to Merton's classic strain theory (1938), society pressures people to achieve certain financial goals. Individuals lacking the means to do so experience a strain (i.e., the uncomfortable disparity between actual achievement and society's expectations). Some of these people respond by committing crimes to ease the negative feelings resulting from the strain.

The classic strain model has been criticized for being classist and androcentric. Many theorists argue that crime can result from the inability to achieve a wide range of aspirations—not just financial success. Additionally, attempts to revise the theory acknowledge that focusing on poverty as an explanation for crime largely ignores the fact that "females constitute the most impoverished group of every Western society, yet females commit by far the least crime" (Faith, 1993).

In response, Robert Agnew developed general strain theory (GST) in 1992, which has since become a principal theory of crime. GST focuses on a wide array of strains, including the inability to accomplish various goals, the loss of assets or possessions, and adverse treatment by others. Strain triggers negative feelings such as frustration, anger, and depression, which, in turn, create the need for the sufferer to ease his or her emotional distress. While there are myriad legitimate and prosocial coping mechanisms available to some individuals, others who lack such resources utilize unhealthy coping strategies, such as engaging in criminal or delinquent behavior. In this way, crime is used to reduce or escape the negative impact of strain. For example, someone who is chronically unemployed may steal or sell drugs to get money, physically aggress against a boss who fired him or her, or abuse drugs as a way of self-medicating. Research supports the idea that the strains identified by GST increase the likelihood of crime (Agnew & Scheuerman, 2015).

Multiple studies propose that general strain theory helps to explain gender disparities in crime. According to Baron (2004), anger is a significant predictor of a vast array of criminal behaviors, ranging from violence to property crimes. Although strain triggers anger in both males and females, females are more likely to experience concurrent negative emotions such as guilt, disappointment, fear, worthlessness, and depression (Broidy, 2001; Ngo & Paternoster, 2013). Depression appears to be more closely related to strains in females than in males; however, males experiencing depression (as a result of strain) are more likely to offend than are their female counterparts (Ostrowsky & Messner, 2005). Additionally, the depression caused by strain in girls predicts suicidal thoughts, regular alcohol use, running away, and violent offenses, but is related to suicidal ideation alone among boys (Kaufman, 2009).

The sources of strain also appear to vary by gender. Girls report more psychological, physical, and sexual abuse and experience more strain surrounding close relationships, while boys experience more stress about external achievement (i.e., material success). Walker and Bright (2009) add that there is a correlation between the strain caused by disrespect and subsequent humiliation and the respondent's use of aggression to regain stature (i.e., "masculinity"). They believe that this accounts for the contradiction of individuals with apparent low self-esteem exhibiting high levels of aggression. Although the researchers do not specify gender differences in this assertion, this perspective is useful for the examination of the connection between humiliation, anger, and violence in females (Belknap, 2015).

Differential Association Theory

Unlike GST, differential association theory (DAT) views deviance from a learning standpoint. DAT proposes that criminal behavior is learned via social interaction. In other words, would-be offenders learn (and replicate) the values, attitudes, methods, and motivations relating to criminal activity. Although DAT itself does not specifically address female offending, the feminist perspective recognizes DAT as positively contributing to the examination of gender differences in delinquency. For example, the social and familial constraints (curfew, expectations to stay close to home, and overall less freedom) imposed on girls, in combination with the fact that girls are more likely to be disciplined for minor infractions and sexual experimentation, may account for the fact they commit relatively fewer crimes as compared with boys. In other words, the gender gap in crime may be explained (at least in part) by the differential opportunities to learn criminal behavior. This significant difference in socialization is thought to result in different (i.e., gendered) behaviors (Hoffman-Bustamante, 1973). It follows, then, that the increase in girls' delinquency rates in recent years may be a result of the increased freedoms experienced by females. According to Cressey (1964), greater equality between the sexes is likely to lower gender distinctions in crime.

Social Control Theory

Social control theory (SCT) stipulates that people engage in criminal behavior when their bond to society has weakened and therefore social constraints have diminished. SCT, developed by Travis Hirschi (1969) and originally called social bond theory (SBT), identifies four categories of social bonds that impose restrictions on people's behaviors: attachment, commitment, involvement, and belief. The theory specifies that an individual's likelihood to offend is related to his or her ties to one of the following: conventional people such as parents, conventional institutions and/or behaviors in his or her employment or recreation, and societal rules (norms) (Belknap, 2015).

Gottfredson and Hirschi (1990) shifted the emphasis from social control to self-control in *A General Theory of Crime*, thus advancing the notion that self-control interacts with criminal opportunity to account for delinquency. That is, people with access to opportunities for offending *and* low self-control are more likely to commit crimes. While the general theory of crime (GTC) suggests that gender disparities result from how the aforementioned characteristics are related to self-control (and social control), it has been widely critiqued for ignoring violence against women, research on gender divisions within families, the role of power/control as it relates to crime, and how social and self-control might interact (Taylor, 2001).

Building on SCT, power control theory (PCT) is one of the few models to explicitly incorporate gender: "A key premise . . . is that positions of power in the workplace are translated into power relations in the household and that the latter, in turn, influence the gender-determined control of adolescents, their preferences for risk-taking, and the patterning of gender and delinquency" (Hagan et al., 1987, p. 812). To further support this hypothesis, research reveals that greater gender differences in delinquency are more prevalent in patriarchal homes (i.e., where the mother assumes a lower status than the father), than in egalitarian homes (i.e., where both parents are equal or the mother is the only parental figure) (Hagan et al., 1985). Therefore, in a home where sexism is not woven into the parents' relationship, there should theoretically be a lower instance of gender differences in the children's behaviors. These findings submit that the power constellation in the parents' relationship specifically influences daughters' potential for engaging in delinquent behavior (Belknap, 2015).

Biological Theories

Biological theories assert that there is a direct correlation between biological risk factors and criminal behavior. In fact, some early researchers believed that a link existed between physique and personality. Caesar Lombroso, often regarded as the father of criminology, held that criminality was an inborn trait and that offenders could be identified based solely on their physical appearance (Bartol & Bartol, 2008).

Twins, Adoption, and Criminal Behavior

Twin studies have been conducted to determine the heritability of criminality. Presumably, if biology is the key determinant of personality and behavior, identical twins should be carbon copies of one another because they share the same genes. Research reveals that identical twins *do* share more personality and cognitive traits than do fraternal twins. However, identical twins with varying environmental experiences (e.g., different prenatal/chorionic environments [Rhee & Waldman, 2002], separate homes, varying peer groups, etc.) go on to engage in different behaviors and to have different criminal outcomes, suggesting that environment can "turn on" or "turn off" genetic influences at different developmental stages. Studies indicate that some combinations of genes do appear to put certain children at risk for engaging in antisocial behavior, but the interaction of that biological risk with the environment is what plays a critical role in whether said criminal behavior will come to pass. Overall, the research supports the heritability of nonviolent crime, but does not favor the same genetic emphasis for violent offending (Bartol & Bartol, 2008).

The influence of biology as compared with environment has also been examined through the use of adoption studies. A review of Danish records specifically focused on the relationship between the criminality of sons and that of their fathers, both biological and adoptive, thus excluding mothers and daughters from the discussion. The researchers found that when the biological father had a criminal history and the adoptive father had none, 22% of adopted sons later went on to have a criminal record. In cases where the biological father had no arrest record, but the adoptive father did, 11.5% of adopted sons engaged in criminal behavior. However, when both the biological and adoptive fathers were offenders, the adopted son's risk of pursuing criminal activity greatly increased. Thus, the researchers determined that although environmental factors do play a role in the development of criminal behavior, genetics do appear to exert an undeniably strong influence (Hutchings & Mednick, 1975).

A more comprehensive and inclusive study involving more than 14,000 European adoptees evaluated the criminal records of biological and adoptive parents and revealed a significant relationship between the criminality of both male and female adoptees and their biological parents. Specifically, if either biological parent had been convicted of a crime, the child exhibited a higher risk of engaging in criminal activity; this risk was especially strong for male adoptees who were chronic offenders. Perhaps unexpectedly, there was no indication that the type of crime committed by the biological parent had any impact on the nature of the offense committed by their biological child. Furthermore, there was no evidence that the children had any knowledge of their parents' offense histories (Mednick et al., 1984, 1987). As a result, Gabrielli and Mednick (1983) stated, "It is reasonable . . . to conclude that some people inherit biological characteristics which permit them to be antisocial more readily than others" (p. 63).

In Utero Experiences/Birth Complications

In addition to genetic markers, certain in utero experiences, including exposure to toxic substances such as opiates and methadone, can put children at risk for behavioral problems later in life. Additionally, fetal exposure to alcohol can cause serious complications. Lead poisoning before and after birth (from hand-to-mouth behavior) is also associated with the development of conduct problems. Although lead paint is not common in many homes today, this continues to be an issue in lower-income areas (Dodge & Pettit, 2003).

Additionally, birth complications, especially when combined with psychosocial risks (e.g., maternal rejection, marital discord, an absentee father, parental mental illness) can lead to antisocial behavior (Raine et al., 1997). However, pregnancy and/or birth complications alone do not to trigger violence or criminality (Bartol & Bartol, 2008). Neurological dysfunction resulting from deficient brain development, on the other hand, is correlated with serious and violent offending (Ishikawa & Raine, 2004). This is especially true if the dysfunction affects the frontal lobe of the brain, which is responsible for the executive functions of organized thought, planning, and self-regulation.

Trait Theory

Trait theorists posit that people's personality traits are inborn and remain constant across time, place, and situation. According to Eysenck (1977, 1996; Eysenck & Gudjonsson, 1989), criminal behavior is the result of an interaction between environment and the characteristics of an individual's nervous system. Therefore, to understand an offender's specific behavior, one must examine his or her neurophysiological composition *and* his or her unique socialization history. Eysenck proposed that various combinations of neurobiological, environmental, and personality elements result in different types of crime (Eysenck & Eysenck, 1970) and that criminal behavior cannot be understood in terms of either heredity *or* environment alone (Eysenck, 1973).

Although Eysenck (1996) did not believe that people are born criminal, his theory places significant weight on a genetic predisposition toward antisocial behavior, as he opined that some individuals are born with nervous system characteristics that predispose them to engage in criminal activity: "It is not crime itself or criminality that is innate; it is certain peculiarities of the central and autonomic nervous system that react with the environment, with upbringing, and many other environment factors to increase the probability that a given person would act in a certain antisocial manner" (Eysenck & Gudjonsson, 1989, p. 7).

According to Eysenck, there are four higher-order factors of personality: general intelligence, extraversion, neuroticism, and psychoticism, all of which describe temperament. Extraversion and neuroticism are the core concepts of the theory. The extraversion dimension reflects the basic functions of the central nervous system (CNS) and is a continuum representing an intensifying need for stimulation. At one end of the spectrum are extroverts who have a high need for excitement and stimulation-seeking, and at the other end are introverts who do not have such needs. Eysenck (1967) believed that people differed along this axis due to genetic variations in their CNS and cortical arousal. Because extroverts get bored more easily, consistently seek stimulation, and have a more intense need for excitement, they are more likely to engage in behavior that is against the law. They require greater levels of excitement/stimulation to feel aroused and thus satisfied (Bartol & Bartol, 2008).

Another core concept is neuroticism or emotionality, which reflects the biological predisposition to respond physiologically to stressful events. A person high on this scale has intense reactions and is likely to be moody, sensitive, and anxious even in low-stress environments. The neuroticism–stable axis deals with innate differences in the autonomic nervous system. Neurotics have an overactive sympathetic nervous system, so they engage the "fight-or-flight" response rapidly; they become emotional quickly and maintain that state for more considerable periods of time than do their stable counterparts. In contrast, stables have an underactive sympathetic nervous system and an overactive parasympathetic nervous system (Bartol & Bartol, 2008).

Psychoticism is the final dimension developed by Eysenck and is most similar to primary psychopathy. It is characterized by cruelty, callousness, lack of emotionality, an attraction to the unusual, disregard for danger, and a dislike of other people. Psychotics are typically hostile and mean-spirited; they enjoy lying and "getting one over" on others. While no neurophysiological mechanism has been identified to explain the development of this trait, it is believed that high levels of testosterone, in combination with low levels of the enzyme monoamine oxidase, along with minimal serotonin, may play a role (Bartol & Bartol, 2008).

Feminist Theories

Feminist theories of crime are a group of related ideas that view the social construct of gender as not only a central organizing feature of social life, but also of both victimization and offending. At the root of these philosophies is the idea that women must not be treated as a homogeneous group. Rather, it is critical to acknowledge each individual's unique set of circumstances (e.g., social strata, privilege, race, culture, victimization history, age, sexuality, etc.) and how these elements shape each woman's experience with criminality (Renzetti et al., 2006). Moreover, feminist theories maintain that because of the patriarchal and sexist nature of the world in which we live, females of all ages have been marginalized not only in society, but also as research subjects; therefore, the feminist literature is in its infancy. This in and of itself creates a plethora of issues, including relatively few female offenders having been used as research subjects (i.e., small sample sizes or case study research design), and thus the inability to generalize from the findings to the larger population of female offenders. In other words, the lack of attention that has been paid to studying female-perpetrated crime has resulted in limitations when attempting to extrapolate larger meaning from the current data.

Masculinization and Opportunity Theories

In its inception, masculinization theory was a groundbreaking feminist viewpoint developed by Freda Adler (1975) in her book *Sisters in Crime*. She hypothesized that women's participation in liberation movements changed their roles in the family and in the workplace as they slowly transformed from submissive and passive to independent, assertive, and aggressive members of society. As a result, widespread changes in socialization began to occur and women underwent a "masculinization" process. In other words, as women fought for the same rights as men, they started to develop personality characteristics and means of interacting that were previously perceived as masculine.

According to Adler, this masculinization process was highlighted by criminal behavior in the 1970s. At the time, although men committed the majority of criminal acts, the female crime rate in the United States was rising faster. Not only were women engaging in more criminal activity, but the nature of their crimes was also becoming more violent—women were committing traditionally male crimes. As women became more progressive in their thinking and approach to the social and professional world with which they interacted, they began to integrate "masculine" characteristics into their personalities (aggressiveness, pushiness, stubbornness, etc.), and they began to use crime as a means by which to achieve their goals. As a result of masculinization, women's rates of both property and violent offenses increased (Small, 2000).

While masculinization theory perhaps offers a viable explanation for the pattern and trends of female offending in first-world nations, it falls short in that it is not inclusive of developing countries where women have far fewer rights than their male counterparts. It has been criticized by feminist scholars because it is based on a male-centric viewpoint (Islam et al., 2014).

Somewhat similar to masculinization theory is opportunity theory. Coined by Rita Simon (1976), this perspective asserts that males are more criminally active because they have greater access to social and professional opportunities than do women. Therefore, it stands to reason that if women's opportunities were to increase, so would their criminal behavior—or at least certain types of it. For instance, if women had more opportunities to become employed, they would also have more opportunities to engage in employment-related offenses (e.g., embezzlement, fraud, etc.). However, where this theory differs from masculinization theory is that it holds that one can logically assume that as women become financially independent, their rates of violent crime would decline, as most such offenses are committed against spouses:

> As women feel more liberated physically, emotionally, and legally, and are less subjected to male power, their frustrations and anger decrease . . . [which results] in a decline in their desire to kill the usual objects of their anger of frustration: their husbands, lovers, and other men upon whom they are dependent, but insecure. (Simon, 1975, p. 40)

Overall, opportunity theory predicts that as women's opportunities increase, so will their propensity to commit white-collar crimes (e.g., larceny/theft, fraud, forgery, etc.), but their violent crime will decrease. As with masculinization theory, opportunity theory has been criticized for its inability to be applied in the global context.

Marginalization and Crime

Viewing female offending from the perspective of the marginalization of women has garnered significant support. Proponents of economic marginalization acknowledge that simply because women have more access to education or to the labor force does not necessarily mean improved financial status (and stability) for the vast array of women (Chesney-Lind, 1997). There is *still* a pay differential between men and women hired into the same positions, with the *average* woman's salary being only 78% of her male colleague's (O'Brien, 2015). According to the economic marginalization perspective, female-perpetrated crime is strongly associated with unemployment, underemployment, inadequate welfare support, and an increase in the number of single female households with multiple children (Small, 2000). These conditions predispose women to commit crimes due to financial necessity—and these factors continue to be an issue today.

However, the marginalization of women is not restricted to the area of economics. From a young age, girls are bombarded with the message that they are peripheral objects in a man's world: not as good as men, not equal to men, and frighteningly vulnerable. Victimization of females of all ages (e.g., trafficking, molestation, sexual torture, domestic abuse, etc.) at the hands of males is widespread. As it relates to crime and deviance, this social marginalization and exploitation of females predisposes them to not only engage in criminal activity, but also to turn to drugs in order to self-medicate as a result of the (often unresolved) trauma (Chesney-Lind & Sheldon, 2014).

The Relationship Between Victimization and Offending. Girls are abused more frequently than boys (Laidler & Hunt, 2001) and have typically endured abuse in at least one sphere (physical, sexual, emotional) prior to the commission of their first offense (Lake, 1993). In a survey of justice-involved girls in California, 92% of respondents reported a history of abuse (Langton & Piquero, 2007).

Research underscores the concept that childhood abuse is a precursor to violence for some females, with one in four violent girls having endured sexual abuse as opposed to one in 10 nonviolent girls (Laub & Sampson, 1993). Why, then, do some female victims of abuse develop deviant and violent behavioral patterns while others do not? While abuse and exposure to trauma as well as other stressors are irrefutably connected with subsequent conduct problems (Lauritsen, 1993), some theorists suggest that dysfunction in violent female offenders' coping mechanisms may intensify the adverse effects of childhood trauma and victimization (Li, 1999). That is, violent female offenders have not only been victimized at higher rates than their nonviolent counterparts, but they also tend to lack adequate coping skills with which to manage various stressors, including past trauma (Loeber, 1996).

Cycle of Violence. The cycle of violence theory builds on the notion that victimization and offending are correlated, and it is perhaps one of the most useful perspectives regarding the development of delinquency in girls and women. According to Widom (1998), a history of childhood victimization "increases the likelihood of delinquency, adult criminality and violent criminal behaviour" (p. 226). Her theory stipulates that childhood maltreatment is a substantial risk factor for subsequent offending. This is critical to viewing criminal behavior through the feminist lens because of the fact that females are abused at much higher rates than males. Therefore, it assists us in understanding one of the unique pathways to crime for women.

Widom's (1998) research indicates that individuals who have endured physical or sexual abuse or neglect as children are nearly twice as likely to be arrested for violent offenses than are same-aged individuals (of the same race and from the same neighborhood) who have not been abused. In fact, people who have experienced childhood sexual abuse in tandem with either physical abuse or neglect are at the greatest risk for running away (considered a juvenile status offense), and victims of child sexual abuse are much more likely to be arrested for prostitution than nonvictimized persons (Belknap, 2015).

Widom's (1998) research implies that maltreated children engage in criminal behavior at an earlier age, are convicted more often, are more likely to reoffend, and are at a greater risk to become habitual offenders than are children who are not abused. Widom (1998) concludes that "childhood victimization significantly increases a person's risk of arrest as follows: by 59% as a juvenile, by 27% as an adult, and by 29% for a violent crime" (p. 226).

Perhaps one of the most comprehensive theories about the development of deviant behavior is Beth Richie's (1996) pathways to crime (for battered women). Through a host of interviews, Richie developed a theory of gender entrapment in order to understand the relationship between intimate partner violence, the cultural concept of gender identity, and female offending. Through her work, Richie was able to identify six pathways to crime: three for African American battered women, two pertaining to African American and Caucasian battered women, and one specific to African American and Caucasian battered women in addition to African American nonbattered women (see Table 2.1 on the next page).

Conclusion

As part of an effort to develop a general theory of crime, criminologists initially conceptualized female offending as an offshoot of male-perpetrated crime. However, this hypothesis was vastly flawed, and subsequently a multitude of theoretical perspectives emerged (e.g., psychological, sociological, biological, developmental), each offering explanations about the etiology of antisocial behavior. While many of these theories were sound and could be applied to female offending, they were initially articulated from a masculine perspective.

It was not until the establishment of feminist theories of criminal behavior that gender was truly recognized as a central feature underlying female offending. Feminist theories explored how the unique nature and impact of gendered experiences, such as the marginalization and victimization of women, can and do shape the types of crimes committed by women.

When analyzing the cases in this book or in society at large, it is common to find that several theories are relevant to the same offender. Individuals who engage in serious criminal behavior often present with numerous risk factors that fall into multiple domains.

TABLE 2.1 Women's Pathways to Crime

Pathways Correlated With African American Battered Women	
Women held hostage	This trajectory involves women whose batterers use violence to isolate them and/or hold them hostage. These women are often charged for the deaths of their own children, when caused by the abuser.
Association and projection	This pathway represents those women who violently aggress against men *other* than their batterer. Their crimes are symbolic revenge, and their victims serve as proxies for their abusers.
Poverty	As economic abuse and hardship are intertwined with domestic violence, women in this category often commit property or other financially motivated offenses (e.g., robbery, theft, forgery, receiving stolen property, burglary, etc.).
Pathways Correlated With *Both* African American and Caucasian Battered Women	
Sexual exploitation	These women are often arrested for prostitution-related offenses after having been forced or coerced to engage in illegal sex work by their abusers.
Fighting back	This pathway involves battered women who commit criminal acts such as arson or assault during an attack; they view their behavior as self-defense.
Pathway Correlated With African American and Caucasian Battered Women *and* Nonbattered African American Women	
Addiction	This pathway takes various shapes. For African American women who are battered, drug use typically follows an abusive episode and is a way for them to emotionally reconnect with the abuser. For African American women who are not abused, drug use is more voluntary. For Caucasian battered women, selling drugs may be a way to achieve financial independence and ultimately the ability to leave the batterer.

Source: Adapted from Richie (1996).

When those offenders are women, those precipitating risks often coincide with gendered events, thus overlapping feminist theories. That is not to say that a biological risk (e.g., exposure to drugs in utero) condemns someone to a future of crime. However, when that risk is combined with a developmental risk, such as insecure attachment, and a gendered risk, such as sexual violence, those multidimensional pressures work together to increase the likelihood of offending.

Part II

Chapter 3

Black Widows

The Archetypal Female Serial Killer

Prediction: Murder

According to legend, Tillie Klimek had psychic powers that enabled her to foresee the deaths of those around her, and thus she was both respected and feared by the people closest to her. Vivid premonitions came to her in her dreams—or so she said. In reality, Tillie only pretended to prophesy death in order to set the stage for her crimes. Once she selected a target and determined when she was going to kill them, she announced her forecast under the guise of having received spiritual guidance; Tillie always made sure that her intended victim knew the details of her "prediction," as she enjoyed inflicting psychological torture.

In 1914, Tillie warned of the impending death of her husband, John Mitkiewicz. At the time, she was 49 years old—significantly older than most black widow murderers when they begin their killing careers. Tillie and John had been married for nearly 3 decades; within weeks, John was dead and Tillie was cashing in on his life insurance policy (Kelleher & Kelleher, 1998).

After receiving her inheritance, Tillie engaged the aid of a marriage broker and soon wed a laborer named John Ruskowski. Before long, Tillie told of an ominous dream about his passing. John died a few months later—and on the exact date that Tillie had predicted. The cause of death was assumed to be heart failure, leaving Tillie as the sole beneficiary to once again collect a large insurance payout. She then married for a third time. Like her second husband, Joe Guszkowski fell ill and died within months of marrying Tillie.

Husband number four was Frank Kupczyk. He survived more than 3 years of marriage before succumbing to an illness similar to that which had killed Tillie's previous spouses. According to several popular Chicago media outlets of the time, Tillie taunted Frank with the idea that his death was imminent and that he surely wouldn't live much longer.

Four times married and four times widowed. The community was growing increasingly suspicious. In fact, the one neighbor who was brazen enough to vocalize the previously unspoken fear that Tillie had killed her husbands for profit turned up dead a few days later. People began to notice that relatives and townspeople who crossed Tillie often ended up dying shortly thereafter.

In 1921, Tillie married for the fifth and final time. Her husband Joseph Klimek fell ill shortly after his new life insurance policy went into effect. During a visit, his relatives became alarmed by his rapidly deteriorating condition and brought him to the hospital where he was diagnosed with arsenic poisoning. Despite having played the doting wife in front of in-laws and doctors alike, Tillie later confessed that she had routinely been dosing Joseph's food with arsenic.

Following an investigation, Tillie was arrested and ultimately convicted of only one murder, that of her fourth husband, Frank Kupczyk. In 1923 she was sentenced to life in prison, which was the harshest sentence leveled against any woman in the history of Cook County, Illinois. The media conjectured that Tillie's conviction and sentence were perhaps more a reflection of her appearance and mannerisms than they were of her crimes. Most journalists held the opinion that because she was a woman, Tillie would have been acquitted had she presented with a feminine figure or porcelain complexion. This point was driven home in Genevieve Forbes's article: "Tillie Klimek went to the penitentiary because she had never gone to a beauty parlor" (as cited by Selzer, 2016).

Although Tillie was ultimately found guilty of only one murder, investigators maintained that she likely killed many other victims, including her previous husbands, other relatives, and neighbors. She had a tendency to exploit her position in relationships to get close to her victims and ultimately murder them. Many estimates total her victim count at close to 20, and therefore popular lore regards Tillie Klimek as a black widow serial killer.

Female Serial Killers: An Overview

Serial murder is defined as the unlawful and intentional killing of three or more victims, with a "cooling-off" period in between (Farrell et al., 2013; Hickey 2010; Holmes et al., 1991). While this reprieve may last only days or weeks, there are more typically months or even years between murders. Serial killers are widely stereotyped as being white males with violent predilection, psychosexual disturbance, and psychopathic personalities who target strangers and who have the means with which to overpower and brutalize their victims. However, statistics indicate that one out of every six serial killers is female (Vronsky, 2004). That said, serial murder itself is an infrequent occurrence, making female serial killers (FSKs) exceptionally rare.

Previously, the crimes of FSKs were misunderstood, underestimated, or disregarded altogether for a multitude of reasons. For example, although people had their misgivings about Tillie Klimek, she was able to lull five men into a deep enough sense of security that they agreed to marry her. Therefore, it stands to reason that despite the fact that so many people around her (several of whom she alone had specialized access to) died *exactly* when she projected that they would, people were reluctant to label her a killer; society was more accepting of her psychic façade than they were of the notion that a woman could be a serial killer.

There has historically been a common misconception that women are somehow incapable of repetitive and grave violence—and therefore do not commit serial homicide. According to Schurman-Kauflin (2000), "No one believes that a woman could kill multiple victims" (p. 13). The very essence of serial murder violates the constructs of femininity and conventional gender roles, which underscores the cultural denial of the phenomenon of the female serial killer. This mindset contributes to the fact that FSKs often go undetected by law enforcement for longer periods of time than do male serial killers (Hickey, 2010; Kelleher & Kelleher, 1998)—and sometimes even get away with murder (Pearson, 1998). Therefore, it is essential to reach an accurate conceptualization of the characteristics and motivations of women who kill repeatedly (Harrison et al., 2015).

Hickey (1991, 2010) published one of the most comprehensive studies of FSKs to date. By reviewing offense details and biopsychosocial histories of 64 such offenders, he was able to discern a general profile of these women. (Note that although this study is broader in scope than others, it only includes a sample size of 64, and thus inferences should be regarded cautiously.) Ninety-eight percent of the included FSKs were white, and the vast majority of them began killing at age 31. They murdered between seven and 10 people, and their victims were most often known to them (Harrison et al., 2015).

It has been suggested that because they often lack the physical strength to overpower their victims, FSKs are known to use "less violent" tactics than men. Overall, FSKs tend to favor covert killing methods, such as poison, suffocation, or staged accidents, and frequently target helpless victims, such as children, elderly adults, and the infirm, in addition to romantic partners or other family members (Harrison et al., 2015). In many such cases, it is the offender's own intimate relationship with or ministering to the victim that gives her unrestricted access to the target but also protracts the victim's suffering as she administers dose after dose of arsenic or strychnine, for example. While these means of murder are indeed considered "neat" and "clean," to call them less violent is misleading. What these methodologies lack in overt violence is translated into prolonged suffering and a purposeful manipulation of the victim's sense of security. The victim is often left to rely blindly upon the killer, growing agonizingly sicker and frequently dying without ever having an identifiable adversary. Therefore, although these discreet (i.e., "less violent") methods of murder are often considered feminine, could the torment of the victim's psychological landscape in fact be a gender-specific expression of sadism?

While poisoning is the primary means of murder for the FSK (Hickey, 1991, 2010; Wilson & Hilton, 1998), this is a generality and does not preclude the possibility that a woman's MO will include shooting, stabbing, or drowning victims. Findings suggest that females are four times more likely than their male counterparts to drug their targets, as this may make it easier for them to subdue their victims (White & Lester, 2012). Schurman-Kauflin (2000) noted that while male serial killers often immobilize their victims by tying or binding them, females are more apt to victimize individuals who are *already* helpless, thus increasing their sense of power and control.

FSKs rarely travel outside of their comfort zone to complete their kills, with 44% committing their murders locally (Farrell et al., 2013). They tend to operate in a specific location with which they are intimately familiar, such as their home or a healthcare facility where they are employed. Unlike men, women typically do not troll for random victims but rather select their targets from within their family or workplace (Bonn, 2015).

While male serial killers typically target unknown victims (or strangers), females are far more likely to dispatch a spouse, boyfriend, or other kin. In fact, Farrell and colleagues (2013) report that 80% of FSKs are acquainted with their victims. Specifically, females tend to target men who are emotionally close to them and to whom they have ready access, such as family members and intimates (Harrison et al., 2015), and do so in order to improve their lifestyle (Bonn, 2015).

After examining 100 FSKs from around the world, Kelleher and Kelleher (1998) found profit to be one of the primary motives for these offenders and noted that those who killed for monetary gain were the most likely to enjoy the longest period of time at large prior to being apprehended (Harrison et al., 2015). FSKs are far more likely than men to kill for financial gain, comfort, or revenge (Bonn, 2015). Due to their desire to attain material things, women who are motivated by comfort/gain often commit theft, fraud, or embezzlement prior to serial murder (Vronsky, 2007). While most FSKs are motivated by profit, some kill for other reasons, such as a pathological need for attention or sympathy (Bonn, 2015).

Perhaps unsurprisingly, a study by Farrell and colleagues (2013) found that the majority of FSKs are not charged with homicide, but rather lesser offenses. This is illustrative of society's reluctance to view women as capable of mortal violence (Kelleher & Kelleher, 1998) and to instead portray them as victims (Pearson, 1998). Despite the inherent generalities in this assumption, research supports the notion that there are differing environmental and psychological risks that underlie female serial murder as opposed to male serial murder—and yes, gender-based victimization is one of them. For instance, women are more likely to kill if they have been battered or if they suffer from a psychological disorder such as postpartum psychosis than as a result of a psychopathic personality constellation or lack of empathic concern for others.

Classifications of Female Serial Killers

Typologies have long been utilized to categorize male serial killers based upon theories about their crime characteristics, motives, and other common sociodemographic features (Hazelwood & Douglas, 1980; Holmes & DeBurger, 1985; Ressler et al., 1988). Holmes and Holmes (1998) attempted to classify FSKs by denoting five distinct types based on their offense patterns and motives (see Table 3.1 on the next page).

The classification of "comfort killer" was the most common, and it encompassed "black widows" or women who killed multiple spouses/paramours. However, this typology is built on an existing framework of male serial murder and thus fails to reflect the distinct experience and gendered nature of violence perpetrated by women (Farrell et al., 2013; Yardley & Wilson, 2015).

To date, only Kelleher and Kelleher (1998) have devised a typology strictly focused on FSKs. They stipulate that these women fall into two main categories: those who act alone and those who kill as part of a team. Of the women who kill solo, they identified five typologies representative of the broad spectrum of potential

TABLE 3.1 Holmes and Holmes's Classification of FSKs

Type of Killer	Characteristics
Visionary	• Kills are spontaneous. • Usually target random victims/strangers. • Suffer from severe psychopathology (psychosis). • Extrinsic motivation, typically a response to auditory hallucinations or delusional beliefs.
Comfort	• Planned and highly organized kills. • Motivated by material gain. • Target people with whom they are acquainted; victims are chosen according to the offender's anticipated gain.
Hedonistic	• Motivated by sexual gratification, sadism. • Acts tend to be planned and organized. • Target strangers, typically with specific characteristics.
Power-seeker	• Intrinsic motivation; the desire to dominate another person. • Crimes are planned and organized. • Murders serve to increase offender's self-esteem. • Most often target strangers with specific qualities (e.g., helpless).
Disciple	• Kill at the behest of a charismatic leader. • Internally motivated by the need for acceptance from this "idol." • Offenses are planned and organized. • Kill strangers who have been selected by the (typically male) leader.

Source: Adapted from Frei, Vollm, Graf, and Dittmann (2006).

(or probable) motives *when the perpetrator is legally sane* (Scott-Snyder, 2016):

- *Black widow*: These women *methodically* kill spouses, paramours, or other family members, and are motivated by financial gain (Vronsky, 2007).

- *Angel of death*: These killers murder people in their care. This typology is frequently associated with mercy killings and Munchausen syndrome by proxy.
- *Sexual predator*: These individuals commit serial sexual homicide. While females do kill for sexual gratification, males are more likely to commit sexually motivated serial murder (Hickey, 2006).
- *Revenge killer*: Revenge killers systematically target and kill people for the purpose of revenge. Jealousy is a common motive in this type of homicidal pattern.
- *Profit or crime killer*: These women kill for financial gain, but do not fall within the classification of the black widow.

Kelleher and Kelleher (1998) differentiate the aforementioned categories from team killers, and note that when a woman kills with one or more associates, her motive often becomes fused with or otherwise comingled with that of her partner(s). The identified subcategories for women who kill in tandem are those whose sanity is questionable, those with unexplained or unclear motives, and those whose crimes remain unsolved. Overall, the researchers found the greatest prevalence of team killers (28%) and black widows (26%).

Black Widows

The image of the beautiful but equally ruthless woman who uses her charm to get what she wants has long been a mainstay of literature and mythology, not to mention our society's collective unconscious. This motif has produced the reluctant belief that *if* a woman *is* in fact capable of killing, this act is limited to those close to her and only under very specific circumstances.

The news media has popularized the cultural icon of the black widow serial killer. These women kill three or more paramours or family members for the purpose of personal and/or monetary gain. Although they focus mainly on killing spouses and family members, they are capable of killing others with whom they have a personal relationship or who hinder their ability to attain their goal, as did Tillie Klimek. Black widows rarely target strangers, as it is their relationship with their victims that affords them the opportunity to kill.

These predatory women are named after the black widow spider because of their MO—their crimes are victim specific and systematic. They prey on the grieving and the lonely, literally and figuratively weaving an intricate web of deceit (Johnston, 2012a). As they lavish their target with affection and gifts, they quietly and steadily plot; they seduce men to render them helpless. Like the *Latrodectus*, these killers lull their victims into a false sense of security and attack when their target is most vulnerable.

Black widows are intelligent, manipulative, and organized. They are charming and socially skilled; their crimes depend on their ability to develop a substantial rapport with their victims, gain their trust, and get close enough to kill them without alarming anyone. They tend to poison their victims little by little over time, causing them to fall increasingly ill. Victims are often misdiagnosed and the black widows are assumed to be concerned caretakers, which, in turn, allows them to continue their attack. Once a victim succumbs, these women remain dormant for a period so as not to arouse suspicion (Kelleher & Kelleher, 1998).

The black widow's crimes are not random or careless. She is driven by a pathological desire to improve her circumstances, which usually translates to killing in order to collect life insurance proceeds or other assets. Such women can be conceptualized as a subtype of profit-motivated murderers—the female equivalent of the male hedonist comfort killer, who views others as expendable, enjoys the act of killing, and is motivated by material gain and a comfortable lifestyle. While people typically think of black widows as profit-motivated, some may kill for other reasons, such as vengeance or control, the acquisition of which improves the killer's lifestyle. In some instances, taking the victim's property or a relatively small sum of money is an expression of control rather than materialistic desire (Vronsky, 2007). Recall Tillie Klimek, who not only poisoned several husbands for profit, but who also killed a neighbor who accused her of said crimes. That particular murder served a dual purpose for Tillie: self-preservation and revenge. As you can see, black widows view murder as a reasonable means by which to better their lives.

The black widow is also driven to avoid apprehension and therefore attacks only when she needs (or wants) more money. If targeting spouses or immediate family members fails to yield the desired results, she may begin killing others with whom she has a personal relationship—and those she knows she can exploit. It is clear that the black widow has no regard for the emotional bond typically inherent in romantic or familial relationships. She enjoys her perceived role as confidante or caretaker and plays on this to escape detection. She is aware that societal bias stereotypes women as incapable of brutal and repetitive violence—and uses this to her advantage (Kelleher & Kelleher, 1998). The black widow carefully and deliberately portrays herself as the quintessential caring, nurturing female.

These women often begin their criminal career in their late 20s or early 30s and are the epitome of organized and successful (Kelleher & Kelleher, 1998). Because they begin killing relatively late in life, they bring with them experience and maturity. Their murders are precise and painstakingly planned, and their crimes reflect patience and draw little attention. On average, they kill for a period of a decade or sometimes more before they are apprehended or their crimes cease for another reason (such as illness, death, or incarceration for an unrelated matter).

Often because they have trusting relationships with their victims and present themselves as devoted caretakers, black widows subsist under law enforcement's radar. They frequently escape detection until the victim count has climbed significantly and/or the number of deaths within their inner circle cannot possibly be viewed as coincidental (Kelleher & Kelleher, 1998). However, even once a black widow is arrested, a conviction is not guaranteed. A 1995 study conducted by the U.S. Department of Justice found that female murder defendants are less likely to be convicted than men, and those who are found guilty typically receive lesser sentences. According to the Death Penalty Information Center (2017), only 16 women have been executed in the United States since 1976 (as compared with 1,427 men), and at least six of them were black widows (Investigation

Discovery Editors, n.d). After completing research that explored the blatant gender disparity in criminal sentencing at the federal level, Professor Sonja Starr noted that these differences could be due to society's perception that women are often more cooperative with the justice system than men, are complicit in their male paramour's crimes without being the principal offender, or are the primary caregiver for their children. Therefore, lengthy incarceration would place an undue burden on the family structure (Starr, 2012).

Risk Factors

Why does a woman become a serial killer—and more specifically a black widow? While there is a plethora of research on the backgrounds of male serial killers, similar literature on women is sparse. However, some investigation has been done into the biopsychosocial composition of FSKs. The profile that begins to emerge from these seminal studies may be applied to the black widow typology *with caution*.

History of Trauma

It is widely believed that a history of abuse is a contributing factor to serial murder perpetrated by men. However, it is unclear as to whether this holds true for females (Hickey, 2010; Keeney & Heide, 1994). In a study by Keeney and Heide (1994), five out of the eight FSKs surveyed reported having endured sexual abuse (rape and/or molestation) and five disclosed physical abuse. As can be inferred from these statistics, some of the women described having been abused *both* physically and sexually. However, a case study conducted by Frei and colleagues (2006) revealed *no* physical or sexual abuse during the subject's childhood, but rather implied that she had instead experienced neglect. Ostrosky-Solis and colleagues (2008) reviewed the case of another FSK who reported having been exposed to both physical and psychological abuse as a child. While generalizability from these small sample studies is severely limited, the findings suggest that the often traumatic disruption to normal development caused by abuse and/or neglect may be a contributing factor to serial homicidal violence by women.

In a larger study by Harrison and colleagues (2015), 20 out of 64 (31.5%) of FSKs examined had a history of physical and/or sexual abuse. In five of the cases, the subject experienced abuse in both spheres. For 70% of these individuals, the trauma occurred during childhood and was perpetrated by parents or grandparents, while the remaining 30% experienced maltreatment during adulthood at the hands of a spouse or other long-term paramour.

Childhood Issues

In addition to past trauma, various childhood issues could play a role in women's risk to commit serial murder. For example, Harrison and colleagues (2015) found that nearly 10% of the FSKs in their study had suffered from severe illness during childhood (including head injury/traumatic brain injury [TBI], scarlet fever, seizures, polio, blood poisoning, measles, or thyroid issues). To give this number greater context, the Centers for Disease Control and Prevention (2009) estimates that over the last 50 years between only 2% and 7% of children have had chronic ailments.

Close to 10% of Harrison's participants exhibited conduct difficulties such as lying, stealing, violent behavior, and cruelty during their formative years. While these girls were not necessarily diagnosed with conduct disorder, the prevalence of these behaviors was nearly one-third higher in this sample than in the general population (Nock et al., 2006). In 5% of cases, the FSK was pregnant and/or wed before the age of 16. Additionally, some of the women reported having had a mother (3%) or father (6%) who struggled with alcoholism; these statistics for males are equivalent to the general population of American men but higher compared to women (World Health Organization, 2012). In addition, significant family issues were highlighted, such as a controlling/coercive mother, an overly controlling father, a verbally or emotionally abusive mother who was insulting, an absent or deceased mother, an absentee father, a mother who was a prostitute, parental abandonment, parental remarriage, being one of five or more siblings, a strict religious upbringing, severe mental and/or physical abuse in the immediate family, and extreme poverty (Harrison et al., 2015).

Mental Health

In general, society believes that only individuals who are psychologically disordered are capable of heinous violence. According to Keeney and Heide (1994), that belief may hold true; in their sample of 14 FSKs, they found that the majority had been diagnosed with personality disorder (histrionic or borderline, specifically), bipolar disorder, or a dissociative disorder. It is important to note that with regard to headline-making crimes, mental illness may only be ascribed *after* the offender has been apprehended and publicly scrutinized.

Harrison and colleagues (2015) found that nearly 40% of the FSKs they studied were afflicted with a "severe mental illness." Specifically, two women had a diagnosis of Munchausen's syndrome by proxy (MSBP), while another had comorbid diagnoses of MSBP and schizophrenia. Two other subjects had a singular diagnosis of schizophrenia. Moreover, two FSKs exhibited symptoms of antisocial personality disorder (ASPD), while another woman was comorbid for ASPD and post-traumatic stress disorder (PTSD). It should be noted that ASPD is relatively uncommon among women, with only 1% of the general public accruing this diagnostic label (American Psychiatric Association, 2000; Lenzenweger et al., 2007). However, nearly 5% of women in this sample presented with ASPD, representing a nearly fivefold risk. Three other women in the study exhibited major depression and/or suicidal ideation. Interestingly, this is below the 6.7% prevalence of major depression among the general population of American women (Kessler et al., 2005), and directly contrasts with the results of Schurman-Kauflin's study (2000), which found that 87% of the FSKs analyzed suffered from depression.

In Harrison and colleagues' research (2015), a total of 25 women had mental health diagnoses, and nine of them had received prior intervention or treatment. Additionally, 23% of the sample had abused substances (illicit or prescription drugs and/or alcohol). Several of these FSKs exhibited evidence of psychological decompensation (e.g., psychotic breaks, suicide attempts, loss of control, dissociative episodes such as fugue states, etc.) just prior to the killings.

Problematic Sexual Behavior

Harrison and colleagues (2015) also noted that 12.5% of the women in their sample exhibited problematic sexual behavior. For instance, one had committed rape, two had engaged in deviant sexual acts such as autoerotic asphyxiation, three were "promiscuous," and another two had employed sex as a means by which to obtain money and drugs. Although data on relationship status was not available for all of the women, the authors determined that, at the time of their crimes, 54% were married, 15% were divorced, 13% were widowed, 8.5% were in committed relationships, and 8.5% were single. For those individuals who were or previously had been married, the women's number of marriages ranged from one to seven, with two being the average. Nearly one-quarter of them had been married three or more times. Additionally, the majority of FSKs studied were considered middle class (55%), with 40% being of "lower" socio-economic status, and slightly over 4% qualifying as "upper class."

Demographics

According to Kelleher and Kelleher (1998), the average age for FSKs at the time of their first kill is 30—2.5 years older than the average age for nascent male serial killers (Kraemer et al., 2004). Per the findings of Harrison and colleagues (2015), FSKs also exhibit considerable variation in academic achievement, with 35% possessing college or professional degrees, 19% having completed some college or other post-high-school training, 15% having graduated high school only, and 31% having dropped out of high school. For those individuals for whom intellectual ability information was available, 50% were of average intellect and 13% were considered highly intelligent. Twenty-nine percent had intellectual deficiencies, resulting in difficulties associated with low IQ. The women's occupations also proved diverse, as they ranged from teacher to caregiver (i.e., nurse, health aid, etc.), to prostitute, to psychic, to waitress, to homemaker.

Triggers/Antecedents

Harrison and colleagues (2015) found various antecedents to the FSKs' crimes, including environmental stressors, such as tension related to their husband's position in society, ridicule by family members, relinquishing of parental rights, and multiple pregnancies within the span of a year's time. Additionally, some of the women reported precursory crises, which may have triggered the murders. These included significant (romantic) relationship difficulties, family problems, unexpected pregnancy, job stress, and financial hardship. Accessible information additionally allowed the researchers to classify the demeanor of 31 FSKs as relevant to their offenses (see Table 3.2).

Case Studies

We've now laid a solid foundational basis for understanding the situational, environmental, psychological, and gender-specific factors that impact a woman's pathway toward becoming a black widow. The following vignettes depict some of the most famous of these killers. Each woman's story highlights her unique risk factors, stress responses, and subsequent acts of cruelty.

Judy Buenoano

Judy Buenoano clutched the hands of two correctional officers—one on each side—as she slowly entered the death chamber at Florida State Prison. Her head had been shaven and she looked almost frail in stark contrast to the life she had led. Crowds swarmed the prison grounds either in protest or support of the execution of "Florida's Black Widow." By 7:15 a.m. on March 30, 1998, the 54-year-old had become the first woman in the state to be put to death by electric chair since the 1800s.

Judy Buenoano (née Welty) was born in 1943 in Quanah, Texas, a small rural city approximately 200 miles north of Fort Worth. World War II began shortly thereafter, and Texas, with its fair climate and abundant resources, became the backdrop for many wartime facilities. Despite the medical advances of the 1930s, infectious diseases, specifically those spread socially and associated

TABLE 3.2 Categorizing the Demeanor of 31 FSKs

Description of Demeanor	Number of Presenting FSKs
Angry	1
Bizarre (e.g., attributing homicidal intent to "the devil" or publicly crying in "mourning" at her own victim's funeral)	6
Depersonalized, claiming to have had no control	1
Flat affect, withdrawn	8
Arrogant/flippant	3
Grandiose, describing herself in highly positive terms	2
Hyperactive	1
Serene	1
Sociopathological (meeting criteria for sociopathy; liking death and/or attending funerals of people with whom she was not acquainted)	7
Unstable	1

Source: Adapted from Harrison et al. (2015).

with war-torn nations (e.g., cholera, polio, malaria, and tuberculosis), were prevalent and resulted in a significant number of stateside fatalities.

During the early years of her life, Judy was raised by both of her parents in a socially conventional household. But when Judy was 4 years old, her mother died from tuberculosis, and she and her baby brother Robert were sent to live with their grandparents, while their two older siblings were given up for adoption. After their father remarried, Judy and Robert returned to live with him and his newly established family. However, it was not a peaceful reunion. Judy endured severe abuse at the hands of her father and stepmother; she was beaten, starved, burned with cigarettes, and forced to do manual labor around the house. At age 14, she was sentenced to 60 days in jail after scalding two of her stepbrothers with hot grease and physically assaulting her father and stepmother.

Rather than return home after completing her sentence, Judy asked the court to send her to a residential reform school.

At the time of her graduation in 1960, women faced a world of restrictions—expectations to marry young, start a family quickly, and resign themselves to being homemakers subservient to their husbands. Those women who did work were employed as nurses, teachers, or secretaries, and Judy was no exception. She became a nursing assistant and subsequently gave birth out of wedlock to a son named Michael.

Judy soon married James Goodyear, who was an officer in the U.S. Air Force. The couple had two children together, and James adopted Judy's son Michael. The family moved to Orlando, Florida, where Judy opened an in-home daycare center, while her husband continued to serve on active military duty. Three months following his return from deployment to Southeast Asia, James fell ill and was admitted to the U.S. Naval Hospital. Physicians were unable to reach a diagnosis, and on September 15, 1971, James died of apparent natural causes. Less than a week later, Judy cashed in his three life insurance policies, and before year's end, her home was destroyed in an "accidental" blaze, earning her another $90,000 in insurance reimbursement.

Less than a year after she was widowed, Judy began a relationship with Bobby Joe Morris. No one questioned her when she quickly decided to uproot herself and her children to move across the country to be with Bobby Joe; financial independence was out of reach for most women of that era, and thus social norms dictated that a woman *needed* a man to support her.

Shortly after Judy moved in with Bobby Joe in Colorado, he began suffering from an unidentified illness and was hospitalized on January 4, 1978. As was the case with Judy's former husband, doctors were unable to find the underlying cause of his symptoms and released him to Judy's care; 2 days later, he collapsed at home and was rushed back to the hospital where he later died. He had named Judy as his heir, and so she collected on his life insurance.

Although the cause of death was officially determined to be cardiac arrest and metabolic acidosis, Bobby Joe's family suspected

Judy of murder. They told of a visit paid to them by Bobby Joe and Judy in Brewton, Alabama, during which a male tourist from Florida was found dead in a nearby hotel. Discovered by police after an anonymous tip, the man had been shot in the chest and his throat had been slashed. After the news broke, Bobby Joe's mother overheard Judy telling her son that the man had gotten what he deserved and should never have shown up in Alabama in the first place. Later, Bobby Joe made a rambling statement on his deathbed in reference to the killing. Despite the circumstantial evidence, there was no concrete proof. Thus, Judy freely moved her family back to Florida, where she legally changed her last name to Buenoano, the Spanish equivalent of "Goodyear," in what some conjectured was a superficial tribute to her first husband and a brazen commentary on her belief that she could outsmart law enforcement.

Although she had successfully gotten away with murder twice, Judy had other challenges; her son Michael was becoming an increasing burden on her. As a youngster, he had exhibited behavioral problems in school and consistently scored in the dull-normal range on aptitude tests. James Goodyear's death had rendered Michael ineligible for benefits afforded to military dependents, including residential treatment, so Judy had temporarily signed him over to foster care. Michael's academic failure eventually led him to drop out of his sophomore year of high school; in 1979, he enlisted in the Army.

En route to his first duty station at Fort Benning, Georgia, Michael stopped to see his mother. The visit was brief, yet within days of his arrival in Georgia, he began to exhibit symptoms of what was believed to be metal toxicity. By the time he received medical attention, his exposure had been excessive and the damage could not be reversed. The muscles in his arms and legs quickly atrophied, causing paraplegia, and he soon required metal braces in order to walk. In 1980, he was discharged from the Army due to disability, and subsequently returned to his mother's home.

Shortly thereafter, Judy planned an outing for herself, Michael, and her other son. The three of them set out on a canoe trip along Florida's East River. Although Judy later offered various iterations of the day's events, including that the small boat suddenly capsized, it is believed that she threw Michael overboard. Weighted down by his leg braces, he was unable to swim ashore and drowned, leaving Judy to collect his $20,000 military life insurance policy.

No one questioned the grieving mother, who appeared the pillar of strength as she moved forward, opening a beauty salon and igniting a romantic liaison with a businessman named John Gentry. Their relationship progressed quickly, and by the fall of 1982 they were planning their wedding. Judy convinced John that they should each take out a life insurance policy—naming the other as the sole beneficiary. She also persuaded him to take "vitamins," but John's health only declined and he was admitted to the hospital.

After receiving treatment for his ambiguous symptoms, John was unsuspectingly discharged to his wife's care. Not long after returning home, he was nearly killed when his car exploded while he was out running errands. During the investigation that ensued, police questioned Judy and ultimately discovered that she had been intent on killing her husband and had been dosing him with arsenic long before she rigged his car. This revelation resulted in the exhumations of Judy's first husband, former lover, and son. Postmortem tissue analysis revealed that all had fallen victim to arsenic poisoning.

Judy was sentenced to death for the 1971 murder of her husband James Goodyear. She was also convicted of the murder of her son Michael Buenoano (1981) and the attempted murder of her fiancé John Gentry (1983). Although she was additionally assumed to be responsible for the 1978 death of her boyfriend Bobby Joe Morris, she was already on death row by the time that authorities connected her to this crime. Her involvement was likewise suspected in several other deaths, including that of another former boyfriend, Gerald Dossett. Judy's prior criminal history consisted of convictions for theft and arson as a means to collect insurance money.

***

Chapter 2 examined criminological theories from various perspectives (e.g., psychological, sociological, biological) in addition to highlighting the gender disparities that exist along the developmental pathways toward offending. A multitude of predisposing risk factors are blatant in Judy Buenoano's story. For instance, she lost her mother at age 4, a time when children are largely reliant upon their primary caregiver. Rather than being comforted and reassured by her father, Judy and her brother were sent away to be raised by relatives. This caused yet another significant loss and major disruption in not only Judy's emotional world, but also her cognitive script. In essence, the death of her mother represented a loss of security and her father's failure to protect her both physically and emotionally from this reshaped her understanding of trust, security, family, and love. She was literally and figuratively stripped of her security blanket at the age of 4.

Judy was then *again* uprooted and reunited with her father—the same man who failed to stabilize her and normalize the universal experience of the death of a parent for her at a young and critical age. This move back to her father's home was likely not only confusing and tumultuous in and of itself, but carried with it additional traumagenic dynamics. Judy's father and his new wife severely abused Judy, reinforcing the message that the world was not a safe and stable environment and that the people society deemed trustworthy in fact were not.

Judy went on to exhibit severe conduct problems, potentially as a result of having observed and modeled violence in her father's home. Her behavior resulted in court-mandated reform school. Children and adolescents with serious behavioral problems (conduct disorder) often feel a lack of control over their own lives and aim to exert control (aggressively) over others. A common theme throughout Judy's childhood and adolescence was a lack of control over her own circumstances. Her entire life, she had been unable to shield herself from the deepest of emotional (and physical) pain. This can cause a person to act out against others while simultaneously stunting their emotional connectivity and empathy; it is a coping mechanism.

As an adult, Judy encountered a parallel scenario in which both her autonomy and security were threatened, when society's gender-specific expectations clearly delineated that women should submit to men and assume submissive roles. She felt the strain of a life in which her material goals and her basic needs for safety and security were thwarted, and she turned to serial murder as the solution. One might view her entire life as a conditioning exercise during which she learned to devalue intimate and familial relationships; mistrust or avoid investing emotionally in others; and use manipulation, aggression, or violence as a means to an end.

Betty Lou Beets

Although we think of black widows as having three or more victims, the story of Betty Lou Beets seems relevant. Betty Lou Beets (née Dunevant) was born in North Carolina in 1917. Her birth occurred in the midst of World War I, 3 years prior to American women gaining the right to vote.

Much like Judy Buenoano, Betty faced significant difficulties at a young age. As a child, she developed the measles, which resulted in hearing loss. Despite being physically attractive, she endured bullying in school and had academic difficulties. Betty also claimed to have been sexually abused by her biological father. When Betty was 12 years old, she was thrust into the role of primary caretaker for her two younger siblings because her mother was institutionalized and her father was consumed with his work.

Betty left home at the age of 15 when she wed her first husband, Robert Franklin Branson. She claimed that their marriage was plagued by domestic and sexual violence, much as her relationship with her father had been. The couple therefore separated, only to reunite following Betty's subsequent suicide attempt. Their reconciliation, however, was not permanent. Six children and 16 years later, Betty and Robert divorced, and Betty began drinking heavily.

A year later, Betty married Billy York Lane. Like her father and ex-husband, Billy was abusive. During the course of one particular altercation, he hit Betty so hard that he broke her nose. In retaliation, she shot him. His wound was superficial, and ultimately the charges against Betty were dropped when Billy admitted that his behavior had precipitated the shooting. The couple soon divorced.

Betty was married a total of six times, twice to the same man. In addition to having shot Billy, she attempted to run down her third husband with her car; he survived the assault, and both men testified against her at trial.

In 1982, Betty married her fifth husband, Jimmy Don Beets. In August of 1983, Betty told Robert Branson (her son from a previous marriage) to leave the house because she was going to kill Jimmy. He obliged and upon his return found Jimmy's lifeless body on the floor; he had been shot to death. Robert helped his mother bury the corpse in the front yard of their Texas home. Betty then strategically called the police to report her husband missing. The next day, Betty planted some of her late husband's heart medication on his fishing boat and abandoned it in a nearby lake. A few days later, it washed ashore near Redwood Beach Marina, suggesting to police that Jimmy had fallen overboard and drowned. They dragged the lake to no avail.

Nearly 2 years later, the Henderson County Sheriff's Department received information that led to the 1985 arrest of Betty Lou Beets. When investigators executed a search warrant on the Beets family property, they found Jimmy's remains in a filled-in well. They also came upon the decomposing body of Doyle Wayne Barker entombed in the garage. Doyle had been Betty's fourth husband. Both men had been shot with a .38-caliber pistol and then stuffed into a sleeping bag.

Although Betty was never tried for the murder of Doyle, she was prosecuted for killing Jimmy Don. Her trial began in the summer of 1985. She pleaded not guilty and claimed that two of her children had in fact committed the murders. Both children ultimately admitted to having played a role in concealing their mother's crimes, and agreed to testify against her.

Betty Lou Beets was found guilty and sentenced to death by lethal injection in October of 1985. As she was remanded to the Texas Department of Corrections to await execution, protests erupted— was Betty a battered spouse or a black widow? Those in opposition to the death penalty, in conjunction with domestic violence activists, argued the former. Betty's lawyer urged the court to grant her clemency because of her history of abuse and the fact that her roster of victims contained only family members. However, this request was denied. When surveyed afterward, the jury supported the imposed sentence and noted: "She knew that her actions would cause Jimmy's death. She did it for the insurance money" (Clark County Prosecuting Attorney, n.d.).

On February 24, 2000, Betty Lou Beets became the second woman to be executed in Texas after the death penalty was reintroduced. She was 62 years old at the time of her death and had six children, nine grandchildren, and six great-grandchildren. Although none of her family chose to witness the execution, Jimmy Don Beets's son was in attendance. He noted that Betty didn't look frightened or remorseful as she was strapped to the gurney (CBS News, 2000).

Like Judy Buenoano, Betty Lou Beets had a history of childhood issues. However, the overriding factor when looking at the big picture appears to be her history of domestic violence. Domestic violence is commonly interlaced with feminist trajectories toward crime and violence. Its very nature is cyclical and it can escalate quickly. Victims are likely to experience ongoing abuse and prolonged trauma, including PTSD. Additionally, as in the case of Betty Lou, bidirectional violence in which both individuals engage in violent behavior is not uncommon. Moreover, it is important to note that mental health symptoms can be related to untreated trauma. In women especially, when (frequently childhood) trauma goes untreated, the individual can develop lifelong maladaptive coping responses akin to borderline personality features (e.g., instability in interpersonal relationships, suicidal ideation/self-harming behaviors, manipulativeness, antisocial behavior, impulsivity, anger, a general sense of discontentment, depression, a distorted self-image, unstable moods, etc.; psychosis may also be a symptom for some people). The timeline in Table 3.3 provides an overview of Betty Lou's trauma history, as well as the frequency of the instances of domestic violence and an outline of the murder timetable. It highlights the risk factors indicating instability during various time periods in Betty Lou's life.

TABLE 3.3 Betty Lou Beets: Life Events Timeline

Date	Age	Event
3/12/1937	0	Born in Roxboro, North Carolina
1940	3	Contracted measles, suffered hearing loss
1942	5	Sexually assaulted by father
1942	5	Moved from North Carolina to Virginia
1949	12	Left to care for younger siblings after mother had a psychotic break/was institutionalized
1952	15	Married first husband, Robert Branson
1953	16	Gave birth to first child (a daughter)
1953	16	Separated from husband
1953	16	Attempted suicide
1953	16	Reunited with Robert
1954	17	Gave birth to second child (a daughter)
1954	17	Moved to Texas
1959	22	Had third child (a daughter)
1962	25	Had fourth child (a daughter)
1964	27	Birth of fifth child (a son)
1966	29	Birth of sixth child (a son)
1969	31	Divorced Robert and began drinking
1970	33	Married for the second time (Billy York Lane)
1970	33	Filed a restraining order against Billy
1970	33	Divorced Billy
1971	34	Altercation where Billy broke Betty's nose
1972	34	Billy threatened to kill Betty and she shot him
1972	35	Remarried Billy; the marriage lasted 1 month
1973	36	Met Ronnie Threlkold
1978	41	Married Ronnie Threlkold
1978	41	Attempted to run Ronnie over with a car
1979	42	Began working as an exotic dancer
Date	Age	Event
1979	42	Divorced Ronnie Threlkold

(Continued)

TABLE 3.3 *(Continued)*

1979	42	Married Doyle Wayne Barker
1980	42	Serious car accident, TBI
1980	42	Divorced Doyle
1981	44	Killed Doyle and buried him in her front yard
1982	45	Married Jimmy Don Beets
1983	46	Murdered Jimmy
1984	47	Burned down Jimmy's house
1985	48	Filed for Jimmy's death certificate
1985	48	Arrested and indicted for Jimmy's murder
1985	48	Convicted and sentenced to death
2000	62	Executed at 6:18 p.m.

Source: Adapted from Beaber, Gomez, and Barber (n.d.).

Nannie Doss

Samuel Doss prided himself on being a strong Christian man who avoided temptation and the near occasion of sin. He was so devout that he forbade his wife from bringing a television or radio into their home for fear that they would be entertained by violent or sexually explicit programming. He even disapproved of his wife's affinity for romance novels. But Samuel was alone in these convictions, and his wife Nannie was quietly bothered by his idiosyncratic rigidity.

Shortly after the two married, Sam developed flu-like symptoms and was admitted to the hospital. He vomited violently, a fact that probably saved his life, at least temporarily. Following a month of emergency medical treatment, he was stable and released into the care of his wife. Within 24 hours, however, he was dead. Given Sam's abrupt decline, an autopsy was ordered. Results revealed large amounts of arsenic in his system.

Once the investigation was underway, police in Tulsa, Oklahoma, received information that prompted them to focus their attention on Sam's wife Nannie. Anonymous tips suggested that Sam was not the first person in Nannie's inner circle to die without any obvious cause or while under Nannie's care. Armed with this new information, investigators questioned Nannie at length. Although she initially denied any involvement in her husband's death, she began to display incongruous behavior as the interrogation continued. For example, she burst into several intermittent fits of laughter and further admitted that she had lied to doctors and law enforcement about multiple aspects of her husband's death. Approximately 7 hours into her discussion with police, Nannie faltered and admitted that she had fatally poisoned Sam. He was annoying, she claimed, and as if it reasonably excused the act of premeditated murder, she noted that she hadn't realized what she was getting herself into when she'd married him.

Once she signed her confession for the murder of Samuel Doss, police guided Nannie in a strategic conversation about the demons of her past, canvassing for information about other murders. It was later noted that her jovial demeanor appeared both to contradict and to make a mockery of the brutality of her crimes. She was nicknamed the "Giggling Granny."

* * *

Nannie was born in Blue Mountain, Alabama, in 1905 and was one of five children (four sisters and one brother). She despised her father, whom she characterized as austere and overly controlling. He forced Nannie and her siblings to work on the family farm in lieu of attending school, so she never learned to read very well. When she was 7 years old, the family took a trip to southern Alabama. During their journey, the train stopped suddenly and Nannie's head hit the metal bar on the seat in front of her, resulting in a TBI. From that point forward, she suffered from headaches, frequent blackouts, and nearly debilitating depression.

As a young child, Nannie was imaginative. She treasured memories of reading her mother's romance novels and, like many little girls, daydreamed about meeting her one true love. However, as she and her sisters blossomed into teenagers, their father refused to allow them to wear makeup or stylish clothing or to attend dances and other social functions. He couched these restrictions in terms of requisite protective measures to prevent the girls from being sexually abused by men. In a time when females were already constrained by gender inequality and social strata, Nannie was even further stifled by her father's strict rules. She was repeatedly sent the message that females were responsible to not only remain chaste and proper, but to also prevent males from victimizing them—a frightening and disheartening message for a young woman whose ambition was to find true love.

When Nannie was 16, she met Charles "Charley" Braggs, of whom her father swiftly approved. The two wed after a brief courtship, and Nannie moved in with Charley and his mother, who was as overbearing and domineering as her own father. Nannie's mother-in-law controlled much of the young couple's life and demanded a startling amount of attention from her newlywed son. Nannie's union with Charley produced four children in rapid succession, and Nannie became progressively stressed. She began drinking and smoking compulsively. Both she and Charley engaged in extramarital affairs, which had a deleterious effect on their marriage.

Within 6 years, the marriage had completely fallen apart. In addition to their unfaithfulness, Nannie and Charley had endured struggles that had further divided them. Two of their children had died from what had appeared to be food poisoning. But when Charley received an anonymous tip warning him not to consume any food that his wife prepared, he thought the worst. Without a word, Charley fled the home with the couple's oldest daughter in tow. He would soon become the only man to survive a marriage to Nannie.

When questioned about Charley, Nannie noted that the two had married at her father's behest. Before she realized what was happening, Charley's mother had completely taken over her life—and she was miserable.

It wasn't long before the dissolution of her first marriage led Nannie to place a personal ad in a "lonely hearts" column. She began corresponding with a factory worker named Frank Harrelson. At first, Nannie found his poetic letters to be charming and romantic, and the two were married in 1929. Like Charley, however, Frank disappointed Nannie.

Marital difficulties erupted in large part due to Frank's alcoholism and violent nature. Prior to meeting Nannie, he had been convicted of assault, which he failed to disclose to her. On one occasion, he forced Nannie to have sex with him against her will. The next day, while tending the garden, Nannie uncovered a jar of moonshine that Frank had hidden. After topping it off with rat poison, she reburied it in its hiding spot, and waited. One can only assume that Nannie found satisfaction in her use of Frank's secret vice as a murder weapon—as though she had beaten him at a game of cat and mouse that he didn't know they were playing. Her tactic was inherently manipulative and covertly callous. The couple's marriage lasted a total of 16 years, and Frank's death was officially attributed to food poisoning.

In 1943, Nannie's eldest daughter Melvina gave birth to a son. While in a state of physical and emotional exhaustion as well as hormonal fluctuation following childbirth, Melvina reported that she thought she had witnessed Nannie puncture her baby's skull with a hatpin. Although the infant was in fact pronounced dead, doctors were unable to confirm the cause. So, while Nannie had reportedly been seen cradling the child's limp body in one hand while holding a hatpin in the other, Melvina's recollection of the events was malleable. Without definitive evidence against Nannie, Melvina quickly repaired her relationship with her mother, so much so that she sporadically relied on Nannie to provide care for her other children. Two years later, Melvina's other son died while in Nannie's charge. Nannie later collected a life insurance policy that she'd taken out on the little boy.

Nannie's third husband was Arlie Lang. Like his predecessor, he was a philanderer who liked to drink. Nonetheless, Nannie played the doting wife. She was so believable in this role that when Arlie died of what was deemed to be heart failure, neighbors turned out in droves at his funeral in support of Nannie. The couple's house, which Arlie had left to his sister, soon burned down, and again Nannie was left to collect the insurance money. Before Nannie could be linked to any wrongdoing, she fled the state (North Carolina) and sought refuge at her sister Dovie's home. Dovie was ill and bedridden and thankful for Nannie's offer to take care of her. Dovie died shortly after Nannie's arrival.

***

Under questioning, Nannie confessed to the killing of 11 people in total—four husbands, two sisters, two children, one grandson, one mother-in-law, and her own mother. Her killings began in the 1920s and spanned 2 decades and four states. Detectives noticed that each time she disclosed a new homicide, she undermined her acceptance of responsibility by denying trivial details about the offense. Although she collected insurance payouts for many of her victims, Nannie maintained that her crimes were not financially motivated. Instead, she reported that the murders had been borne of marital boredom and her desire to fulfill an evasive romantic fantasy: finding her true soul mate.

In the case of Nannie Doss, it is impossible to ignore the fact that she suffered a TBI as a child and thereafter exhibited drastic changes in personality, mood, and impulse control. She also had a history of childhood issues; her father was overbearing and stifled her access to social opportunities, which were important to Nannie as she romanticized her future husband and often fantasized about what her life would become once she met him. Children, especially those who have experienced trauma, sometimes use fantasy as a means of escape; it is a coping strategy.

The way that Nannie was socialized—because she was a girl—directly conflicted with her unrealistic (and young-minded) dream of meeting her true love, whom she believed would be the picture of perfection. It is worth noting that because Nannie's access to education was also obstructed, and she was forced into overwhelming adult situations for which she was ill-prepared (e.g., marriage and motherhood) during her teen years, she was not afforded the opportunity to achieve emotional maturation. In other words, her romantic ideals were childlike and fantasy driven; she had a "happily ever after" vision of her future and likely never gained adult perspective. This fact, coupled with the lasting effects of her brain injury and the trauma of domestic violence, likely left Nannie to view anyone who stood in the way of her fantasy as threatening and thus dispensable.

TABLE 3.4 A Comparison of FSK Risk Factors

	Judy Buenoano	Betty Lou Beets	Nannie Doss
Risk Factors			
Childhood sexual abuse		X	
Physical abuse	X	X	
Psychological abuse	X	X	X
Conduct difficulties	X		
Pregnant or wed prior to age 16			
Alcoholic parent		X	
Domineering mother			
Controlling father		X	X
Childhood illness/TBI		X	X
Early school failure		X	
Peer rejection		X	
Absent or deceased mother	X	X	
Absentee father			
Parental remarriage	X		
One of five or more siblings			
Strict religious upbringing			
Triggers/Antecedents			
Educational deficit		X	
Domestic violence		X	X
Sexual violence		X	
Alcohol/drug abuse		X	
Relationship difficulties	X	X	X
Job loss			
Financial hardship			

Conclusion

As a result of gendered stereotypes, women have long been regarded as incapable of serious and repetitive violence. The idea of a woman committing serial murder was almost inconceivable because the very nature of serial homicide violated the convention of femininity; women were *supposed* to be inherently nurturing. They were society's caretakers.

Even once the anomaly of the female serial killer was recognized, her sheer cunning and brutality was lost, muddled among minimizations of her killing methods as "neat" and "clean." She was widely characterized as less brutal than her male counterparts because of her lack of overt violence, when in reality her tactics only served to protract her victims' suffering.

The black widow, perhaps the most iconic of the female serial killer subtypes, has been a fixture in film and television for decades, and with good reason. She is perhaps the most frightening of all serial killers, male or female. Unlike male serial killers who target strangers, the black widow kills people close to her. She manipulates their perception of her to gain access to them and to earn their trust; she often uses gender expectations to her benefit and ultimately lures her victims into her literal and psychological web. She creates a very personal and intense world of suffering for her victims, who often die without the closure of knowing that she breached their trust in the most vile way.

Munchausen Murders and Angels of Death

Chapter 4

Garnett's Journey

"I love children," Lacey Spears told *48 Hours* in her first postconviction prison interview. "They're our future. They should be loved and cared for." One year prior, Lacey had been found guilty of murdering her 5-year-old son Garnett.

Garnett Spears was born on December 3, 2008, in Decatur, Alabama. According to Lacey, he was a sickly baby who suffered from ear infections, and rarely ate but yet vomited regularly. He spent the better part of the first 2 months of his life in the hospital, where he was diagnosed with failure to thrive.

At 9 weeks old, Garnett underwent his first stomach surgery, but his improvement was brief and he struggled with severe dehydration. When he was 9 months old, he had another surgery, this time to insert a feeding tube (G-tube) to pump nutrients directly into his stomach. However, Garnett's condition failed to make steady improvement. As a result, his doctor and hospital visits became routine. However, because Lacey frequently relocated them, Garnett was often forced to change doctors, and thus his treatment providers never got the full picture; he lacked critical continuity of care.

When Garnett was 2 years old, he and Lacey moved to Florida. By the time he was 3, they were living in New York. Throughout this time, his health had continued to deteriorate, and Lacey sought treatment for him from an entirely new group of New York–based medical specialists. Among them was a pediatric gastroenterologist who asked Lacey to provide all of Garnett's medical documentation; she never did. Additionally, the doctor recommended that a battery of tests be run to see whether Garnett's feeding tube could be removed. Although Lacey agreed to some of the more invasive tests, she refused to allow Garnett to undergo basic nutritional testing. The doctors began to question whether Lacey herself had induced Garnett's illness.

Then, in January 2014, Garnett came down with a headache and fever. Lacey rushed him to the pediatrician, but no underlying medical issue was found, and within a few days he seemed better. But his condition once again worsened as suddenly as it had eased, and he was rushed to New York's Nyack Hospital with seizure-like symptoms. Although Lacey reported that Garnett had seized while in the hospital waiting room, not a single person had witnessed it. Physiological examination concluded that no seizure activity had occurred. Nonetheless, Garnett was admitted.

Shortly thereafter, Garnett coded. Emergency testing revealed that while his sodium level had been 138 upon admission, it had skyrocketed to 182. He was airlifted to the children's hospital at Westchester Medical Center, but the damage was permanent. His brain had swelled, and within 48 hours he was brain dead and on life support. Doctors determined that the only way Garnett's sodium level could have gotten so high was if someone had purposely administered large doses of table salt to him—directly through his feeding tube. They quickly realized that Lacey had remained by Garnett's bedside throughout the duration of his hospitalization. On January 23, 2014, Garnett died and authorities began to unravel a highly publicized tale of mental illness and deception.

* * *

Throughout Garnett's life, Lacey had frequently taken to social media to chronicle his medical issues and the difficulties of being a single mother. To many, her rhetoric was heartbreaking, but to others, it seemed to be a cry for attention. On September 18, 2012, she posted the following passage to her blog entitled "Garnett's Journey" (2012): "We have together survived nearly 365 days, a complete year without Blake, my soulmate and Garnett's Daddy." On its face, it was a benign message. However, no one outside of Lacey's online followers had ever heard of Blake—not her friends and certainly not her family. Garnett's biological father was Chris Hill, a neighbor with whom Lacey had had a brief sexual relationship. When Lacey became pregnant, Hill proposed marriage, but she abruptly ended the relationship. Despite his repeated attempts to reconnect with her and Garnett, Lacey cut Hill out of her life. It was not until the day after Garnett passed that Lacey even accepted a friend request from Hill on Facebook.

* * *

During the course of the investigation, Lacey's neighbor Valerie Plauche came forward with damning evidence. In an attempt to help soothe Lacey's grief following Garnett's death, Valerie had offered to help out in any way necessary. Lacey subsequently asked her to dispose of the feeding bags she'd used to feed Garnett through his G-tube. Of course, Valerie complied, assuming that seeing them was too painful for Lacey, but she had second thoughts when she learned of the suspicious circumstances under which Garnett had died. Valerie turned the bags over to investigators, who found high levels of sodium in them.

* * *

Perhaps if Lacey and Garnett had not moved from place to place (and doctor to doctor), the red flags would have come to light earlier. For instance, investigators discovered a medical report that noted that Lacey had disclosed that she wanted to harm her child. Another report indicated that Garnett's symptoms included bleeding from his eyes and ears—sans medical causation. And then there was his unexplained high sodium level on more than one occasion. However, because Lacey made certain that none of the doctors had consistent contact with Garnett, her pattern of abuse did not emerge until it was too late. To the outside world, Lacey maintained the appearance of a concerned and doting mother.

* * *

Following a 14-day trial, Judge Robert Neary sentenced Lacey to a custodial term of 20 years to life. In his ruling, he said that it was clear Lacey suffered from a mental illness known as Munchausen syndrome by proxy, and he therefore did not impose the maximum sentence. To this day, Lacey maintains her innocence, denies having a psychological disorder, and is adamant that her son's death was the result of a medical mishap.

Munchausen and Munchausen by Proxy

Factitious disorder (imposed on self) is a psychological disorder in which someone deceives others by feigning illness, purposely making him- or herself sick, or inflicting self-injury. Symptoms can be mild (e.g., slight exaggeration of physical ailments) or severe (e.g., purposely eating contaminated food to cause food poisoning). Those people presenting with the latter extreme are often considered to have Munchausen syndrome. Although not a formal diagnosis, Munchausen is viewed as a subclassification or extreme variant of factitious disorder. Some individuals who fall into this category may go so far as to tamper with medical tests, purposely endanger themselves by making themselves sick, or undergo unnecessary and risky medical procedures to convince others of the existence (or severity) of their condition (Mayo Clinic Staff, 2017). Richard Asher (1951) named the constellation of aforementioned symptoms after the legendary Baron von Munchhausen, who was known for fabricating stories and telling tall tales. His fictional concoctions, although overly dramatic and illusory, were jarringly convincing.

When a person with factitious disorder makes *someone else* sick, as did Lacey Spears, it is referred to as factitious disorder (imposed on another), previously factitious disorder by proxy. As with Munchausen, the severe form of this ailment is commonly referred to as Munchausen syndrome by proxy (MSBP). People with MSBP typically induce symptoms of illness in children or others under their care, and for that reason it often manifests as a form of child abuse. In such instances, the child may have a history of numerous hospitalizations, multiple treatment providers in multiple locations (usually in different cities and/or states), symptoms that are reported by the perpetrator (usually the mother) but not witnessed by hospital staff, and/or clinical test results that conflict with the reported ailments. These child victims often receive extensive and unnecessary medical care because the person with MSBP misrepresents symptoms to healthcare professionals, manipulates test results, or purposely harms (poisoning, suffocation, etc.) to create an onset of symptoms (Stirling, 2007).

Differentiating Factitious Disorders

Factitious disorders are particularly difficult to diagnose because they involve inherently deceptive behavior. Unlike with some somatic disorders, such as hypochondriasis, individuals with a factitious disorder are aware that the medical condition (in themselves or their victims) does not actually exist. However, they may be unaware as to their motivation(s) for fabricating said illness (Mayo Clinic Staff, 2017). For instance, Lacey Spears blogged about her son's fabricated illness. She used society's gender role expectations to exploit her position as a single mother and "caretaker" to garner sympathy from her online following. The question is whether her pathological need for attention was a conscious one.

Before the differential diagnosis of factitious disorder can be made, delusional disorder must be ruled out. Individuals with a delusional disorder hold one or more non-bizarre delusions, such as the belief that they (or someone close to them) are being poisoned or have an illness, despite evidence to the contrary. Factitious disorders may also be confused with malingering, which is the intentional exaggeration or fabrication of symptoms to reap a material benefit. Some common external motivations that drive people to malinger include insurance fraud, obtaining prescriptions for controlled substances (often to sell on the street or to fuel an addiction), worker's compensation, or the avoidance of incarceration for criminal activity. People with a factitious disorder do not appear to be motivated by such material gains. Rather, their behaviors are frequently associated with attention seeking. It is of note that malingering, unlike factitious disorders, is not in and of itself a mental illness, but rather a purposeful act of deception. Table 4.1 provides further comparison among factitious disorders, malingering, and delusional disorder.

TABLE 4.1 Differentiating Factitious Disorders

	Factitious Disorders	Malingering	Delusional Disorder
Results in the reporting of illness that does not actually exist	X	X	X
The exaggeration or feigning of illness/injury in self	X	X	
The exaggeration or feigning of illness/injury in another	X		
The production of symptoms in self or others (inducing illness)	X		
Examinations do not yield an underlying medical cause	X	X	X
Behavior is inherently deceptive	X	X	
Involves the belief that the illness is real			X
Behavior is motivated by material gain		X	
Behavior is motivated by the need for attention	X		
Considered a mental illness	X		X

Correctly attributing a child's symptoms to MSBP can be challenging. Before a conclusion regarding the presence of MSBP can be drawn, actual physical illness of the child must be ruled out.

Similarly, so should a delusional disorder of the caregiver. The physician must question whether the child's medical history as well as the signs and symptoms of disease are credible. Additionally, it must be determined whether the child is receiving unnecessary medical treatment and, if so, who is requesting or initiating those procedures (Stirling, 2007). With the attention given to cases like that of Lacey Spears, a cluster of potential indicators of MSBP has come to the fore. For a list of factors that may create suspicions about the presence of MSBP, see Table 4.2.

TABLE 4.2 Indicators of MSBP

Suspect that a child is an MSBP victim when . . .
• A child has a history of hospitalizations due to strange or unexplained symptoms.
• One or more children in the same family have died from or presented with an unusual or unexplained ailment.
• Medical tests indicate that there are chemicals in the child's blood, stool, or urine.
• The child's symptoms improve during hospitalization but recur or worsen after returning home to the mother/caretaker.
• The child's lab tests are tampered with (e.g., a blood sample positive for a specific disease does not match the child's blood).
• The child's symptoms don't match the test results or seem to fit any known disease.
Suspect that a caretaker is an MSBP offender when . . .
• She reports symptoms that do not align with test results, medical observation, or collateral information.
• She starves the child based on the claim that the child has severe food allergies, none of which the child has tested positive for.
• She repeatedly reports that the child has been sexually victimized despite any evidence to support such abuse.
• She engages in attention-seeking behavior.
• She appears self-sacrificing and devoted, and refuses to leave the child.
• She is overly involved with doctors and medical staff and appears to enjoy the hospital environment/attention given to her and the child.

Prevalence of MSBP

Reliable statistics on the prevalence of MSBP are not available due in large part to its duplicitous nature. People with this illness do not typically admit that they have it. Complicating matters is the fact that caretakers with the disorder tend to seek treatment for their victims at a variety of healthcare facilities, making it difficult to cross-reference. However, the Cleveland Clinic estimates that roughly 1,000 of the 2.5 million cases of child abuse that are reported each year may be related to MSBP. In 10% of these cases, MSBP leads to the death of the victim (Pietrangelo & Krucik, 2016).

Because parents and caretakers often seem concerned with and invested in the child's treatment, cases of MSBP are likely underestimated. Moreover, the disordered individuals often possess the ability to manipulate others, including doctors, nurses, and psychologists. In fact, approximately 25% of MSBP offenders meet criteria for Munchausen, having previously induced illness in themselves (Pietrangelo & Krucik, 2016).

The vast majority of child abuse stemming from MSBP is perpetrated by women, specifically mothers. The frequency of maternal perpetrators is likely linked to the fact that they more often assume the role of primary caretaker; however, there is not believed to be a gender-based predisposition to MSBP. Individuals with MSBP target both male and female children, usually under the age of 4. It is probable that the rate at which MSBP occurs is miscalculated because the disorder often is not accurately identified in association with someone's first victim. From the time of onset, it may take upwards of 2 years for the behavioral pattern associated with MSBP to be properly classified. Once a diagnosis is made, it is common to discover that siblings of the known victim have died from unexplained or atypical causes or have experienced similar abuse (Dryden-Edwards & Shiel, 2016).

Theory

MSBP is a controversial and poorly understood phenomenon. Although the exact cause is unknown, various theories about its etiology have emerged. Similar to the broader spectrum of criminological perspectives presented in Chapter 2, most of these models view biological, psychological, and environmental factors as critical in the development of MSBP and its resulting offense behavior. For instance, some researchers suggest that situational elements, such as child abuse/neglect and the early loss of a parent, may be relevant (Table 4.3). Some evidence supports the idea that the presence of major stressors, such as marital discord, can trigger the onset of MSBP. Theories about what the MSBP offender gains by assuming the sick role through their child highlight this perpetrator's pathological need for attention, possible addiction to interactions with high-ranking physicians, and need for control, likely as a result of a constellation of psychological, environmental, and emotional risk factors.

TABLE 4.3 Risk Factors for the Development of MSBP

• Childhood trauma (e.g., emotional, physical, or sexual abuse), causing them to see the hospital as a safe space • Serious illness during childhood (that they are reliving through factitious behavior) • History of factitious behavior
• A relative with a serious illness (with whom they identify) • The loss of a loved one through death, illness, or abandonment in childhood • Exposure to a parent's factitious behavior

• Poor self-esteem or lack of self-identity
• Depression or substance abuse
• Personality disorder (especially borderline)
   o Risks for borderline personality disorder include the following:
     ■ History of abuse
     ■ Abandonment in childhood or adolescence
     ■ Disrupted family life
     ■ Lack of communication in family of origin

• Unfulfilled desire to be a doctor/nurse • Inability to trust authority figures such as doctors • Career in the healthcare industry

Individuals with MSBP are considered vulnerable to other psychiatric conditions and may present with one or more comorbid illnesses, including depression, anxiety, or a personality disorder (frequently borderline). People with personality disorders engage in a persistent pattern of maladaptive behaviors, which often correlate with an inability to form healthy social bonds. Similarly, persons with MSBP have difficulty forging and maintaining relationships and utilizing adaptive coping mechanisms. Some individuals with MSBP may additionally present with psychopathic personality features (Proops & Seibert, 2009).

MSBP perpetrators experience difficulty forming an appropriate attachment to their children and managing negative emotions, such as anger and frustration. They have the ability to overcome their instinctual maternal (or caregiver) tendency to protect the children under their care.

While acknowledging psychopathologic comorbidity, some theorists posit that MSBP is most accurately described as medical abuse (Boros et al., 1995; Lesaca, 1995), wherein perpetrators "engage in the behavior willingly, not under the influence of some uncontrollable impulse and with full knowledge that it is wrong" (Boros et al., 1995, p. 773). Clearly, MSBP offenders *do* commit medical abuse. But is it that simple?

Psychodynamically oriented researchers have sought to explain the motivation of these perpetrators in terms of the child victim as the object through which the MSBP offender regulates an "intensely ambivalent but often destructive relationship with a physician" (Schreier & Libow, 1994, p. S110). Bursten (1965) suggests that the Munchausen patient is acting out sexual and aggressive impulses due to unresolved Oedipal conflicts, which easily lend themselves to the doctor–patient relationship. That is, to resolve early frustration and trauma, the MSBP patient seeks love and approval from the symbolic object (i.e., the physician) "as well as revenge through superiority and hostility expressed by the knowledge of the deception" (Spiro, 1968). The individual reasserts (her) control by producing and then terminating symptoms. While this framework was developed specifically to address Munchausen syndrome, it can be assumed that a sufferer of MSBP would reap the same emotional and psychological benefits by inducing illness in her child (Riser, 2011).

MSBP: An Evolutionary Perspective

Saad (2010) describes the existence of MSBP from an evolutionary stance. According to the parental investment hypothesis, mothers are more heavily invested in providing for their offspring and therefore should logically be more vested in the well-being of their children than their mates. This theory supports the idea that a mother's love for her children is interminable and her drive to protect them insurmountable. However, for a small portion of women who suffer from specific personality disorders *and* who lack the requisite support from their husbands/male partners, maternal instinct is subverted by a narcissistic need for attention—particularly from high-status male physicians. The fact that the sex-specificity of MSBP persists across time and culture lends credence to this theory.

MSBP: A Developmental Deviation

Some theorists view factitious illness as a deviation from the normative developmental progression. As humans, we initially focus on "taking and self" and then mature to focus more heavily on "giving and selflessness." However, MSBP offenders use deception as a way of taking—by forcing others to give them the attention they crave. According to Meadow (1993), some MSBP mothers harbor feelings of hatred toward their own children. This resentment stems from the contrast between the child's happiness and the mother's history of suffering, abuse, or distress during childhood. The mother's focus on self allows her to view this disparity as an indication that the child is purposely hurting her in some way. Other MSBP mothers view their children as imposing limitations on their own personal or professional lives, which is also an example of emphasizing self over selflessness (Rand & Feldman, 2001/2002).

The social narrative dictates that a woman's developmental trajectory *should* include motherhood. Women are socialized to prioritize having children over having successful careers, and women who do not wish to become mothers are often labeled selfish or otherwise reproached by society. For women with unresolved childhood trauma, the thought of such rejection is particularly painful. They may therefore give in to this pressure and become mothers despite wanting to pursue other avenues. Their feelings of powerlessness and regret may manifest as resentment and hatred toward their children and symptoms of MSBP may begin to emerge. From this perspective, the gender specificity of MSBP is almost unavoidable.

MSBP: A Learned Behavior

While acknowledging the popularity of other theories, Rand and Feldman (2001/2002) suggest a behavioral approach to understanding MSBP. By broadening the scope of more conventional schemes, they place the emphasis on observable behaviors and verifiable background factors. In their research, they spoke with a woman, whom we'll call "Ms. A." She reported having engaged in factitious behavior during childhood and early adulthood as a means of escaping from problems that were too difficult to confront. In her case, she enjoyed the attention that she received from assuming the sick role, but also felt that the painful medical procedures were punishment for past wrongs.

When Ms. A. went on to have children, she bore a daughter, followed by twin sons, one of whom was stillborn. She was paralyzed by the fear that her other children were going to die, so she began to emotionally detach herself from them. This lack of emotional connection allowed her to do things to make them sick. She reportedly believed that if her children were admitted to the hospital, they would be safe. The authors submit that Ms. A.'s mother likely modeled medical deception, which Ms. A. was rewarded for participating in beginning at a young age. She learned that she could benefit from using similar factitious presentations with her own children (Rand & Feldman, 2001/2002).

Conditioning plays a significant role in the concept of learned factitious behavior. For example, when a child feigns illness and is rewarded with attention from the parent, caretaker, etc., said behavior is reinforced. The individual's needs (for attention, love, control, relief from certain responsibilities, etc.) are met through playing the sick role. In some instances, the afflicted person feels empowered by her ability to trick high-ranking physicians. The correlation between these behaviors and positive gain lays the foundation for future MSBP (Artingstall, 1999).

MSBP: A Three-Part Behavioral Model

Based on their research, Rand and Feldman (2001/2002) propose a behavioral model of MSBP consisting of three parts: drive, breakdown of internal inhibitions, and neutralization of external inhibitions. Drive refers to the intent to ameliorate negative feelings, known as dysphoric drive states (e.g., anger, anxiety, envy, loneliness, inadequacy, resentment, and fear). Relief is achieved by harming the child (i.e., making him or her sick), and then concealing the abuse. Drive states may be heightened by or associated with both positive and negative feelings that mothers typically have toward their children. This intensity can create cognitive and perceptual distortions.

A breakdown of internal inhibitions refers to the fact that the MSBP offender lacks the maternal instinct that would typically prevent her from harming her child. Due to a deficit in empathic concern or attachment, the MSBP perpetrator is able to depersonalize the child. Factors that contribute to this collapse include the offender's experience of self-harm, factitious illness behavior, antisocial behavior, and the intensity of the drive to commit the abuse (Rand & Feldman, 2001/2002).

In addition to internal inhibitors, people in the child's life (such as the child's father or primary care doctor) might act as external inhibitors of MSBP abuse. However, MSBP offenders carefully select people whom they view as vulnerable to their manipulation in order to fulfill these roles. If we refer back to the Lacey Spears case, it is clear that she chose Chris Hill to father her child because she knew that she would be able to easily control how much (if any) access he had to their son. The neutralization of external inhibitions is a hallmark feature of MSBP behavior.

The researchers posit that each time the MSBP offender experiences the drive, surmounts internal and external inhibitions, achieves the desired emotional release, and successfully manipulates others to get away with the abuse, the MSBP behavior is reinforced. In other words, they hypothesize that these three factors reinforce each other, thus creating "habit strength" (Hull, 1943, 1951), or the likelihood that the behavior will persist due to successive reinforcement.

Marybeth Tinning and MSBP

As she stood before the parole board for the sixth time, 74-year-old Marybeth Tinning was asked how the deaths of her children had impacted her. "It's just made me hollow inside," she said. Marybeth was convicted of the December 20, 1985, murder of her 3-month-old daughter Tammi Lynn—the ninth of the Tinning children to die within a 14-year span. She is currently serving 20 years to life at the Bedford Hills Correctional Facility for Women where she was again denied parole (Cook, 2017).

**

Marybeth (née Roe) and her husband Joseph Tinning met on a blind date in 1963 and were married 2 years later. Together, they had eight biological children and adopted another. During their first 5 years of marriage, Marybeth gave birth to a daughter Barbara and a son Joseph. Then, in December of 1971, she bore a third child, Jennifer. Jennifer was only a few days old when she was diagnosed with meningitis; she died without ever leaving the hospital. She is the only one of the Tinning children thought to have died from natural causes.

Less than 1 month after Jennifer's death, Marybeth brought 2-year-old Joseph to the hospital claiming that he'd had a seizure. Doctors monitored him, but found no underlying medical issues and sent him home. Within hours, Marybeth returned to the emergency room with the toddler, who was dead on arrival. According to Marybeth, she'd put him to bed, but when she returned to check on him he was blue. Without the benefit of an autopsy, doctors determined that the cause of death had been "seizure disorder" brought on by acute infection.

Six weeks later, Marybeth was back in the emergency room, this time with Barbara. Although doctors wanted to keep the child overnight for observation and testing, Marybeth took her home. A few hours later, Marybeth returned with Barbara, who was rapidly declining; she died later that day.

Having lost three children in 3 months, Marybeth garnered the sympathy and support of friends and neighbors and she appeared to bask in the attention.

In November of 1973, Marybeth gave birth to her fourth child; within a month he was dead. Then, in the spring of 1975, she birthed her fifth child, and by the fall of that same year he also died without warning or explanation. People began to question whether there was something genetically wrong with the Tinning children that caused them to die suddenly and at such an early age. Marybeth and her husband submitted to numerous medical tests, despite the fact that there was no known genetic condition to cause such problems. Rumors even surfaced that there was a curse—a "death gene"—in the Tinning lineage.

In late 1978, the Tinnings adopted an infant son named Michael, and Marybeth birthed another daughter in rapid succession. As if following a script, their daughter died within months and Marybeth once again became pregnant. Shortly after that child was born, she brought him to the hospital, where doctors revived him. Due to the lengthy history of inexplicable infant deaths in the Tinning family, a detailed examination was performed. Experts found no underlying medical cause for the baby's presenting problem and sent him home with a clean bill of health. However, a few days later he was brain dead.

Then, in March of 1981, Marybeth wrapped an unconscious Michael in a blanket and brought him to the pediatrician's office. When the doctor pulled back the cloth, he saw that the child was dead. Since Michael had been adopted, the theory that there was a genetic predisposition triggering the deaths was discarded.

After Michael's death, Marybeth gave birth to Tami Lynn. On December 19, 1985, the Tinnings' neighbor Cynthia Walter, a nurse, received a phone call from Marybeth. Tami Lynn wasn't breathing. Cynthia rushed to Marybeth's house and found Tami Lynn lying on the changing table. She wasn't moving and Cynthia couldn't get a pulse. Tami Lynn was pronounced dead at the emergency room and an investigation into the overwhelming number of deaths at the Tinning residence commenced.

A postmortem evaluation determined that Tami Lynn had been smothered to death. Under questioning, Marybeth told investigators, "I got up and went to her crib and tried to do something with her to get her to stop crying. I finally used the pillow from my bed and put it over her head. I held it until she stopped crying" (Fisher, 2016).

She also confessed to having murdered two of her sons, but later recanted. Authorities suspected that Marybeth suffered from mental illness, specifically MSBP, and began to question the deaths of her other children. The remains of three of the Tinning children were exhumed. However, two of the bodies were too badly decomposed to offer any answers, and the third had been taken from the wrong grave. Lacking evidence, authorities were only able to charge Marybeth with the murder of Tami Lynn.

Despite the actual charges against Marybeth, those close to the case regarded her as a serial killer. The story sent shock waves through the community. People responded with anger, but also confusion. How could a mother kill her own children?

* * *

Marybeth Tinning was born on September 11, 1942, in Duanesburg, New York, a small town just outside Schenectady. As a child, she was isolated, with few friends or social attachments. She desperately craved attention from her father, who frequently ignored her. In fact, he would lock her in a broom closet when she cried, which only reinforced her feelings of rejection. Marybeth also claimed that her father was physically abusive, a statement which she has changed multiple times over the years. Despite inconsistencies in her account of her own childhood, it appears likely that her murder of Tami Lynn paralleled her interactions with her own father—frustration with and disregard for the child led to an abusive response from the parent. Additionally, it is possible to view Marybeth's crime(s) from a developmental perspective. Her own abuse and attachment issues (which we know from Chapter 2 can have a longstanding and detrimental impact), may have led her to resent her children.

Alternatively, they may have resulted in her inability to shift focus from self to selflessness.

Moreover, Marybeth married a man who mirrored her father in many ways. Joseph Tinning has been characterized as cold, distant, and disconnected. He and Marybeth lived very separate lives. Not only did Joseph never once question *why* the Tinning children were dying, but some people have said that he didn't he even seem to notice. It is possible and even probable that Marybeth killed her children as a way to generate an outpouring of attention and affection from friends and neighbors in order to fill the void begun by her father's lack of attention and continued by her husband's.

As with many people afflicted with MSBP, Marybeth suffered a catastrophic event that triggered the onset of MSBP symptoms. Shortly before the death of her first child, Marybeth's father passed away suddenly, leaving her with unresolved feelings about their relationship. Only a few weeks later, her daughter Jennifer died of meningitis. Whether Marybeth felt fearful that all of her children would be cursed (as she stated in some interviews) or was struggling to make sense of the loss of her father, the close succession of these events, followed by the addictive attention she received, may have acted as her trigger. This line of reason underscores the applicability of the behavioral model to Marybeth's offense history (see Table 4.4).

As of this writing, Marybeth Tinning has been formally diagnosed with MSBP.

MSBP in Medical Professionals

Although most MSBP offenders are mothers who target their own children, individuals in caretaking roles (such as doctors and nurses) have also exhibited symptoms resulting in harm to their patients. In such instances, there is a significant uptick in cardiopulmonary arrests or deaths in the office or on the hospital unit where the individual practices. As with MSBP maternal offenders, there are often numerous victims, and it is the pattern of illness or death that draws the attention of authorities.

For example, Kristen Gilbert was a Massachusetts nurse convicted of murdering four patients; however, she was thought to

TABLE 4.4 The Application of Rand and Feldman's Behavioral Model to Marybeth Tinning

Drive	• Negative feelings about marriage • Poor self-worth • Rejection from husband and father • Narcissistic tendencies • Negative emotions amplified by irritation caused by children
Breakdown of internal inhibitions	• Lack of maternal instinct • Lack of attachment to children • Depersonalization of children
Neutralization of external inhibition	• Social isolation • Selection of an uninvolved, detached man to father the children • Selection of an easily manipulated husband

Source: Adapted from Rand and Feldman (2001/2002).

be involved in 37 suspicious deaths. Kristen was married and was also having an affair with a security guard who worked at the same hospital. Facility protocol dictated that security had to respond to all cardiopulmonary arrests, so Kristen began injecting her patients with epinephrine to induce such episodes, thus allowing her to call a code and see her paramour under the guise of work. An investigation proved that suspicious codes occurred only when both she and the guard with whom she was involved were working the same shift (Yorker et al., 2006).

Other such offenders have admitted to causing life-and-death medical crises in their patients because they enjoy the admiration given to them by colleagues when they are able to save a patient. Still others are motivated by the excitement of urgency. Professor Roy Meadow labeled this as a professional form of Munchausen syndrome by proxy due to the motivation of secondary gain. This conceptualization was the foundation for his testimony in the Beverly Allitt case (Davies, 1993; Yorker, 1996).

Beverly Allitt

"The trouble is, the more you knew Beverly Allitt the more normal she appeared in every way."
　　　　　　　　—Eileen Jobson, the mother of Allitt's lover
　　　　　　　　　　　　　　　　(St. Estephe, 2016)

In 1991, Beverly Allitt took the lives of four children and was suspected of causing over 20 suspicious health emergencies in a total of 13 victims. Her first victim was 7-month-old Liam Taylor. Liam was admitted to Grantham and Kesteven Hospital's children's ward (Ward 4) in Britain with a respiratory infection. On the surface, Beverly was an exemplary nurse—reassuring Liam's parents, pulling extra hours to watch over the boy, and so on. The infant had two respiratory crises on the night that he was admitted to the hospital, both of which he pulled through. However, once left in the sole care of Beverly, his condition worsened. He grew pale and developed red blotches on his face. Beverly called the emergency resuscitation team, but Liam had suffered brain death.

Two weeks later, 11-year-old Timothy Hardwick was admitted. He had cerebral palsy and had suffered an epileptic fit. Once again, Beverly took over the case in the chronically understaffed hospital. While alone with Timothy, she again called for the resuscitation team, who found the child without a pulse. They were unable to revive him. Although an autopsy failed to provide definitive answers, the cause of death was officially thought to be complications related to epilepsy.

Three days later, 1-year-old Kayley Desmond went into cardiac arrest and was rushed into Ward 4. However, she was quickly transferred to another hospital where doctors found a puncture hole in her arm with an air bubble beneath her skin. It was attributed to an accidental injection and never investigated.

Beverly's crimes were becoming more frequent, and the children under her care were experiencing unexpected life-threatening emergencies at an unusually high rate. Still, she managed to remain undetected. A child admitted for a bronchial infection suffered a coma due to fluctuating insulin levels, and another being treated for pneumonia went into cardiac arrest, also as a result of unstable insulin. Still a third suffered an unexplained heart attack, while a fourth stopped breathing altogether; his symptoms were attributed to a fractured skull, the result of a fall.

In the spring of 1991, 2-month-old twins Katie and Becky Phillips were under observation following their premature birth when gastroenteritis landed Becky on Ward 4 with Beverly. In short order, Beverly reported that Becky was hypoglycemic and cold to the touch. However, no medical causation was ever found and the baby was sent home with her mother. During the night, Becky cried and went into convulsions. Her parents called for a doctor who suggested that Becky had colic; she was dead by morning. The autopsy was unable to yield any clear answers.

Beverly then targeted Becky's surviving twin, Katie. The baby was hospitalized as a precaution only, but within a few hours, she had stopped breathing. Although she was revived, she had a similar "episode" 2 days later, which caused her lungs to collapse. She was transferred to Nottingham, where it was discovered that she had five broken ribs and had incurred serious brain damage due to oxygen deprivation. As a result of the lack of oxygen, Katie was left with a host of ailments, including partial paralysis and impaired hearing and vision. In a heart-wrenching twist of irony, Katie's mother felt indebted to Beverly for saving the little girl's life and named her as Katie's godmother—a distinction Beverly readily accepted.

Beverly had four more victims in rapid succession, but it was the murder of 15-month-old Claire Peck on April 22, 1991, that brought Beverly's killings to an abrupt end. Claire was asthmatic and required a breathing tube. While in Beverly's care, she quickly suffered a heart attack. Although the resuscitation team revived her, she had a second heart attack when again left alone with Beverly; this time she could not be saved.

Although the autopsy suggested that Claire had died of natural causes, it triggered an inquiry by a consulting physician, who was disturbed by the uncharacteristically high number of juvenile cardiac deaths on Ward 4. Initially, an airborne virus was thought to be the culprit, but when a curiously high level of potassium was found in baby Claire's blood, the police initiated an investigation. Claire's body was exhumed and the medical examiner found traces of lignocaine, a drug used to restore rapid or irregular heartbeats in cardiac patients, but never intended for administration to an infant. The police suspected foul play and began to delve into the other equivocal deaths at Grantham and Kesteven.

Dangerously high levels of insulin were found in most of the children who had experienced unexplained illness or death. The investigation further revealed that Beverly herself had reported the key to the insulin refrigerator missing. There were also missing nursing logs that corresponded to periods of time when suspected victims had been on Ward 4. The only common denominator among the more than 20 suspicious episodes, 13 victims, and four deaths was Beverly Allitt. A search of her home uncovered the missing logs, and an examination of her past pointed to vital warning signs that had somehow been overlooked.

As one of four children, Beverly was used to vying for attention. As a child, she wore bandages and casts over "wounds" that didn't actually exist as a way of getting sympathy, lending credence to the theory that MSBP is a learned behavior. When she became overweight in her teen years, her attention-seeking behaviors intensified and she began exhibiting aggression. Beverly displayed more consistent factitious behaviors, showing up in various hospitals and seeking treatment from an array of physicians. She reported excruciating gallbladder pain, ongoing headaches, urinary tract infections, vomiting, back problems, ulcers, and blurred vision. She was so adept at manipulating medical personnel that she convinced a surgeon to remove her completely healthy appendix, which was then slow to heal because she refused to leave the surgical scar alone.

In addition to feigning illness, Beverly inflicted violent self-harm. In one instance, she used a hammer to bruise herself, and in another, she cut herself with a shard of glass. She even attempted to inject herself with water. Such self-injurious behaviors can be symptomatic of borderline personality disorder (BPD), which is often comorbid with factitious illness. Although Beverly's self-induced ailments triggered the sympathetic response she desired, she craved more and turned her efforts outward, victimizing others. It is worth noting that antisocial behaviors may be indicative of antisocial personality disorder, which, like BPD, is often diagnosed in those with Munchausen or MSBP.

Beverly went on to attend nursing school. During an internship at a nursing home, she was suspected of smearing feces on the walls and hiding them in the refrigerator to garner attention. She was also frequently absent due to a host of "illnesses." Her boyfriend at the time claimed that she was aggressive, manipulative, and deceptive—having professed to be pregnant when in fact she was not, and having fabricated a rape allegation.

Despite her chronic attendance issues and failure on her board examinations, Beverly was offered a position at Grantham and Kesteven in Lincolnshire. The hospital was consistently starving for medical professionals, and there were only two nurses on the day shift and one assigned to the night shift, which offered the perfect opportunity for Beverly's crimes to go undetected.

* * *

Beverly Allitt was arrested in November of 1991, at which time she denied any involvement in the attacks. While awaiting trial, she refused to eat and lost 70 pounds, which resulted in her being diagnosed with anorexia nervosa. While in jail, she stabbed herself with paperclips and poured boiling water on her hand to create burn marks.

The trial lasted several months, although Beverly only showed up intermittently due to "ongoing illness." Dr. Meadows testified that Beverly exhibited various symptoms associated with Munchausen and MSBP, citing her childhood and adolescent behaviors, offenses, and postarrest behaviors. Despite her psychiatric difficulties, Beverly Allitt was convicted on May 23, 1993, and given 13 life sentences, with a stipulation that she had to serve at least 30 years in prison. It was the harshest sentence ever handed down by the High Court to a female perpetrator.

Angels of Death

Although we address the overarching typology of angels of death separately from those healthcare providers who kill as a result of MSBP, there is an overlap between the two. The angel of death is an iconic serial killer who represents the final companion to the vulnerable; she is the lethal caregiver who targets the weak individuals under her care who are reliant upon her for both life-sustaining needs as well as for comfort. She selects defenseless victims who are unable to ward off an assault. Therefore, those victimized are almost always the very young, the very old, the frail or the ill, and her crimes occur nearly exclusively within institutional settings such as hospitals or nursing homes. It should be noted that although these killers are typically thought to be female, there have been documented instances of male nurses committing such homicides (Kelleher & Kelleher, 2008).

Some serial killers who fall within this category are driven by the professional manifestation of MSBP. In part, these individuals are compelled to engage in criminal behavior to attract attention from other medical professionals, usually for their heroic life-saving efforts (Kelleher & Kelleher, 1998). Beverly Allitt is such an example. Such women have typically engaged in prior factitious behavior, often have a history of pathological lying, and may meet criteria for hypochondria (Beine, 2003). It is not uncommon for these healthcare providers to falsify their credentials or fabricate significant events such as sexual assault before committing their murders (Yorker, 1996). People with MSBP are often drawn to helping professions. The serial killer nurse motivated by factitious illness falls under the umbrella of "angel of death."

However, not all angels of death are driven by MSBP; some kill for reasons other than attention. Take French nurse Christine Malevre, who confessed to killing more than 30 terminally ill patients and claimed to be motivated by compassion. Mercy killers such as Malevre believe that they are performing an act of kindness by killing because death ends their victims' suffering. Of course, this thought may very well be delusional, and death may be at odds with their victims' desires (Yorker et al., 2006).

On the opposite end of the spectrum are those angels of death who are sadistic and use their position as healthcare providers to inflict pain and suffering. They are driven by a compulsive need for dominance and enjoy wielding the power of life and death over their victims. They not only relish exerting physical control, but also savor the inherent psychological manipulation in securing their victims' trust before killing them (Kelleher & Kelleher, 1998). Similar to the psychological torture inflicted by the black widow, one can question whether this is a gender-specific expression of covert aggression and sadism.

Waltraud Wagner is a prime example (Yorker et al., 2006). She was a nurse's aide in Vienna, Austria, and worked the night shift on a geriatric ward, a place where people died from natural causes on a rather regular basis. Although Waltraud's first kill was a mercy killing—a patient who asked for her help in passing on—she realized very quickly that she enjoyed the act of killing. Waltraud recruited three colleagues, and together the four women killed between 42 and 300 patients. They did not limit themselves to those with incurable diseases, but rather killed individuals who annoyed them or were hard to care for. The women later admitted their own involvement in some of the murders and implicated one another in the rest.

In another case, Honora Kelley (aka Jane Toppan), a nurse in Boston, Massachusetts, killed more than 30 victims in the years between 1887 and 1901. Unlike Waltraud, she didn't limit her victim pool to her patients—she also targeted relatives. She injected her victims with poison (morphine and atropine). When she was arrested, Honora told investigators that her ambition was to kill more people than any singular individual, male or female, ever had.

Some view her crimes as sadistic, while others view them as the result of mental illness. Honora had a difficult life. Her mother died of tuberculosis when she was still a baby, and her father, a tailor, was confined to an asylum after he tried to sew his own eyelids shut.

After a brief stint at the local orphanage, Honora was sent to live with the Toppan family of Lowell, Massachusetts, as an indentured servant. Although they never formally adopted her, she took their surname and became known as Jane. Jane Toppan did well in school and seemed well-adjusted until her fiancé left her; she attempted suicide twice and began to exhibit peculiarities, including magical thinking.

Once stabilized, Jane began nursing training at Cambridge Hospital, where she began to experiment with poison and dosages. She altered medication dosages for those patients whom she chose as her victims. Then, as they neared death, she climbed into bed with them. Jane later said that she derived sexual pleasure from being close to her victims as they were dying. She enjoyed experiencing their last breath.

Jane's deviant interests soon drew the attention of her classmates and instructors. Those around her were disturbed by her morose obsession with autopsies, and she was discharged after two patients died under her care. She went on to work at another prestigious hospital, where she claimed more victims and was ultimately fired. But Jane didn't let that stop her; she forged her credentials and went on to find work as a private nurse for homebound patients—many of whom she is thought to have killed. Jane Toppan was found not guilty by reason of insanity and was remanded to the Taunton Insane Hospital, where she died peacefully at the age of 81.

When analyzing Jane's lengthy criminal history, it is clear that she reveled in portraying the image of the self-sacrificing caretaker, while slowly and surreptitiously poisoning patients to whom she ministered. One would assume that she also enjoyed the acknowledgment she may have received from patients' grateful relatives (Johnston, 2012d). However, Jane's profile is more complex than that.

Given her childhood and upbringing as an indentured servant in the Toppan house and the fact that she assumed their last name despite never having been adopted by them, it is likely that Jane carried with her a deep sense of inadequacy, which caused her to develop an intense need for control over others. This likely resulted in a self-serving (i.e., manipulative and coercive) interpersonal style. Because she failed to achieve emotional maturation due to experiences during her formative years, Jane also came to view those around her through an exploitative lens and thus without empathy.

Chapter 2 discusses the psychodynamic perspective on values. It appears that Jane was developmentally stunted and therefore never acquired a moral compass; her actions were guided by principles such as greed and lust rather than morality. Jane also had strong fantasies rooted in wish fulfillment (Johnston, 2012d) as a means of (maladaptive) coping, as evidenced by the sexual deviancy involved in her kills. Such escapist fantasies are often seen in individuals who have unresolved childhood trauma. Finally, we can examine Jane's crimes from a behavioral stance. Poison often eludes immediate detection. Therefore, each time that Jane was able not only to get away with a murder but to achieve sexual gratification while doing so, her feelings of power and control in addition to her deviant fantasies were strengthened, thus reinforcing her overarching behavior: serial murder.

Conclusion

Social norms demand that women be cast in caretaking roles in society. They are expected to become mothers and to protect their children at all costs. Therefore, when a mother kills her child, it is seen as an act of evil—rather than of mental illness. The same can often be said of how healthcare workers who murder their patients are regarded. The common thread that links the offenses committed by MSBP mothers and angels of death is the poorly understood diagnosis of Munchausen syndrome by proxy.

Various theories about the etiology of MSBP have been put forth, ranging from evolutionary to behavioral to developmental. However, while both fathers and mothers murder their offspring at comparable rates, and both male and female healthcare workers have committed (serial) murder targeting their own patients, research has consistently shown that there is sex-specificity among MSBP patients. Why are MSBP offenders mostly female? These women lack emotional support from their male partners, which results in a pathological and narcissistic need for attention—specifically from high-ranking male physicians. This need overrides their maternal instinct and they sacrifice their own children.

While there are a multitude of predisposing risks for MSBP, we must consider the role of the male-centric narrative in putting these women at risk for this illness. Did they receive the message that their worth is based on being with a man—or a man of status, such as a doctor? Does society need to accept any responsibility in the deaths of these innocent children?

Chapter 5

Domestic Homicide

Jodi Arias

Jodi Arias first made headlines in 2008 when she was arrested for the murder of her boyfriend Travis Alexander. Her dramatic trial received round-the-clock coverage, and by the time that she was convicted in 2013 she had become a household name. Jodi again garnered media attention in 2016 when she announced that she planned to get married despite serving a life sentence.

Media outlets from tabloids to TV news stations ran various versions of the story: "Jodi Arias prison bombshell: She stole another woman's boyfriend—from behind bars" (*In Touch Weekly*, 2016). "Jodi Arias planning dream wedding?" (ABC15). "Jodi Arias has fallen in love with one of her many admirers," she "hopes to wed the man, who hasn't been named, wearing a fitted dress, diamond and gold wedding band and holding a bouquet" (Parry, 2016). One write-up quoted one of Jodi's friends as saying, "It will be a fairytale wedding to a man she loves" (*In Touch Weekly*, 2016).

The media's approach to the topic elevated Jodi to Hollywood-celebrity status and treated her vision of a prison wedding as not only newsworthy, but enthralling, thus trivializing the sheer brutality of her crime. By focusing on romantic wedding details, they undermined the pain that she had caused Travis, his friends, and his family. This fact is glaringly emphasized in a piece run by the *Daily Mail* in which a bullet-point list outlining Jodi's wedding plans, dreams for the future, and prison wedding regulations was released. Only in the last two lines of the article is the heinous nature of Jodi's crime addressed (Parry, 2016):

- "The 35-year-old was sentenced to life in prison in 2013 for boyfriend Travis Alexander's murder in 'a jealous rage.'"
- "Alexander was stabbed 30 times, slit in the throat, and shot in the forehead."

Despite Jodi's crime, the media circus attempted to capitalize on the female stereotype of the blushing bride, which raises the question if the media treatment would have been the same (or even remotely similar) had the gender roles been reversed. Had Travis Alexander slain Jodi Arias and then proposed to a female admirer from behind bars, would the media have been so enamored with the situation—and with him? Probably not. Perhaps the larger question is, what role does gender play in domestic homicides and in society's perception of them?

* * *

June 4, 2008. It was a grisly scene, wall-to-wall blood. Travis Alexander's body lay slumped in the shower at his Mesa, Arizona, home. His throat had been sliced from ear to ear, nearly decapitating him, and he had been stabbed 29 times (not 30, as reported by the tabloids) before being shot in the head (Owens, 2013). His hands were marred with defensive wounds.

Upon finding the body, Travis's friends phoned the police. They immediately told them that before he died, Travis's ex-girlfriend, Jodi Arias, had been stalking him. After their breakup, Jodi and Travis had continued to maintain a sexual relationship, which consisted of exchanging explicit messages and meeting only in secret. However, Jodi wasn't satisfied with this arrangement, and upon learning that Travis was involved with someone else, became wildly jealous; she slashed his tires, hacked into his Facebook account, and overtly threatened him. She also broke into his house in the middle of the night by crawling through a doggy door. Travis awoke to find her in bed next to him. A few days before the murder, Travis had reportedly told Jodi that he wanted no further contact with her.

When investigators combed through the crime scene, they found Travis's badly damaged digital camera—it was in the washing machine. They recovered photos of Jodi and Travis in sexually suggestive poses, several of which had been taken just hours before his body was found. The last picture of Travis alive was taken at 5:29 p.m. on June 4, 2008; he was in the shower. Minutes later, another series of shots was taken. They depicted a person—assumed to be Travis—bleeding out on the bathroom floor and another—assumed to be Jodi—fleeing the scene. Upon further investigation, police learned that a bloody handprint on the bathroom wall contained DNA from *both* Jodi and Travis. Jodi Arias was arrested for the murder of Travis Alexander on July 15, 2008.

Under questioning, Jodi offered multiple accounts of her involvement in Travis's death. She initially reported that she had not seen her estranged lover in nearly 2 months and had not been anywhere near his home on the day of the killing. She later revised her story, placing herself at the crime scene. However, she claimed to have barely escaped with her life when two masked intruders broke into the house and brutally attacked Travis. It wasn't until years later that Jodi admitted to having committed the murder.

Jodi then painted a sympathetic picture of herself as an abused woman who snapped in the face of a deadly threat. She claimed that after a long day of rough sex with Travis, she playfully took erotic photos of him with his new camera. When she accidentally dropped it, he became enraged and lunged at her. Fearing for her life, she killed him in self-defense. Prosecutors, however, didn't believe Jodi's version of events, in part because of her previous lies, but also because the scene reflected significant overkill. They suspected that she had deliberately carried out the murder and that her motivation was rooted in pathological jealousy.

Psychological Evidence in the Arias Case
Jodi Arias was born on July 9, 1980, in Salinas, California, to William Angelo and Sandra Arias. She often spoke fondly of her "ideal"

upbringing as one of five siblings. However, in contradictory statements, she alleged that both of her parents began physically abusing her when she was only 7 years old. Jodi's parents, on the other hand, were vocal about their belief that their daughter was mentally unstable. Her father described her as dishonest, a character flaw with which she'd struggled since her teen years. He even indicated that friends of Jodi had implored him to get her psychiatric help for what he assumed to be bipolar disorder. According to her mother, "Jodi has mental problems" (Associated Press, 2013).

When it came to evaluating Jodi's mental state at the time of her crime, experts lined up on both sides of the aisle. The prosecution's expert, Dr. Janeen DeMarte, diagnosed Jodi with borderline personality disorder (BPD), describing her personality profile as hostile, aggressive, immature, emotionally labile, and desperately fearing abandonment. Dr. DeMarte noted that individuals with BPD typically function well in their day-to-day lives, hiding their negative emotionality from others. However, when they feel as though they have been wronged or hurt, they have a tendency to externalize blame and often react violently, with inappropriate bursts of anger. In other words, they justify their treatment of others because they perceive those people as having "deserved it."

Dr. DeMarte pointed out that Jodi had engaged in bizarre, clingy, and desperate behaviors to mitigate her fear of abandonment. For instance, when Travis initially broke up with her, she moved to Mesa, Arizona, to be closer to him. She began violating his privacy by checking his Facebook and text messages without permission. While these behaviors were motivated by Jodi's intense need to keep Travis close, they were intrusive in nature and pushed him further away.

Jodi had an extensive history of instability in romantic relationships, and she moved from boyfriend to boyfriend very quickly. Despite transgressions committed by her partners, she idealized them, which highlights her desperate desire to avoid abandonment. In one particularly disturbing instance, Jodi dyed her hair, bought a new car, and adjusted her attitude to mimic a previous boyfriend's ex-wife. This frantic effort to keep him close alludes to her unstable sense of identity—her willingness to change herself to please others and keep them from leaving her.

Defense witness Ms. Alyce Laviolette, however, testified that Jodi was a battered woman. She viewed Travis as a domestic violence perpetrator and Jodi's actions as a result of trauma stemming from a pattern of severe abuse. Ms. Laviolette noted that Travis was not the first person to abuse Jodi. She reported that Jodi had informed her that her mother had beaten her with a spoon and failed to protect her from her abusive father. Jodi's father had allegedly beaten her and on one occasion pushed her into a piece of furniture, causing her to lose consciousness. Feeling abused and controlled, Jodi left home at an early age, only to move in with a boyfriend who berated and physically abused her. According to Ms. Laviolette, Travis was the last in a long line of people who abused Jodi. Similarly, defense psychologist Dr. Richard Samuels, who many regarded as a "hired gun," noted that Jodi suffered from PTSD due to past trauma and amnesia related to the violent and disturbing act of killing Travis. Taken together, one could infer that Dr. Samuels believed that Jodi's history of abuse had caused her to be hypervigilant (a symptom of PTSD), react violently toward a perceived threat (i.e., Travis lunging at her), and then blackout or have difficulty recalling her actions (due to the emotional turmoil involved in the incident). The jury had to decide.

Jodi took the stand in her own defense, an act that defendants are typically advised against. She admitted to having killed Travis and described her actions as an impassioned and frenzied attempt to save her own life from an abusive and controlling boyfriend. She was forced to confront the various versions of events she'd previously given and stated, "Lying isn't typically something I just do. The lies I've told in this case can be tied directly back to either protecting Travis's reputation or my involvement in his death . . . because I was very ashamed" (Biography.com, n.d.).

Jodi had difficulty when questioned about evidence that she had turned off her cell phone prior to nearing Travis's house on the day of the crime and had not turned it back on until 6 hours after he was dead. By that time, she was hundreds of miles away and her cell signal couldn't be used to triangulate her location, thus ensuring that she didn't leave a digital fingerprint at the crime scene. On the surface, this all seemed rather circumstantial until Jodi called Travis's voicemail and left a detailed message during which she explained that her phone battery had died, so she'd been off the grid for several hours, but wanted to make plans with him. Phone records revealed that Jodi had actually dialed his number numerous times and accessed his voicemail to delete and rerecord this final message. During cross-examination, Jodi conceded that she wanted the voicemail to sound believable because she was trying to cover her tracks. Jodi Arias was convicted of murder in the first degree on May 8, 2013. She was sentenced to life without parole.

This case begs the question: Why do women kill intimates? Is it symptomatic of a pervasive mental illness, or is it a trauma response to prolonged abuse? The answer is that it depends on the case; crimes motivated by both factors have occurred and continue to occur.

Borderline Personality Disorder and Violence

Borderline personality disorder, or BPD, is defined as a pervasive pattern of instability in interpersonal relationships, ineffective emotional regulation, distorted or unstable self-image, and pathological fear of abandonment. A person with BPD is likely to experience intense episodic anger, rapid mood fluctuations, and recurring suicidal ideation, and to present as impulsive and manipulative. He, or more typically she, will often go to extreme lengths to avoid real or imagined abandonment.

Approximately 1.6% of U.S. adults have been diagnosed with BPD, and 75% of those individuals are women. However, recent studies suggest that BPD *may* be more prevalent than originally thought (with up to 5.9% of the population meeting diagnostic criteria) and may actually affect men almost as frequently as it does women (National Association on Mental Illness [NAMI], 2017).

While the exact causes of BPD are not well understood, experts agree that it is the result of a combination of genetics, environmental influences, and brain function. Although no causal link has been identified between a specific gene and the development of BPD, twin studies suggest that the heritability of this disorder is clearly apparent.

People with a first-degree relative with BPD are five times more likely to have the disorder as well. Additionally, people who have suffered severe trauma, such as physical or sexual abuse during childhood, are at an increased risk for the development of BPD. Studies also reveal that the brains of people with BPD often function differently than the brains of people without the illness; specifically, the parts of the brain that govern emotions and judgment do not communicate well with one another in affected individuals, thus indicating that there may be a neurological basis for at least some of the symptoms (NAMI, 2017).

BPD is oftentimes associated with self-harm, such as cutting or burning. With a suicide rate of nearly 10%, individuals with BPD pose the greatest risk of physical harm to themselves. While self-harm is the most common concern, people with this disorder may also externalize their aggression, resulting in violence toward others. Sometimes, even threats of suicide are utilized as a passive form of external aggression, wherein the afflicted person attempts to manipulate and psychologically injure others by blaming them for potential self-harm: "Look what you made me do!" "If I kill myself, my blood will be on your hands." It is a form of psychological warfare (Sansone & Sansone, 2012).

BPD is highly correlated with verbal, emotional, psychological, and physical abuse as well as domestic violence. Less frequently, it is related to familicide and/or serial murder (Kreisman, 2013; Sansone & Sansone, 2012). The proclivity for this abusiveness in people with BPD is triggered by the narcissistic injury that is central to their fear of abandonment.

People with BPD lack a consistent concept of self and struggle with abandonment issues because they incurred an acute psychic injury (wound of abandonment) very early in life. This unresolved pain leaves them unable to interact in healthy ways; they develop maladaptive coping responses specific to emotional intimacy. Their fear or panic surrounding abandonment causes them to develop an approach–avoidance conflict, whereby they engage in behaviors that push people away as a means of developing closeness. This "get away closer" style is rooted in the borderline sufferer's internal "I hate you—don't leave me" struggle, wherein they perceive any withdrawal or lessening of intense intimacy or attachment as an actual threat to their safety and potentially to their entire psychological existence. In other words, they idealize their partner—and come to view and understand themselves in terms of said partner. Therefore, emotional intimacy triggers a fear of abandonment in them, and they will go to extreme lengths to escape that abandonment (Mahari, 2009).

Jodi Arias and BPD

Jodi Arias is not the first high-profile offender to be given the BPD label. In fact, Casey Anthony, Adam Lanza, and James Holmes all received this diagnosis. According to the *DSM-5* (American Psychiatric Association, 2013), an individual must meet at least five of the following criteria in order to be eligible for a diagnosis of BPD (Archer, 2013a):

- *Frantic efforts to avoid real or imagined abandonment*: When Travis threatened to break up with Jodi, she uprooted herself and moved closer to him, stalked him, hacked into his social media, and even broke into his home. Experts have even speculated that she recorded sexual conversations with Travis as collateral in the event that he tried to leave her. Her fear of abandonment was pathological and drove her to behave irrationally.
- *A pattern of unstable and intense interpersonal relationships, characterized by extreme fluctuation between idealization and devaluation*: According to the prosecution, Jodi had a history of failed relationships. Perhaps more telling is the fact that although she idealized Travis while he was alive, despite the fact that he had cheated on her, she described him as abusive and pedophilic after his death.
- *Unstable self-image/identity disturbance*: As Dr. DeMarte pointed out, Jodi was in the habit of changing herself—physical appearance, demeanor, attitude, etc.—in order to please the man in her life. This indicates instability of self-image.
- *Self-damaging impulsivity*: People with BPD often exhibit impulsive behaviors such as irresponsible spending, indiscriminate

and/or unsafe sex, reckless driving, binge eating, and substance abuse. By any definition, Jodi was impulsive, as evidenced by her intense sexual practices with Travis and the fact that she threw the digital camera (which contained photographic evidence) into the washing machine following the murder. She was also in the habit of calling Travis from work. If he didn't answer, she would reportedly drop everything to go find him. During fits of rage, she slashed his tires, broke into his email account, and sent threatening messages to other women with whom Travis had contact. Jodi was even physically aggressive toward her mother and the family dog. Police video revealed that following her arrest Jodi was left alone in the interrogation room, during which time she kicked chairs, sang, did yoga stretches including a handstand, and scolded herself for not having worn makeup to the police station. Jodi clearly exhibited impulsivity across time and circumstance.

- *Recurrent self-mutilation or suicidal ideation, gestures, or threats*: While in police custody, Jodi made several suicidal gestures, such as making superficial cuts on her wrists.
- *Affective reactivity and instability (i.e., intense episodic mood disturbance)*: Jodi's mood changed—and changed quickly. During her testimony, Dr. DeMarte noted that Jodi's rapidly fluctuating moods were apparent in her journals; within a matter of hours, her tone would change from euphoric to hopeless to anxious to irritable.
- *Chronic feeling of emptiness*: This symptom is unclear in Jodi's history.
- *Intense bursts of anger/difficulty controlling anger*: Jodi often became quickly enraged, especially when her relationship was threatened. Aside from murdering Travis, she slashed his tires, threatened him and his female companions, and had even kicked her own dog. These incidents are indications that Jodi had difficulty managing her emotions and controlling her anger.
- *Stress-related paranoia or dissociation*: This symptom may or may not apply to Jodi. Although she claimed that Travis

was abusive, this appears to have been a result of her fear of abandonment and not paranoid ideation. However, one could look at her behavior on the interrogation tapes (referenced previously) and wonder whether it was the result of dissociation or psychosis.

Spontaneous Domestic Homicide as a Result of BPD

Jodi Arias's offense certainly appears to reflect characteristics of BPD. Although she was convicted of first-degree murder, which indicates that premeditation was involved, research by Hanlon et al. (2016) illuminates qualities of offenders who commit what is known as *spontaneous domestic homicide*, or the unplanned killing of an intimate or family member. Aspects of their work may offer new insights into Jodi's crime.

According to Hanlon and colleagues (2016), spontaneous domestic homicide (SDH) offenders are more likely to manifest psychotic disorders and have more severe neuropsychological impairments than other homicide offenders. These individuals have typically had nearly twice the amount of treatment with antipsychotic medication than other killers, which suggests that serious mental illness plays a significant role in spontaneous domestic homicides. SDH offenders are also less likely to achieve a diagnosis of antisocial personality disorder or to use a firearm, indicating a more affectively driven and less organized crime. They additionally exhibit greater deficiencies in executive functioning than do others who commit murder. Taken together, this information may represent the existence of a discernible criminal phenotype.

If we apply these findings to Jodi Arias, we might conclude that she did *not* plan the murder of Travis Alexander. Rather, as a result of his decision to end their relationship, she felt deeply threatened and panicked; this pathological fear of abandonment is symptomatic of BPD. This, coupled with the impulsivity that is also inherent to BPD, resulted in her lashing out and killing Travis in a frantic and angry outburst. The murder was extremely personal and thus involved over-kill. Although Jodi did use a gun during the commission of the crime, testimony at her trial revealed that it was Travis's weapon, which he stored in his closet. Therefore, one could argue that Jodi retrieved it in the heat of an emotional crisis brought on by mental illness.

Moreover, Jodi's bizarre behavior during her interrogation cannot be ignored. Was it a sign of psychological instability? Of trauma following her crime? Of dissociation? Psychosis? Could, or should, Jodi be classified as a SDH offender?

Domestic Violence and Domestic Homicide: The Connection

Not all domestic homicides are underscored by mental illness; many are part of a larger pattern of abuse. Therefore, to fully understand domestic homicide, we must discuss it within the context of domestic violence. According to the U.S. Department of Justice's Office on Violence Against Women (2015), domestic violence can be defined as follows:

> A pattern of abusive behavior in any relationship that is used by one partner to gain or maintain power and control over another intimate partner. Domestic violence can be physical, sexual, emotional, economic, or psychological actions or threats of actions that influence the other person. This includes any behaviors that intimidate, manipulate, humiliate, isolate, frighten, terrorize, coerce, threaten, blame, hurt, injure, or wound someone.

Domestic violence, or DV, as it is often referred to, includes not only abuse within the context of romantic relationships, but also abuse between ex-spouses, former paramours who have or are expecting a child together, and members of the same household (i.e., parents, children, siblings, or roommates). Violence between intimate partners tends to follow a general pattern or cycle in which the severity of the abuse escalates over time and the periods of reprieve become shorter as the intervals of acute violence become incrementally larger (Scott-Snyder, 2016). This pattern, known as the *cycle of violence*, has three phases, defined by their behavioral and relational dynamics (Walker, 1979):

- *Tension-building phase*: During this time, the victim feels tension mounting within the relationship. She reacts by acquiescing and trying to please the abuser. She may feel as though she is "walking on eggshells" in order to avoid a confrontation. Eventually the emotional pressure erupts, and violence ensues.
- *Battering or explosion phase*: This is the actual occurrence of violence. Although it is most often physical, it can be sexual, emotional, etc. The abuser's explosive behavior is not caused by the victim's behavior and is therefore unpredictable and out of the victim's control. Rather, it is triggered by either something in the batterer's environment (an external stimulus) or a change in the batterer's mood (an internal event).
- *Honeymoon phase*: During this part of the cycle, the abuser apologizes and attempts to make amends, often promising that the abuse will end. The batterer may act lovingly toward the victim or shower her with gifts. As this period of time is often peaceful with romantic interludes, it offers the victim relief from the anxiety and hostility that built up during the previous two phases. Oftentimes, this convinces the victim that she no longer has a valid or pressing need to end the relationship. This phase gives way to the tension-building phase, and the cycle continues to repeat itself.

In its most extreme form, physical abuse between intimates manifests as domestic homicide (Scott-Snyder, 2016). Such murders account for nearly half (40% to 50%) of all femicides in the United States. This jarring statistic means that more American women die at the hands of a lover or a spouse than as a result of violence perpetrated by a stranger or an acquaintance (Bachman & Saltzman, 1995; Bailey et al., 1997). But what about when men are murdered by their female partners?

Male victims of domestic violence, and by extension domestic homicide, are statistically rare. One in four men is physically victimized by an intimate partner, and one in seven endures severe physical violence. One in 18 men is stalked by a current or former paramour to the point of fearing that they or someone close to them will be hurt or killed (Centers for Disease Control and Prevention, 2011). Seventy-two percent of all murder-suicides involve a romantic partner, and in only 6% of those is the perpetrator female (National Coalition Against Domestic Violence, n.d.).

Perhaps unsurprisingly, men and women who perpetrate intimate partner violence do so for different reasons and engage in different patterns of behavior. The relative proportion of men and women who are violent with a romantic partner is directly related to situational context, for instance situational violence, abuse, or responsive violence. Table 5.1 summarizes how often and under what circumstances men and women employ domestic abuse in heterosexual relationships (New York State Office for the Prevention of Domestic Violence, 2016).

TABLE 5.1 Domestic Abuse in Heterosexual Relationships

	Percentage of Cases	What It Looks Like	Context
Domestic abuse (coercive and controlling)	97% of perpetrators are male.	Ongoing, one-sided, control-oriented, and motivated; severe abuse with a pattern of escalation.	Significant power imbalance; the abuser has a need to dominate his partner.
Responsive violence	96% of perpetrators are female.	Occasional, one-sided; a less severe (and nonescalating) form of self-defense.	A physical attempt to ward off an attack, defend self or others, or to control the (volatile) situation.
Situation-specific fights	56% of perpetrators are male; 44% are female.	Occasional and mutual, with no pattern of control, domination, or escalation.	Conflict within the relationship that becomes physically aggressive and violent.

Source: Adapted from New York State Office for the Prevention of Domestic Violence (2016).

Domestic abuse committed by heterosexual men is grounded in misogynistic and sexist views about male–female relationships, a sense of male entitlement, and the historically inherent power imbalance between the sexes. While women's violence in relationships is more typically reactive in nature, domestic violence perpetrated by men is more likely to be a pattern that remains stable from one relationship to the next, rather than being situational and specific to a single relationship (Worcester, 2001).

Domestic abuse is not constrained to male–female relationships; it also occurs within same-sex couples. As this chapter focuses on female-perpetrated domestic homicide, we will place emphasis on lesbian partner violence. Domestic violence among lesbian couples involves physical, psychological, sexual, digital, or financial abuse, as it does with heterosexual couples. Approximately 17% to 45% of lesbians report having been the victim of at least one act of violence at the hands of a same-sex partner. In fact, according to the National Coalition of Anti-Violence Programs (NCAVP, 2014), lesbian women are more likely than women in heterosexual relationships to experience domestic abuse. Although abuse within lesbian relationships is not motivated by misogyny, it does share other similarities with heterosexual partner violence. For instance, the cycle of violence is vividly present and the frequency of domestic abuse is comparable (Burke & Follingstad, 1999). Additionally, lesbians abuse their partners to gain or maintain power and control in the relationship, part of which is often the incessant manipulation of their partner. Additionally, lesbian abusers fear abandonment, as do heterosexual male batterers (NCAVP, 1999), and thus many violent incidents are triggered by the victim's attempt to end the relationship.

In addition to these fundamental similarities, basic differences between heterosexual partner violence and lesbian partner violence inform lesbian domestic homicide. Perhaps the most notable fact is that lesbian women are more likely than straight women to fight back against the abuser. However, due to this, these altercations are more often mislabeled as "mutual battering situations." Also, it is not uncommon for the lesbian who batters to be acutely aware that gender myths are at her disposal and that society assumes that power imbalances do not exist within a same-sex couple, and therefore she can claim to be the victim. In a male–female couple, if a man makes this assertion, it is most often challenged based on the size and strength differential (WomenSafe, 2002).

Research by Mize and Shackelford (2008) examined the effect of gender and sexual orientation on characteristics of intimate partner homicide by reviewing more than 51,000 such cases. They found that lesbians commit intimate partner homicide less often than do heterosexual women. However, when they do, they do so in a more brutal manner. Despite this, the authors found homicide rates among lesbian couples (9.07 per million per year) to be lower than among heterosexual couples (21.25 per million per year). However, these numbers contradict statistics released by the NCAVP that indicate that lesbian women disproportionately fall victim to intimate partner homicide. According to a 2014 NCAVP report, lesbians accounted for 19% of intimate partner homicide victims in 2013 despite the fact that only 1.5% of American women identify as lesbian and another 0.9% as bisexual (Ward et al., 2014). Current research continues to suggest that same-sex couples are at a higher risk for both domestic violence and domestic homicide, in large part due to the consistent strain of societal pressure, social stigma, and marginalization by society, as well as by the justice system.

History of Domestic Violence

Domestic violence has deep roots, which have inevitably been woven into the fabric of the modern world. Historically, a woman was considered to be her husband's property and was therefore required to obey his demands. If she committed any transgression that besmirched his honor or threatened his property rights, he could legally beat, divorce, or even murder her. Because women were not viewed as independent human beings deserving of equal rights, these instances of domestic abuse were considered private family matters and were not publicly scrutinized (Swisher & Wekesser, 1994).

The history of battering in Western culture highlights our society's pattern of pervasive sexism. Whenever a woman is regarded as *belonging* to a man, it paves the way for violence to be employed as a method of intimidation and, ultimately, control. Such "legitimate control" tactics have been codified by various civil and religious laws (WomenSafe, 2011).

In 1800 BC, the Code of Hammurabi decreed that a wife was subservient to her husband, and therefore he was entitled to punish her (as he saw fit) for any disobedience. Similarly, the Roman code of paterfamilias stated, "If you should discover your wife in adultery, you may with impunity put her to death without a trial, but if you should commit adultery or indecency, she must not presume to lay a finger on you, nor does the law allow it." Roman law additionally permitted a husband to murder his wife for other offenses, including walking outside without her face covered or attending a public event without his express permission.

Medieval canon law encouraged husbands to publicly admonish and humiliate noncompliant wives, including using devices such as iron muzzles.

During the Renaissance in France, so many women were being beaten to death and their economic contributions lost that lawmakers enacted what was considered a progressive statute for the time. It restricted the punishment of wives to "blows, thumps, kicks, or punches on the back . . . which did not leave any marks." It was later revised so that all men "have the right to beat their wives so long as death does not follow" (WomenSafe, 2011).

In the 1700s, English common law dictated that a husband could "chastise his wife with a whip or rattan no bigger than his thumb, in order to enforce . . . domestic discipline." This became known as the "Rule of Thumb" (WomenSafe, 2011). During the 1800s, the colonial courts in America were heavily influenced by English law. While the Puritans openly disparaged and banned family violence, these doctrines were rarely enforced. It was not until the 1870s that the first states outlawed wife beating: "The privilege, ancient though it may be, to beat her with a stick, to pull her hair, choke her, spit in her face or kick her about the floor or to inflict upon her other like indignities, is not now acknowledged by our law" (*Fulgham v. State of Alabama*, 1871). However, these laws were only moderately enforced until the feminist movement of the 1960s, when activists began bringing issues of domestic abuse to the attention of the media. Then, victim-witness programs began to emerge. However, ambivalence still surrounded the issue of criminalizing domestic violence, and the police response continued to focus on avoiding arresting batterers. Through most of the 1970s, women continued to face other barriers within the legal system as well. It wasn't until the reforms of the late 1970s that a woman could apply for a restraining order against her violent husband without also having to file for divorce at the same time (U.S. Commission on Civil Rights, 1982). By the 1980s most states had drafted legislation banning domestic violence (Swisher & Wekesser, 1994).

Sweeping changes continued throughout the 1990s. Twenty-three states elected to permit officers to make an arrest based on "probable cause" in cases of simple or minor assault within the home, while a few other states instituted a mandatory arrest policy *requiring* police to arrest batterers in such instances. In California, judges were obligated to consider the presence of spousal abuse prior to making a determination about child custody and/or visitation. Also in California, individuals under a domestic violence restraining order were prohibited from possessing a firearm. Additionally, the first same-sex domestic violence (SSDV) case was successfully tried, and battered woman syndrome (BWS) was officially permitted to be used as evidence in court in the state of California. The U.S. Surgeon General also listed abuse by husbands as the leading cause of injury to women aged 15 to 44, and the United Nations named domestic violence an international crisis (Indiana Coalition Against Domestic Violence, 2009).

In 1994, Congress passed a watershed piece of legislation known as the Violence Against Women Act (VAWA). The initial iteration of the bill was the first comprehensive legislative package aimed at addressing violence against women at the federal level. It granted funding for victim services and preventative education and included sexual assault, domestic violence, and stalking under the umbrella of violence against women. The bill also included the first federal criminal law against battering and required that every state honor orders of protection issued elsewhere in the United States. VAWA was reauthorized in 2000 and then again in 2005. The bill expired in 2011, and a subsequent political battle ensued. It was again reauthorized in 2013, at which time its provisions and protections for survivors were expanded. This version of the bill marked the first time federal nondiscrimination protections were expressly extended to LGBTQ survivors of domestic and sexual violence.

Abuse as a Motive for Murder

It is often difficult for society to conceptualize how domestic abuse escalates into a situation where the abuser is killed by the domestic violence victim. Such scenarios open the battered woman to public scrutiny, and she is often blamed for taking matters into her own hands. In some instances, she is vilified and characterized as vengeful. The victim—because one cannot lose sight of the fact that that's what she is—is commonly shamed for having stayed in the relationship. Society sends the antiquated and simplistic message that if the abuse had really been that bad, she simply would have walked away from the relationship, thus making the killing inexcusable and incomprehensible. Of course, this insinuation doesn't take into account the lack of options at her disposal. Therefore, to fully grasp the fatal escalation that occurs in these cases, we must first understand why victims stay.

Society assumes that the best course of action for any victim is to unequivocally leave the abuser and never look back; if she doesn't, the assumption is that on some level she gets what she deserves. In other words, if she were really interested in preserving her own well-being, she would take action. While the plan to walk away from an abusive partner seems logical on the surface, many victims are aware that there is an increased risk to their own safety should they attempt to leave the relationship. Abusers often fear abandonment and will go to extreme lengths to prevent their victim from leaving. They will threaten violence or even murder as a way to coerce their victim into staying. If the victim then leaves, the abuser is more likely to carry out these threats as separation initiated by the victim is a documented precipitating factor for domestic homicide (femicide) (NCADV, 2014).

In addition to fearing for her own safety, a victim may remain in an abusive relationship because she believes that her abuser will make good on threats to harm her (or their) children, pets, or other family members. According to a 2007 analysis of domestic violence fatalities, in 20% of cases the murder victim was not the domestic violence victim, but rather a friend, relative, bystander, responding police officer, or other person attempting to intervene (Rothman et al., 2007). It is critical to acknowledge that a victim is the best and only expert on her own relationship. She alone knows how far the abuser will go and what they are capable of. If she believes that the abuser will kill her or someone else should she leave and that she therefore cannot safely exit the relationship, that must be respected.

Aside from the threat of physical harm, numerous emotional and psychological factors impact a victim's decision to remain in an abusive relationship. For example, she may lack the requisite support system to allow her to escape. Many victims have been socially isolated by their abusers and therefore fear becoming homeless or having no means with which to support themselves. They may have nowhere to go if they leave the shared (or marital) residence or may lose access to shared finances. It is not uncommon for abusers to forbid their victims from working and to control financial assets, leaving victims destitute in the event of a split. Moreover, because the emotional and/or physical violence in these relationships is intermittent, the victim may truly maintain positive and even romantic feelings for the abuser. She may feel that the batterer fulfills her needs at times and therefore has mixed feelings about ending the relationship (NCADV, 2014).

Beyond the practical barriers involved in ending the relationship, cultural and religious hindrances also are strongly tied to social stigma. For example, some religious and cultural values support male-dominated households or strictly forbid divorce, causing victims to feel trapped in abusive marriages. Some religious organizations place their sole focus on reconciliation between spouses rather than helping victims terminate abusive relationships and begin healing (Scott-Snyder, 2016).

As you can see, the very nature of domestic violence truly is cyclical, and many victims become trapped in what becomes a continuous pattern of abuse. When viewed this way, it is easier to understand how these scenarios escalate and can result in domestic homicide. Women who kill their (male) abusers tend to fall into two categories: (1) those who kill in the midst of a violent confrontation and (2) those who kill while the abuser is asleep, seemingly posing no immediate threat (Edgely & Marchetti, 2011). It is not uncommon for women in both groups to present with features of battered woman syndrome (BWS) or to utilize psychological evidence of BWS in court. BWS is a group of symptoms resulting from psychological and/or physical abuse by an intimate partner that is endured over a length of time. Hallmark facets include learned helplessness, hypervigilance, and impaired functionality (Scott-Snyder, 2016). However, as BWS is multisymptomatic, victims may experience several of the following symptoms:

- *Re-experiencing the abuse when it is not recurring*: This frequently takes the form of flashbacks and nightmares.
- *Avoidance of the abuser*: As with persons with PTSD, individuals with BWS engage in avoidance behaviors so as not to feel triggered.
- *Hypervigilance*: This is a form of hyperarousal experienced by abuse victims. Often, victims maintain a heightened situational awareness as a defense mechanism; they learn to interpret behavioral cues and even facial expressions from the abuser as indicative of a potential threat. It is important to note that others do not perceive these same gestures as threatening or dangerous.

- *Disrupted interpersonal relationships*: Victims often experience difficulty in interpersonal relationships correlated with the abuser's violent and coercive power and control tactics.
- *Negative body image*: It is not uncommon for domestic violence victims to struggle with poor body image because abusers often make disparaging and damaging comments about their looks. This is a way for batterers to diminish the victim's self-esteem and keep them trapped in the relationship (e.g., "You're a fat ugly bitch that no one else could ever love.").
- *Sexuality and intimacy issues*: As a result of the abuse they have endured, BWS sufferers often have difficulty building healthy intimate relationships in which they expect themselves and their boundaries to be valued.
- *History of being battered*: To meet criteria for BWS, a person *must* have been abused. Without a history of abuse, any overlapping symptoms do not add up to BWS.

Thus, it bears revisiting the previous statement that Jodi Arias's defense team proposed that she was suffering from BWS when she killed Travis Alexander. Note that the testimony in the case proved that Jodi had no documented history of injuries, ER visits, or 9-1-1 calls. Moreover, she never disclosed abuse to anyone close to her, nor did her friends or family ever see any bruises or broken bones. Therefore, one can conclude that while Jodi did commit an act of domestic homicide, it was not motivated by her own trauma or abuse, and was therefore not correlated with BWS. Her attempted use of BWS as a defense only sought to undermine other victims who have struggled against and ultimately killed their abusers.

Beverly Ibn-Tamas

Beverly and Yusef Ibn-Tamas married in 1972. In the years that followed, their relationship was marked by frequent bouts of physical abuse separated by brief and peaceful reprieves. Yusef often beat Beverly, not only with his fists but also with other objects. In one instance, he pinned her to the floor and thrust his knee into her neck until she blacked out.

On February 23, 1976, the couple had another fight, one that was particularly violent. Yusef punched Beverly in the face repeatedly. He then ordered his bloodied, bruised, and dazed wife to pack her bags and move out immediately. At the time, Beverly was pregnant with the couple's unborn child—she refused to leave.

As the altercation escalated, Beverly ducked into the study where she knew her husband kept his gun. She grabbed the weapon, crouched, and hid—waiting for him to continue his attack. When Yusef entered the room, Beverly fired once—the bullet hit him in the head and killed him. As a result, Beverly Ibn-Tamas was arrested and convicted of second-degree murder—without the jury ever hearing about the abuse she'd endured or its psychological impact on her. In other words, the court omitted any mention of battered woman syndrome.

Chamari Liyanage

In a similar case, Sri Lanka–born doctor Chamari Liyanage killed her husband in their home in Geraldton, Australia, in June of 2014 following years of abuse. According to news reports, Din, as she called him, beat Chamari with a wooden rolling pin, forced her to perform sexual acts as strangers watched her over Skype, and subjected her to continued emotional abuse. As a doctor, she knew what domestic violence was, but when confronted with it in her own life, Chamari felt isolated, ashamed, and afraid. She was also torn because she'd seen the good in Din and secretly hoped that he would revert back to the man she'd met years ago.

The abuse escalated to the point that Chamari was living in constant fear. Din's blatant threats and manipulation tactics became overwhelming; her anxiety worsened until she snapped. On the night of the murder, Chamari awoke in the middle of the night and bludgeoned her husband to death with a mallet. When police arrived, they found her cowering on the couch, visibly shaken. Din was lying on the bed in a puddle of blood. There was a pillow covering his face and the mallet was beside him. Chamari told police that she didn't know what had happened. She also indicated that she couldn't imagine having hurt him because she truly loved him (Day, 2017).

Two days later, Chamari was arrested and charged with the murder of her husband. After the jury heard evidence about the extensive abuse that Din had inflicted on Chamari, she was convicted of the lesser offense of manslaughter and sentenced to 4 years in prison. She later told friends that she felt more free while incarcerated than she ever had in her marriage; prison was a safe haven for her (Day, 2017).

Battered Woman Syndrome in the Courtroom

"A woman who defends herself against a man's violence is either a criminal or crazy; our society is very reluctant to say that she is ever justified."

—Cynthia Gillespie (1989)

There is an apparent lack of understanding about the connection between BWS and women who kill their abusers—especially women like Chamari Liyanage who do so when the abuser is not in the midst of a physical assault. BWS contextualizes this type of homicide as reasonable and not a result of malice, but rather a desperate act of self-defense because the battered woman is conditioned to always view her abuser as a real and potentially fatal threat. Therefore, killing him, although illegal, is somewhat understandable. However, self-defense laws are couched in terms of *men* who respond to violence committed by other men; women killing men isn't part of the equation. In many ways, women who kill their abusive husbands are regarded as traitors; their actions are presumed to be unreasonable, often because they are blamed for their batterers' violence to begin with (Wimberly, 2007).

A woman who attributes the murder of her abuser to BWS is effectively mounting a partial defense (referred to as a *diminished capacity defense*). In other words, she is offering a defense by excuse; although she broke the law, she is asserting that she should not be held criminally responsible for her actions because her mental state was affected by the trauma inflicted on her by her abuser.

Expert testimony on BWS was initially introduced into courts across America as a means of explaining the collective experiences of and impact of abuse on battered women. Such expertise was used to assist jurors in determining whether a battered woman's actions could—or should—be construed as "reasonable." However, testimony on this matter is implicitly laden with the notion that (1) a battered woman's voice alone is not strong enough to be heard or understood by a jury of her peers and (2) only psychological experts can bridge the gap between a battered woman's experience and the jury's realm of understanding, given the patriarchal demands governing appropriate behavior by women in relationships and in society in general (Wimberly, 2007). For these reasons, testimony regarding BWS has been quite controversial.

The Criminalization of Battered Women

Jacqueline Sauvage and Norbert Marot married as teenagers and settled in a small village south of Paris, France. By all appearances, they were the perfect couple and had built the perfect life together; 47 years later, Jacqueline shot Norbert dead with a hunting rifle. She explained to authorities that she'd killed her husband to put an end to decades of domestic abuse. Nonetheless, Jacqueline was convicted of murder and sentenced to 10 years in prison (Jeltsen, 2016a). The case drew national attention to the inadequacy of laws surrounding domestic violence, not only in France but around the world. It also raised the uncomfortable and disputed question: Should victims of domestic violence go to prison for killing their abusers? In a progressive and groundbreaking move, President Holland gave Jacqueline a full pardon and set her free in December of 2016. She had served over 3 years in prison (Larimer & Zauzmer, 2016).

According to the American Civil Liberties Union (ACLU), women typically receive harsher sentences for killing their male partners than do men for murdering their female partners;

women's custodial sentences average 15 years, while men's average between 2 and 6. This stark disparity becomes even uglier when we consider that nearly 90% of women who are incarcerated for killing a male paramour were physically abused by their victim. Some people subtly (or not so subtly) blame these women for taking matters into their own hands and performing renegade justice. However, 85% of them sought help from the police at least once before killing their mate, and 50% called the police at least five times (McCray, 2015).

Unfortunately, calling the police doesn't always help; in some instances, law enforcement response and intervention can escalate an already volatile domestic situation. Even in cases where the domestic violence victim is granted a restraining order, she is not necessarily protected. Such orders are only pieces of paper—they are not bulletproof. In fact, being served a restraining order can act as a catalyst for increased violence on the part of the batterer. Therefore, the battered woman often finds herself in a damned-if-you-do, damned-if-you-don't conundrum; if she cannot safely exit the relationship, she can either remain trapped and subject herself to continued (and potentially fatal) abuse, or she can kill her abuser and be subjected to the legal consequences. Neither alternative is adequate.

BWS as a Defense of Duress

Traditionally, BWS has been used not only to demonstrate the impact of domestic violence on the victim, but also to characterize the act of killing one's abuser as understandable. However, more recently, defendants have begun to introduce psychological evidence to support claims that they committed crimes against third parties under duress by the abuser and as a result of prolonged abuse (Long & Wilsey, 2006). When used this way, BWS evidence must satisfy the general requirements for duress (*Dixon v. U.S.*, 2006): reasonableness, imminence (of threat), and lack of opportunity to escape. Such a defense would likely try to persuade the jury to view the woman's fear of her abuser as reasonable, perhaps due to an escalating history of violence; her danger as imminent due to the cyclical nature of domestic violence and her perception of the batterer as an ever-present and grave threat; and her belief that she had no choice but to be complicit in the charged crime and could not escape as a very real result of learned helplessness (Wilsey, 2006).

Consider the application of a BWS duress defense in the case of a young boy who was scalded to death by his father. Both of his parents were subsequently charged with murder. His mother pled no contest and argued that she *could not* report the abuse or try to get help for her son because his father—her husband—literally and figuratively beat her into submission (Dore, 1995). She felt helpless, as though she had no recourse other than to sit idly by. In a similar case, a mother in Virginia was seemingly complacent and perhaps compliant as her boyfriend repeatedly raped, tortured, and eventually murdered her 12-year-old daughter (Wilsey, 2006).

Conclusion

While the statistics on domestic homicide committed by men against women are staggering, the number of men and women who die at the hands of a female paramour is relatively small. Women who commit domestic homicide do so for a few identifiable reasons. Some are pathologically driven and their crimes are spontaneous. Research indicates that severe mental illness may be a significant contributing factor to such crimes. It also stands to reason that some women's offenses, while also motivated by mental illness, may involve an element of planning.

Other female-perpetrated domestic homicides are the culmination of a lengthy cycle of domestic violence. These homicides tend to occur under one of two circumstances: (1) in self-defense during a confrontation or (2) while the victim is asleep. Both scenarios can be explained when viewed through the lens of trauma, and therefore battered women who kill abusive partners may present psychological evidence of BWS in court. However, it remains a frustrating commentary on gender inequity and the inherent power imbalances within the criminal justice system that the same women who present evidence of BWS—a syndrome that stems from severe abuse inflicted on them by their abusers (and murder victims)—will still likely serve time in prison. For the majority who sought help from police before being forced to take matters into their own hands, the system failed them. The justice system often leaves battered women without any recourse and then subsequently punishes them when they are left with no "reasonable" options.

Chapter 6

Andrea Yates

It was a hot Texas afternoon, June 20, 2001. The bodies of Paul (age 3), Luke (age 2), John (age 5), and Mary (6 months) had been carefully laid across their parents' bed. Seven-year-old Noah was still floating face down in the bathtub when the police arrived. The children's mother, Andrea Yates, greeted authorities and readily confessed that she had drowned all five of her children. She believed that the devil had put his mark on her underneath her hair where no one else could see and that killing her children was the only way to save their souls.

Andrea Yates's path to becoming "the most hated woman in the world," as she called herself, involved mental illness, fundamentalist religious beliefs, and a general underestimation of the dangerous consequences of postnatal disorders (McLellan, 2006).

After she had her first child, Andrea began to experience hallucinations. By the time she was recovering from giving birth to her fourth child, she had suffered a nervous breakdown and attempted suicide. As a result, Andrea was psychiatrically hospitalized and diagnosed with postpartum psychosis, which is a postnatal mental illness characterized by a woman's difficulty in responding emotionally to her child; it involves hallucinations and delusions and may include thoughts of harming the child. Andrea was urged by her psychiatrist not to have any more children, as doing so would almost certainly trigger another psychotic episode. However, being religious, Andrea and her husband Rusty had vowed to have as many children as nature would allow, and therefore chose not to heed this warning. Mary, their fifth and final child, was conceived less than 2 months after Andrea was discharged from the hospital.

Mary Yates was born in March of 2000, 8 months after Andrea stopped taking Haldol (an antipsychotic medication prescribed for her). Andrea appeared to be doing well until the death of her father in March of 2001. That loss triggered a downward spiral, during which Andrea stopped taking the rest of her psychotropic medications and began to self-mutilate and read the Bible compulsively. She was again hospitalized.

According to testimony during Andrea's trial, she and her family lived in a cloistered household, replete with fervent religious ideologies. They maintained traditional gender roles, leaving Andrea entirely responsible for caring for the children and maintaining the household. They held what some viewed as eccentric beliefs, as they frowned on the use of medication, found the school system unacceptable, and characterized institutional religion as evil. Additionally, Rusty Yates was a follower of evangelist Michael Woroniecki, who issued stark and hysterical warnings about hellfire and brimstone. As a result, the Yates family often received leaflets in the mail that told of demonic influences that could threaten young children. Following the murders, a former follower of Woroniecki came forward and explained how Woroniecki's teachings were akin to brainwashing—and could have easily overwhelmed and dangerously influenced someone who was vulnerable due to suffering from episodes of psychosis and depression.

In what was perhaps one of the most psychologically complex filicide cases in the United States to date, Andrea Yates was initially convicted and sentenced to death. Then, however, the Texas Court of Appeals overturned the verdict. Andrea was afforded a second trial, at the conclusion of which she was found not guilty by reason of insanity.

Filicide: An Overview

Society subscribes to the belief that women should be intrinsically and biologically driven to protect their children *at any cost*. It is this ubiquitous schema that provokes outrage toward women who either fail to safeguard their children or who are otherwise complicit in the abuse of their children at the behest of an abusive lover. While many find such action—or inaction—to be abhorrent, there is practically no one in our society who is regarded with as much disdain as women who purposely harm or kill their own children when *not* under extreme duress—as Andrea Yates herself recognized.

History of Filicide

Filicide, or the killing of one's own child(ren), is a theme that is referenced throughout history, culture, and literary tradition. Such allusions span all eras and motivations and range from biblical (e.g., Abraham's plan to sacrifice his son Isaac) to mythological, as in the story of Medea, who killed her children to punish her husband for his infidelity. Even fairytales written for children, such as *Snow White* and *Hansel and Gretel*, have a blatant filicidal premise, with evil (step)parents wanting to kill their (step)children (West, 2007).

Filicide has been in existence since the beginning of mankind and has been motivated by reasons ranging from the child's disability or gender to a lack of resources with which to raise the child. While those reasons still hold true today, current systems of documentation, such as birth and death records, make it more difficult for parents to kill their children without coming to the attention of law enforcement. In earlier times, not only was it easier to conceal such acts, but even if the authorities found out, they may have been inclined to turn a blind eye in an effort to strike a balance between available public resources and population growth (or overgrowth) (West, 2007).

It was not until the turn of the 16th century that filicide began to be criminalized in Europe. Both France and England established directives that made filicide punishable by death. In both countries, a mother who killed her children was presumed guilty until proven innocent, which resulted in her having to prove that her child's death was not the result of foul play (Wrightson, 1971). It was not until the passing of the Infanticide Acts of 1922 and 1938 in England that the legal system recognized the potential severe effects of giving birth on a woman's mental health. Therefore, the death penalty was replaced by custodial sentences. Several other Western countries followed suit (West, 2007).

Filicide Statistics

Child homicide rates have tripled since 1950, and homicide is one of the top five causes of death for children between the ages of 1 and 14 years (Centers for Disease Control and Prevention, 2006). In 2004, American research found that nearly 54% of the 578 deceased children studied (all of whom were under the age of 5), had been murdered by their parents. Between 1976 and 2004, 30% of all child murder victims younger than age 5 were killed by their mothers, and 31% were killed by their fathers. These numbers highlight what is perhaps a surprising truth, that women *are equally as capable* as men of killing their young. Additionally, studies show that while male and female children are killed at comparable rates, fathers may be more likely to kill sons, whereas mothers more frequently kill daughters (Rodenburg, 1971).

Classifications of Filicide

In an effort to clarify why parents kill their children, various typologies have been developed based on the offense character- istics and the gender of the perpetrator. The first categorization system was developed in 1927 and divided filicidal mothers into two groups: those motivated by hormonal changes and stressors related to childbirth and those who were not (d'Orban, 1979). In 1969, Philipp Resnick developed one of the most influential classi- fications of filicide based on the parent-killer's apparent or inferred motivations (Bourget & Bradford, 1990). After reviewing 131 such murders, he cited the following five categories of parent-perpetrated child murder: (1) altruistic, (2) unwanted child, (3) spousal revenge, (4) accidental, and (5) psychotic. It is of note that although these typologies have utility with regard to identifying and describing filicide, they are limited due to the significant overlap between groups. See Table 6.1 for a detailed overview of Resnick's typologies.

TABLE 6.1 Filicidal Typologies

Typology	Motivation
Altruistic	• Parent perceives death to be in the child's best interest. • Often done to relieve what the parent views as the child's unbearable suffering, especially in cases of disability or illness (real or imagined). • May be associated with parental suicide because the parent believes that the world is too cruel and it is wrong to leave his or her child behind.
Psychotic	• Response to parental psychosis; devoid of any other rational motivation.
Unwanted child	• Parent views the child as a hindrance. • Includes parents who benefit from their child's death (through an insurance payout or the ability to marry a partner who does not want stepchildren).
Accidental	• Results when the parent accidentally kills the child as a result of abuse. • Includes deaths resulting from Munchausen by proxy.
Spousal revenge	• One parent kills the child as a way of exacting revenge on his or her spouse (the other parent). • May be a response to infidelity or abandonment.

Source: Adapted from Resnick (1969), as cited in Bourget et al. (2006).

If we consider d'Orban's (1979) work with regard to Andrea Yates, she would certainly fall into the group of maternal filicide offenders motivated by postnatal hormonal change given that she was diagnosed with postpartum psychosis. Similarly, if we apply Resnick's (1969) framework, she most obviously meets criteria for the psychotic typology, as she was acting under a religious delusion at the time of the murders. However, her offense also overlaps the altruistic classification, as she believed that killing her children was the only way to save their souls from damnation.

Risk Factors for Maternal Filicide

According to the theory of evolution, the goal of every species is procreation. Therefore, maternal filicide is a difficult phenomenon to wrap one's head around. It has been suggested that children who are the product of rape and/or incest are more likely to fall victim to filicide because they were not created with a carefully selected mate (Daly & Wilson, 1988). Additionally, younger offspring are more likely to be targeted, as less time, energy, and resources have been invested in their rearing. Finally, younger mothers who have a significant period of fertility remaining are more likely to eliminate offspring than are older females. It has been suggested that mental illness and the chaos and disruption it can create in the sufferer's life is one of, if not the main, factor causing mothers like Andrea Yates to not follow evolutionary trends (Stone et al., 2005).

According to an extensive analysis of maternal filicide among the general population, psychiatric population, and correctional population, Friedman, Horwitz, and Resnick (2005) determined that the strongest risk factor for mothers to kill their children was a history of suicidality and depression or psychosis, in addition to previous psychiatric care. Those mothers considered at the highest risk of committing filicide were frequently socially isolated, indigent, and responsible for the full-time care of their children. They had also likely been the victims of domestic abuse themselves.

Women in psychiatric hospitals who had committed filicide were typically married and unemployed with a history of substance use and abuse, while women incarcerated for filicide were more often unmarried, with a lack of social support. The women in the latter category were also unemployed and uneducated and had a history of substance abuse. Studies also suggest that younger children are at greater risk for fatal maltreatment (accidental filicide), while older ones are more likely to be the victims of purposeful homicide.

Research on this subject matter highlights the importance of the mother's own childhood with regard to the crime of filicide. A significant portion of women who went on to kill their own children had received inadequate maternal care secondary to their own mothers being unable to parent them due to alcoholism, abuse, or mental health issues (Crimmins et al., 1997). Friedman, Hrouda, Holden, Noffsinger, and Resnick (2005) determined that 38% of women studied who were deemed legally insane following the murder of their children had a history of physical and sexual abuse (with 5% being victims of incest). Another 49% had been abandoned by their own mothers.

Several studies have identified certain characteristics common among mothers who commit filicide. According to a study by Stone and colleagues (2005), the average perpetrator of maternal filicide was 29 years old and married. Victims were approximately 3 years of age. The vast majority of the women studied had psychiatric diagnoses. Mothers with mental illness were generally older when they committed their crimes, as were their child victims. More than one-third of filicidal women attempted or committed suicide, and up to 29% of these offenders killed themselves following the commission of the filicidal act (Nock & Marzuk, 1999). The most common methods of murder involved in maternal filicide were head trauma, drowning, suffocation, and strangulation. In addition, Rouge-Maillart et al. (2005) found that women who accidentally killed their young children during an abusive episode were often young, poor, unemployed, single, and not suicidal, all traits shared with women who commit neonaticide.

Infanticide and Neonaticide

Filicide is a broad term that refers to the murder of a child up to the age of 18 years committed by his or her parent(s), stepparent, or guardian. Infanticide is used to describe the murder of a child younger than 1 year of age by his or her parent(s), and neonaticide refers to the killing of a newborn by his or her parent(s) within the first 24 hours of life (Resnick, 1970).

Relatively little research has focused solely on child murders committed during the first year of life. A seminal study conducted by Overpeck et al. (1998) reviewed 2,776 such homicides that occurred in the United States between 1983 and 1991. Although the perpetrator was not often specified in the data, the mothers of the infants were largely young, single, poorly educated women who lacked prenatal care. Approximately 25% of the murders were committed prior to the infant's second month of life, with 50% occurring by 4 months. Battering was the most common means of killing the children (West, 2007).

Building on this research, Meyer and Oberman (2001) developed a classification system for distinguishing the underlying causes of maternal infanticide. They identified the following four typologies: (1) women who kill in tandem with abusive male partners, (2) neglect resulting from distraction or preoccupation, (3) harsh discipline gone wrong (i.e., child abuse), and (4) purposeful infanticide, often secondary to mental illness. They also specified denial/ dissociation and deliberately concealing the pregnancy as contributing motives to neonaticide.

In the literature, neonaticides stand in stark contrast to other filicides. Based on his review of 37 such cases spanning international borders and decades, Resnick (1970) rendered the most well-known dataset to date concerning newborn murders. He found that neonaticide is most often committed by a young mother who acts alone. She is frequently unprepared for the birth of the child and typically lacks a history of psychiatric disturbance. Her crime is most often motivated by the fact that the child is unwanted, perhaps because she is unmarried or married to a man who did not father the baby. She most frequently employs suffocation as the method of murder. Unlike in cases of filicide, where 40% of the crimes are brought to the attention of the treating physician, the mother who commits neonaticide rarely seeks prenatal care.

Studies reflect that neonaticides comprise about 5% of all infanticides. Concealment of the pregnancy appears to be common among women who commit neonaticide, and therefore it logically follows that 95% of these newborn victims are not born in a hospital

(Overpeck et al., 1998). Given the secrecy inherent to these offenses, it is likely that some instances of neonaticide never come to the fore.

Passivity appears to be a key element that distinguishes mothers who commit neonaticide from those who terminate their pregnancies (West, 2007) or kill their older children. Neonaticidal moms assume that the hindrances caused by the pregnancy will just go away; they often anticipate a miscarriage or a stillbirth. They do not make plans for the baby's arrival, but they also don't foresee themselves harming or killing the child (Resnick, 1970). It is as if birthing a living breathing child is an unexpected event, after which reality sets in and prompts them to kill the infant.

Previously, neonaticides were not necessarily associated with psychiatric issues, but rather were more commonly influenced by social problems, such as the fear of stigmatization for having a child out of wedlock. Such crimes may even have been a form of resource allocation or family-size control. Resnick (1969) explains:

> Historically, Eskimos living in harsh environments would have twins and send one away on an ice float to die, because the mother may not have enough milk to support two. . . . If the circumstances are such that someone does not have the finances or the wherewithal to raise a child, they may kill that child—that is a social problem in contradistinction to a psychiatric problem.

Today, single motherhood is not only part of the broader social narrative, but it is also becoming more widely respected; it no longer carries the same shameful social stigma that it once did, and therefore one must consider whether present-day neonaticides are more likely to be psychologically or sociologically motivated. Of course, the phrase "single mom" is not entirely devoid of negative connotation, and thus the feelings associated with the single mom stereotype *could* potentially drive certain women to kill their children under the wrong set of circumstances. Some people still incorrectly associate single motherhood with women who rely on welfare, are destined to raise juvenile delinquents, or who engage in indiscriminate sex.

However, the fact is that many young women become single mothers because the fathers of their children, men whom they trusted, bail when they become pregnant. Moreover, with more and more women opting to postpone marriage (or forego it altogether) in favor of pursuing a career, many are choosing to become single parents while they are still within their prime fertility window.

Despite these sociological progressions, the line of Darwinian thinking alluded to by Resnick (1969) carries through research conducted by Mariano et al. (2014). After examining more than 94,000 cases of filicide in the United States, they determined that infants are at the greatest risk of being murdered by a parent or guardian. Is this perhaps because more resources have been invested in raising older children than in raising infants? Or, can we glean insight from Meyer and Oberman's (2001) categorizations of infanticide offenders and assume that neglect by young inexperienced parents or abusive discipline due to parental frustration resulting from a baby's incessant crying plays a more significant role?

Take the case of a Utah woman named Megan Huntsman (age 39) who hid seven consecutive pregnancies from her family. She confessed to having strangled six of her babies and claimed that one had been stillborn. Megan's estranged husband found one of the bodies in a plastic bag in the garage of the home he had previously shared with her.

Similarly, Dominque Cottrez (age 45) dominated headlines in Lille, France, after she confessed to killing eight of her newborn babies. She put two of the bodies in plastic bags before burying them in the garden, and hid the other six in shoeboxes in the garage of the home she shared with her husband. Dominique later testified that she feared the children were the products of an incestuous relationship with her own biological father. Consider the implications of both mothers having discarded their babies' bodies in the garage, which is typically considered a "masculine" domain.

Megan and Dominique each confessed to having committed multiple neonaticides, which although not unheard of, is a statistically rare occurrence. "Repeated neonaticide usually occurs where a woman has not had her earlier crimes discovered . . . it is a relatively uncommon phenomenon to [commit neonaticides] repeatedly, especially as a married woman" (Resnick, 1969). While one could argue that each woman's first victim was the result of social pressure, it is unlikely, given the number of victims, that psychiatric disturbance did not play a role. Regardless, whether their motivations are classified as psychiatric or social, the fact remains that the choice to kill any child involves a very conscious—and unhealthy—decision-making process.

Conclusion

When a woman commits an act of filicide, it is viewed by society as unfathomable and in glaring conflict with her maternal instinct. However, statistics indicate that men and women are equally capable of committing these offenses. Historically speaking, and perhaps counterintuitively, it was maternal instinct that sometimes led women to commit acts of infanticide or neonaticide. For example, when they only had the resources to support three children and a fourth was born, mothers often killed the fourth baby in order to spare the three in which they had already invested time and energy. However, as society has evolved and access to resources has increased, this animalistic approach has become regarded as barbaric.

Four categories of infanticide have been identified: (1) women who kill with an abusive male partner, (2) neglect resulting from distraction or preoccupation, (3) death stemming from harsh discipline (i.e., child abuse), and (4) purposeful infanticide, often related to mental illness. Similarly, the most relevant reasons why women commit filicide have been divided into five categories: (1) altruistic, (2) psychotic, (3) unwanted child, (4) accidental, and (5) spousal revenge. All of the aforementioned typologies are consistent with psychological, biological, and sociological theories of crime, with the exception of accidental, which, as the name indicates, does not meet criteria for a criminal offense.

Chapter 7

Sex Offenders and Madams

Joyce McKinney and the Case of the "Manacled Mormon"

She was a former beauty queen and he was a Mormon missionary. The tabloids hailed it as the "greatest love story of the year." Of her overtures toward Kirk Anderson, Joyce McKinney said, "Yes I tore off his pajamas, but that was because I wanted to please him. . . . It was bombs, firecrackers and the Fourth of July every time he kissed me" (Anderson, 2015). She made this statement in a British magistrates' court after having been charged with kidnapping and repeatedly raping the man whom she characterized as her soulmate.

***

Joyce McKinney was born in 1949 and raised in a small town in North Carolina. Her parents were both teachers, and she had an IQ of 168. She completed an accelerated program in high school while also keeping herself busy with extracurricular activities, including cheerleading and drum corps. She went on to earn both a bachelor's and a master's degree in theatre arts. During college, Joyce lived with a Mormon family. She was so taken by their loving interactions, something she'd not had as a child, that she converted and joined the Church of Jesus Christ of Latter Day Saints. She had high hopes that her newly found affiliation would help her to meet marriage-minded men.

Joyce first met Kirk Anderson at Brigham Young University in 1975. The son of a janitor, he stood 6 feet 4 inches. Slightly pudgy and bespectacled, Kirk had a shy disposition and was also several years her junior. He was not the first missionary to whom Joyce had been attracted, but he was perhaps the only one who'd rebuffed her sexual advances. And for that, Joyce blamed the very Mormon roots that she'd found so appealing. Joyce considered Kirk to be sexually repressed. As she tried to push his boundaries, he began to struggle with the moral conflict between his desire for her and his devotion to his faith. He sought counsel from a bishop, who advised him to terminate the sinful relationship. Kirk did, and quickly embarked on a mission that would take him around the country and, ultimately, the globe.

As Kirk moved from state to state, Joyce's infatuation grew into an obsession, and she pursued him. He began using aliases to escape her. Kirk eventually fled to Britain in September of 1976. By February of 1977, Joyce had employed the services of a private detective to track him down. Once she learned of Kirk's whereabouts, Joyce placed a personal ad for a companion to join her on a "free trip to Europe." One Keith May answered the ad.

Using bogus passports, Joyce and Keith traveled to the Church of Latter Day Saints in Ewell Surrey in the United Kingdom. Under assumed names, they posed as potential Mormon converts and made an appointment with Kirk, who was assigned there. When he showed up to meet them, Keith used a fake revolver to force Kirk into the car where Joyce was waiting. Joyce and Keith then drove their hostage to a rented cottage. Once there, Joyce chained Kirk to the bed using mink-lined handcuffs and forced liquor down his throat. She had sex with him against his will multiple times over the course of several days, reportedly in an effort to become impregnated with his child. She professed her love for him, and only after Kirk agreed to marry her did Joyce untie him, thus enabling his escape.

* * *

When Joyce McKinney was arrested on September 19, 1977, she denied allegations of having kidnapped and held Kirk hostage.

To the contrary, she told authorities that Kirk was her lover and had gone with her willingly. She described having worn a negligee to seduce him as part of an attempt to deprogram him from the influence of the Mormon "cult," as she referred to it. However, Kirk insisted that he had never been a willing participant in bondage sex and had in fact been sexually victimized by the former Miss Wyoming.

To many, Kirk's disclosure was bizarre and preposterous, while to others it hinted at an exciting if not taboo and risqué role-play fantasy. The public failed to regard Kirk as a victim of sexual assault and to understand how his ordeal could have been traumatic. The media dramatized the story and splashed it across the headlines with a *Fifty Shades of Grey*–esque fascination. Newspapers reeled in readers with a tawdry glimpse into BDSM culture and its clash with religious tenets; Kirk became known as the "manacled Mormon." The assault—because that's what it was—was regarded by men and women alike as Kirk's forbidden fantasy because of the implicit (and often explicit) distortion that men *cannot* be sexually victimized and women cannot be sexually predacious. Had the gender roles been reversed, this case would have been regarded differently. Consider how the media would have responded to a man who stalked, kidnapped, and raped a woman repeatedly over the course of several days in an attempt to force her to marry him, and then characterized his offense as consensual; he would have been publically condemned. However, because the cultural narrative has traditionally stipulated that men are the sexual aggressors, Kirk Anderson was victimized not only by Joyce but also by the way that the case was misrepresented by the media as a sex scandal rather than a sex crime.

On numerous occasions, Joyce publicly undermined Kirk's accusations by claiming that they were lovers. Whether she was manipulative or delusional, there were gender myths and stereotypes at her disposal. She was a pathological adversary who knowingly or otherwise played the gender card brilliantly, thus resulting in the muddling of the true dynamics of the case within the vastly misunderstood matrix of social constructs.

Joyce McKinney and Keith May were eventually indicted for their crimes but jumped bail and fled to the United States before they could stand trial in the UK. They were later found in Atlanta, Georgia, but England declined to extradite them. Joyce McKinney has never been punished for her crimes against Kirk Anderson.

Female Sex Offenders: A Sociocultural Overview

The term *sex offender* typically conjures images of masked men assaulting unsuspecting damsels in dark alleyways or perhaps luring small children. These images represent the concept of the *symbolic assailant*, a term first coined by Skolnik (1966). The symbolic assailant is a fictitious offender who meets specific demographic and behavioral criteria: He is a young black male who lurks in the shadows waiting to abduct, rape, or murder unsuspecting victims. His crimes are unprovoked, his victims are unknown to him, and he is difficult to apprehend; he poses a serious risk to the entire community as he could attack at any time.

The idea of the symbolic assailant is particularly salient when it comes to sexual violence, as many victims do not self-identify as such because their assailant was a family member, friend, or acquaintance (i.e., in contrast to their preconceived notion of the symbolic assailant). Female sexual offenders are perhaps even further removed from the collective image of the symbolic assailant. Rarely, if ever, do people associate women with the commission of sexual violence. While anyone can be a sex offender, society has historically viewed sex crimes as a male domain, one that is largely untouched by even the most devious and dangerous of female offenders.

Social and cultural stereotypes, professional and personal biases, and unique dynamics surround female-perpetrated sex crimes. At the macro level, gender stereotyping has caused women to be viewed as nurturers and caretakers whose very nature makes them inherently incapable of purposely harming others (Denov, 2004; Hislop, 2001). Additionally, sexist beliefs depict men as dominant, with women being the submissive recipients of sexual behavior (Denov, 2004). The impact of these pervasive sociocultural beliefs, in concert with emotional factors (e.g., shame, guilt, fear, etc.) that frequently dissuade victims from disclosing such offenses regardless of the sex of the assailant, mean that sexual assaults committed by females are severely underreported. Also adding to this under-awareness are misperceptions about the physical ability of women to sexually victimize unwilling males, which represents a clear lack of knowledge about physiological responses (Center for Sex Offender Management [CSOM], 2007).

On a more micro level, it appears that the responses of various criminal justice agencies to both victims and offenders of female-perpetrated sexual violence can reflect these broad and distorted views. These reactions often take the shape of officers doubting victims who report having been assaulted by a woman, minimizing these victims' experiences, regarding female suspects as less dangerous, and labeling these cases as "unfounded" (Denov, 2004). As a result, such cases are less likely to be reported and/or pursued aggressively by the justice system.

The Extent of Sex Offending by Women

Due to the fact that sexual victimization is significantly under-reported overall, reliable information about the incidence of sex crimes committed by women is difficult to acquire. Despite this, synthesizing statistics from a host of sources, such as arrest records, census and caseload data from criminal justice agencies, sex offender treatment program information, and victimization surveys, can provide a working estimate of the scope of female-perpetrated sexual violence. Collectively, national crime statistics indicate that females comprise the minority of sex offenders, as they account for less than 10% of all adults and juveniles who come to the attention of law enforcement for sex crimes (Federal Bureau of Investigation [FBI], 2006). Specifically, women comprise only 1% of all adults arrested for forcible rape and only 6% of all adults arrested for other sexual offenses (CSOM, 2007).

In comparison to the approximately 140,000 men who are imprisoned for sex crimes in the United States, only 1,500 women are incarcerated for such offenses (Harrison & Beck, 2005). Women represent 1% of all adults behind bars for crimes of a sexual nature. It follows that women account for less than one-quarter of all adults on probation and approximately 12% of all adults on parole supervision (Glaze & Bonczar, 2006). Because sex offenders comprise only a small fraction of adults on community supervision, the number of adult female sex offenders on probation or parole for a sex crime is minuscule. It is important to keep in mind that the data are likely reflective of not only an underoccurrence of female sexual offending, but also the underrecognition of these crimes and underrepresentation of these perpetrators in the justice system (CSOM, 2007).

When reviewing these statistics, we must bear in mind the "dark figure of crime," or the volume of unreported or undiscovered offenses. This has significant implications when the perpetrator is female. Owing in large part to victims' reluctance to come forward, sex crimes are the single most underreported category of crime. Even when the victim is female and the offender is male, survivors regularly face victim-blaming if they choose to report. However, when the gender roles are reversed, victims may face more daunting repercussions, such as not being taken seriously or facing public humiliation, as evidenced by the Joyce McKinney–Kirk Anderson case. It is also possible that as a result of expectations relating to the symbolic assailant, cultural distortions, or gender stereotypes, victims (both male and female) may not even recognize an incident as sexual assault when the offender is female. Alternatively, if they do, they may feel too ashamed to tell anyone.

Distinguishing Female Sex Offenders

Perhaps it's unsurprising that given the nature and dynamics of their crimes, both male and female sex offenders possess *some* of the same features. For instance, many sexually abusive men and women exhibit a dearth of prosocial coping mechanisms, interpersonal and relationship difficulties, evidence of cognitive distortions, and a lack of victim empathy. Women in particular tend to share some of the following characteristics: a history of childhood maltreatment, including sexual abuse; mental health difficulties, especially personality disorders and substance abuse; problems developing or maintaining intimate relationships; a tendency to victimize primarily children or adolescents (but rarely other adults); and a propensity to target relatives or persons close to them, as opposed to strangers (CSOM, 2007).

Female sex offenders have a lower risk to sexually recidivate than do their male counterparts. However, the most palpable distinction between male and female sex offenders is that females are more likely than males to offend with one or more partners. According to Vandiver (2006), in a study consisting of 227 female sex offenders, nearly half (46%) worked with another person, and the majority of the women's co-perpetrators (71%) were male. Some women also work with a group of co-offenders and may take either an active or passive role in the crime (Grayston & DeLuca, 1999; Nathan & Ward, 2002). Female offenders who assume an active role in the assault engage in direct sexual contact with the victim while those who passively participate do not. Instead, these women may procure victims, expose children to pornographic materials, or fail to intervene during a sexually exploitative event (Grayston & DeLuca, 1999).

Typologies of Female Sex Offenders

Typologies have been developed to describe and categorize female sex offenders based on the presence or absence of a co-offender, the age of the victim, and the offense motivation. In their seminal work, Mathews et al. (1989) developed an influential framework for categorizing female sex offenders based on their clinical observations of 16 women. As the researchers acknowledged, because the primary classifications that emerged (i.e., male coerced, predisposed, teacher/lover) were not statistically generated due to the small sample size, they lacked generalizability. However, subsequent research has supported their initial findings (Matthews, 1998; Nathan & Ward, 2002; Vandiver & Kercher, 2004).

The women who were classified as male-coerced offenders were characterized as passive and had endured significant abuse. Due to their fear of abandonment, they were pressured by male partners to commit acts of sexual violence. They were dependent upon these partners and typically aggressed against their own children. Women who met criteria for the predisposed typology often acted alone and victimized either their own children or other children in their family. They had frequently suffered childhood sexual abuse (specifically incestuous victimization), presented with psychopathology, and had deviant sexual fantasies. The women in the teacher/lover classification tended to struggle with age-appropriate relationships and often believed that they had a romantic or mentoring relationship with their adolescent victim. Because of this distortion, they often failed to view their offense as criminal (CSOM, 2007).

These categories were further expanded into a more extensive classification composed of two broader groupings: accompanied offenders and self-initiated (or solo) offenders, each of which contained specific subtypes (Turner et al., 2008). Women who offend in tandem with a male partner (i.e., accompanied abusers) have been described as emotionally dependent and socially isolated, and they frequently struggle with poor self-esteem (Matthews et al., 1991; Nathan & Ward, 2002). These women can further be distinguished based on whether their male accomplice employed coercion. Those individuals pressured or intimidated into committing sex crimes (i.e., male coerced) tend to be motivated by fear, which is underscored by dependence on their co-perpetrator (Matthews et al., 1991). Although these women initially offend under duress, some later go on to initiate sexually abusive behavior (Saradjian & Hanks, 1996). In contrast, women who work with a male accomplice and who, of their own volition, take an active role in the abuse are typically motivated by jealousy and anger; their offenses are retaliatory in nature and are often indicative of significant psychological distress (Nathan & Ward, 2002).

Female sex offenders who act alone (i.e., self-initiated abusers) are further classified based on the age of their victims and the motivation for their crimes (Nathan & Ward, 2002). One typology, the teacher/lover or heterosexual nurturer, refers to women who sexually abuse adolescent boys within the context of an acquaintance or supervisory relationship (Matthews et al., 1991; Vandiver & Kercher, 2004). These offenders present as dependent and often abuse alcohol and/or drugs. Their offenses stem from the entwinement of dysfunctional age-appropriate relationships and attachment deficits and are an inappropriate attempt to meet intimacy and/or sexual needs.

Those self-initiated female offenders who sexually offend against prepubescent children, and who are considered intergenerationally predisposed (in that they come from a family where sexual abuse has been perpetrated across several generations), may view sexual abuse as normative and often exhibit significant psychopathology (Matthews et al., 1991). In fact, they are more likely than other categories of female sex offenders to be diagnosed with post-traumatic stress disorder (PTSD; Foa et al., 2000) or depression. These women also report having endured extensive physical and sexual abuse at the hands of caregivers, and therefore are often motivated by power and control (i.e., to reenact their own trauma, this time as the assailant), as well as sexual arousal.

As a group, female child molesters are more similar to the general population than they are different; aside from their abusive behavior, it is the disturbing frequency of physical, sexual, and emotional abuse common among their histories that sets them apart (Grayston & DeLuca, 1999). Physical and psychological abuse are almost always evident in these offenders' relationships with their own mothers. Perhaps as a result, some studies have found that these women exhibit significant deficits in self-esteem and are often involved in domestic violence (Hendriks & Biileveld, 2006; Tewksbury, 2004).

Recently, these categorical conceptualizations of female sex offenders have been broadened to include women who sexually violate other women, specifically adults or postpubescent females (Vandiver & Kercher, 2004). This classification includes women who engage in the exploitation or forced prostitution of other women for financial gain. These individuals also typically have multiple arrests for nonsexual crimes. Those women who take an active role in the sexual abuse of other adult females often commit acts of abuse within the context of an intimate same-sex relationship and are motivated by anger, retaliation, and jealousy. Table 7.1 summarizes the typologies of female sex offenders.

TABLE 7.1 Conceptualizing Typologies of Female Sex Offenders

Accompanied offenders	• Male-coerced; act under duress, dependent • Psychologically disturbed; act of their own volition, jealous
Self-initiated offenders	• Teacher/lover; attachment deficits • Predisposed; may view sex abuse as normal and have mental health issues
Women who target other females	• Exploitation; may be motivated by money • Direct sexual violation accompanied by domestic violence; motivated by anger, retaliation, jealousy

Source: Adapted from Matthews et al. (1991); Nathan and Ward (2002).

Co-Offending vs. Solo-Offending Women

Although research has found that a substantial portion of female sex offenders commit their crimes alongside a co-perpetrator, there is some debate about *exactly* how often such women work with an accomplice (Becker et al., 2001). Specifically, studies show that anywhere from 22% to 96% of these women have at least one male or female co-offender (Vandiver, 2006). Cases such as that of Joyce McKinney, wherein the woman initiates the assault of her own accord, are few and far between. In the most common co-perpetrator scenario, the female sex offender works with a male accomplice with whom she has a romantic and/or sexual relationship (Syed & Williams, 1996). Often, this relationship is abusive and coercive in nature, and the woman has been threatened, enticed, or otherwise encouraged to participate in the abuse of the (typically) female victim, who is of the male offender's choosing (Lewis & Stanley, 2000; Vandiver, 2006). It is not unusual for this type of offending duo to be married or living as common-law spouses.

Muskens et al. (2011) examined 60 women convicted of sex crimes, most of whom had at least one accomplice. The researchers investigated the similarities and differences between the accompanied and self-initiated offenders in their sample. Unsurprisingly, they found that the women who worked with a partner, and particularly a male partner, were more likely to victimize other women, while the women who offended alone more often targeted men, which was consistent with previous findings by Vandiver (2006). Moreover, solo offenders were more likely to target someone who was unrelated to them, while co-perpetrating women more frequently offended against family members.

With regard to the comparative personality pathology between these offender profiles, Muskens and colleagues (2011) found that the solo offenders were significantly more likely to present with a mood disorder. Prior studies have drawn the conclusion that female sex offenders as a group tend to experience bouts of major depression or depressive symptoms (Kaplan & Green, 1995; Lewis & Stanley, 2000) and have noted that severe depression can often motivate violent behavior (Steffensmeier & Allen, 1996). In contrast, personality disorders were more prevalent among the co-offending women. The solo offenders who did present with disordered personality features exhibited fewer antisocial, avoidant, and/or dependent traits and more borderline personality traits than their co-offending counterparts (Muskens et al., 2011). Experts have theorized that female sex offenders in general are more likely to demonstrate traits associated with borderline and/or dependent personality disorders (Green & Kaplan, 1994; Kaplan & Green, 1995; Mathews et al., 1989). In an early study of female sex offenders who had an accomplice, Kaplan and Green (1995) found that several of the women met criteria for a diagnosis of dependent personality disorder, suggesting that dependent personality traits may be an underlying characteristic of women who co-offend.

Janice Hooker

Janice was 15 years old when she began dating 19-year-old Cameron Hooker. She was a plain-looking girl who boasted little self-confidence. As a result, she had a rather long history of chasing after boys (and men) who mistreated her; the worse they treated her, the more she seemed to clamor for their attention. And Cameron knew it.

At first, Janice was impressed with Cameron. He had a car and seemed respectful—something she wasn't used to. He showered her with compliments and gave her the affection she so desperately craved. Janice quickly made him the center of her world and looked to him to define her own self-worth. It was not until after their relationship had been solidified and Janice was emotionally and psychologically dependent on him that Cameron made his sexual expectations known to his young and vulnerable girlfriend.

Cameron initiated Janice into BDSM culture—bondage, domination, sadism, and masochism. Although she found the idea aberrant, Janice feared losing the relationship, so she complied. Despite the shame, distress, and pain that it caused her, she allowed Cameron to do things such as hang her from a tree and beat her. As time went on, Cameron's sadistic fantasies became more violent and he began introducing torture and erotic asphyxiation into his repertoire. Regardless of Janice's discomfort with Cameron's inclinations, the couple wed in 1975.

Shortly thereafter, the two developed marital difficulties. Janice had grown tired of her husband's fetishes and wanted nothing more than to be a mother, so the two struck a deal. Cameron would father a child and in return Janice would help him abduct a slave with whom he could act out his most deviant and brutal fantasies. Janice hoped that the girl would be a diversion and offer her a reprieve from Cameron's abuse; her only stipulation was that he could not have intercourse with the slave.

In 1976, Janice became pregnant with the couple's first child. That same year, she and Cameron kidnapped a young woman named Marie Elizabeth Spannhake. Marie, who went by the nickname Marliz, was hitchhiking home from a flea market in Chico, California, following a fight with her fiancé. Instead of taking her back to her apartment as they'd promised, the Hookers brought Marliz to their house. There, the seemingly nice couple, who'd seemed so eager to offer a helping hand, imprisoned her. Cameron stripped her and then used leather straps to hang her from the rafters. Marliz screamed and cried, which enraged him. Deeming her uncooperative, he slit her vocal chords and shot her multiple times with a pellet gun, but when she survived, he strangled her. Janice dutifully helped him bury the body in the woods.

Then, in May of 1977, the Hookers, with their infant daughter in tow, abducted another hitchhiker, Colleen Stan, and she remained with them until 1984. During her 7-year captivity, Colleen was beaten and molested daily. Cameron used medieval torture devices to inflict physical pain on her and homemade contraptions to disorient her. He quickly broke his promise to Janice and raped Colleen. Still, Janice stayed. Cameron even went so far as to build a coffin-shaped box, in which he locked Colleen. He kept it underneath the bed that he and Janice shared. Cameron took pleasure in having sex with his wife while Colleen was constrained and forced to listen; he took equal pleasure in violating the sanctity of the one thing—marital intercourse—that Janice viewed as sacred.

Janice would certainly be considered a male-coerced offender, and although she reluctantly participated in the abduction of both of Cameron's victims, she stood passively by, perhaps out of fear of rejection or separation, or maybe as a result of her desire to please him, while her husband committed acts of sexual violence. Ironically, it was Janice who reported Cameron to the local authorities after she developed strong religious convictions and confessed to her pastor what had been going on inside her seemingly conservative home.

Educator-Perpetrated Sex Crimes and Gender Bias

It's every teenage boy's dream. Really, who's she hurting? He's the envy of all his friends. It was consensual—he wanted it. Teachers didn't look like that when I was in high school. Sound familiar?

As headlines about female teachers having sex with (male) students continue to flood the media, so do comments that reflect gender bias. In response to cases such as those involving Mary Kay Letourneau, Debra Lafave, and Stephanie Ragusa, websites and blogs entitled "Teacher Sex Scandals" and "Hottest Teachers to Sleep With Students" have cropped up, serving only to minimize the severity of such sexual offenses (Albrecht, 2012). The public, or at least a portion of it, tends to view female teachers as sympathetic and benign caretakers, and therefore their offenses against those entrusted to them are often portrayed as harmless or accidental slips into sexual activity (Denove, 2001).

However, these crimes don't "just happen," and they certainly aren't innocuous. These offenses are sometimes driven by the offender's desire to care for a male student, typically one from a troubled home, which becomes commingled with her need to feel attractive and desired. She may crave the feeling of being wanted by the student whom she has selected, even though the child may likely lack the capacity to give that love. However, he has the physical capability to provide sex, so the educator-offender substitutes physical closeness for emotional intimacy, and thus the relationship devolves into sex. Another potential motivating factor is to gain revenge against an uncaring or unsupportive husband. In either case, such assaults are not slip ups, accidents, or mistakes—they are crimes. Teachers are warned over and over again not to cross physical or emotional boundaries with their students. They know what they are doing, and regardless of a lack of judgment or emotional maturity, these offenses are purposeful (Albrecht, 2012).

Nonetheless, research indicates that when female teachers commit these indiscretions they are viewed less harshly by society and sometimes even by the criminal justice system. Female teacher–male student sexual encounters are viewed more positively (and are characterized as less criminal) than male teacher–female student sexual interactions (Fromuth & Holt, 2008; Fromuth et al., 2001). It is also not uncommon for other sex crimes committed by women to be viewed as less serious than those committed by men (Knoll, 2010). Thus, it appears that there is a rigid and pervasive sociocultural subtext surrounding sexual abuse, gender roles, and victimization—yet it is one to which many people remain oblivious.

Profiling Teachers Who Sexually Offend

Limited information is available regarding educator-perpetrated sexual assault; the majority of documentation comes from newspaper reports of these incidents. In one of the most comprehensive probes to date, Shakeshaft (2003) synthesized data collected from 80,000 schools for the American Association of University Women (AAUW, 2001). According to the research, 9.6% of students in grades 8–11 reported having been sexually abused by a teacher. A study conducted in Israel yielded similar results, finding that 8% of secondary school students had endured sexual mistreatment by school staff, thus indicating the global nature of this issue (Khoury-Kassabri, 2006).

Teachers Who Molest Prepubescent Students

Meta-analytic research reveals that educator sexual abusers generally fit one of two profiles: (1) those with victims younger than seventh grade and (2) those with victims in late middle school and/or high school (Shakeshaft, 2003). Perpetrators who abuse the younger set of victims depict a drastically different public persona in addition to employing a dissimilar modus operandi to those who target older students. Teachers who abuse elementary-aged school children are high achievers within their profession, and have often been recognized with awards for teaching excellence (Shakeshaft, 2004). These individuals are frequently viewed as popular and trusted, which can lead to allegations being downplayed, ignored, or otherwise overlooked; similarly, the disparity between their salt-of-the-earth façade and the heinous nature of such accusations almost always leads to confusion among school officials. It has been theorized that this type of offender works so hard to secure public trust and build an impeccable reputation as a means of furthering her goal of sexual offending (Knoll, 2010).

Teacher/Lovers and Heterosexual Nurturers

Female educators who sexually offend against older students fall into the typology known as teacher/lover or heterosexual nurturer. In contrast to those who offend against prepubescent children, these women may strive to be overachievers but may also be satisfied with professional mediocrity. Their sexual offenses are often less about premeditation and more commonly the result of a combination of negative emotionality and poor judgment (Shakeshaft, 2004). For example, a female teacher who is having marital difficulties may find herself feeling flattered by attention from a teenage male student and may act on those feelings as a way of soothing an emotional and/or sexual void. The teacher/lover views herself as emotionally equal to her victim (Matthews et al., 1991), who is most often a troubled adolescent male seeking reassurance, nurturing, and attention. She views the offense as a consensual romantic affair.

Grooming

Regardless of which of the aforementioned profiles an educator abuser fits, grooming is part of her crime. Grooming is the purposeful furtherance of the offender's aim to perpetrate sexually offensive behavior. During this process, adult would-be offenders (both male and female) initiate, establish, and maintain relationships with the child(ren) they wish to target. They establish emotional connections in order to earn the child's trust and lower his or her inhibitions. Grooming is a deliberate and elaborately orchestrated approach, the goal of which is to allow the sex offender to get close enough to the child to commit a sexual act (or several sexual acts) *and keep the abuse a secret.*

Grooming involves a variety of methods to build rapport between child and offender and to exploit the power imbalance inherent in the child–adult relationship. It additionally utilizes multiple tactics to ensure the complicity and secrecy of the victim, including systematic separation from family and peers (Lawson, 2003), threats (including being taken away from parents or getting parents into trouble), and coercion.

When the abuser is a teacher, she often recognizes the significance of the violation of student-teacher boundaries—prior to her offense and prior to the onset of grooming behaviors (Barrett et al., 2006). For educator sexual abusers, grooming begins with victim selection and subsequently involves various tactics to "seduce" the student (Robins, 2000). Victims are often children who are not only compliant but most likely to keep the offender's actions a secret. Therefore, students who are from broken homes, are estranged from their parents, or have emotional vulnerabilities are commonly targeted (Shakeshaft, 2003). Because most minors are responsive to positive attention from authority figures, the teacher often uses praise, which can be extremely influential (Nicaise et al., 2007). She may then progress to giving the "chosen" student special attention and keeping them after class for mentoring, special projects, rewards, etc., which have a critical impact on the student's motivation and cognition—and all play into the offender's aim of sexual and psychological exploitation (Davis et al., 2006).

As the teacher is deepening this rapport with the student, who is likely craving positive reinforcement due to a lack of attention at home, she begins to slowly introduce overnight outings and sexual discourse, followed by touching. All the while, she is monitoring the victim's compliance and ability to maintain secrecy while desensitizing the child to progressively more intense sexual behaviors. The teacher may strive to gain the trust of the victim's parents so that she can have greater access to the child and further isolate the student during outings. Additionally, as part of maintaining the grooming process, offenders will try to provide victims with experiences and/or rewards that are valuable to them so that they will remain compliant and dependent and ultimately be reluctant to lose the relationship (Knoll, 2010); this can cause significant and damaging psychological turmoil for the victims.

TABLE 7.2 Warning Signs for Teacher Sexual Abuse

- Preferential treatment of a particular student or students
- Inappropriate/excessive time spent alone with a student
- Time spent alone with a student outside of class
- Offering to drive a student to/from school, extracurricular activities, etc
- Befriending parents and visiting their home to "check in" on the student
- Assuming the role of confidante for a particular student or students
- Bestowing gifts, cards, letters, or tokens upon a student
- Being physically affectionate with a student
- Being flirtatious or making off-color comments around, about, or toward a student

Source: Adapted from Shakeshaft (2004); Sutton (2004).

TABLE 7.3 Sex Offender Grooming Strategies

- Target vulnerable children (e.g., low self-esteem, turmoil at home, etc.).
- Target socially isolated, emotionally needy children.
- Target children whose parents are uninvolved.
- Seek out and assume caretaking roles (e.g., teaching, tutoring, coaching).
- Form "special" relationship or bond.
- Gain trust of parent or guardian.
- Give gifts and privileges, create special outings, etc.
- Isolate child.
- Shower child with attention, playing on his or her desire for affection.
- Desensitize the child to sex (sexual conversation, pictures, pornographic video).
- Employ sexual pretense (i.e., "teaching," "exploring," "closeness").
- Exploit victim's sexual curiosity.
- Bribe the victim to ensure continued compliance and secrecy.
- Threaten consequences of divulging the offense, including blaming the victim.
- Threaten the loss of the "loving" relationship.

Source: Adapted from Elliot et al. (1995).

Mary Kay Letourneau

Mary Kay Letourneau mingled with the crowd; she was the center of attention, and she knew how to work a room. The star of a popular Seattle nightclub promotion audaciously titled "Hot for Teacher," she signed autographs for eager fans. Both she and the DJ, Vili Fualaau, who was her victim-turned-husband, were swarmed by paparazzi. Mary Kay first came into the media spotlight in the 1990s when she had sex with her (then) 12-year-old student. Nine years and two children later, she and Vili married in one of the most reviled and controversial relationship stories in recent history.

***

The daughter of a politician, Mary Kay Letourneau (née Schmitz) was familiar with public scrutiny. She was 2 years old when her father began his (ultraconservative) political career and successfully claimed a seat in the California State Legislature. He went on to become a senator and then a U.S. congressman.

The fourth of seven children, Mary Kay was born in Tustin, California, in 1962 and was raised in a very strict household where Catholic ideals were paramount. She often accepted responsibility for her younger siblings, and in 1973, when her 3-year-old brother accidentally drowned in the family pool, she blamed herself, as she had promised to watch him. The guilt haunted her.

During her high school and subsequent college years, Mary Kay pulled away from the rigid values that her family had instilled in her; she began to test boundaries as a means of self-exploration. She quickly found herself focused on boys and partying. As she worked to lay the personal and academic foundations for her future, her father's political aspirations were crumbling. In 1978, Mary Kay's image of her larger-than-life father was shattered when it was discovered that he'd fathered two children with a student at Santa Ana College, where he'd previously taught. The news not only caused irreparable damage to his career, but it left Mary Kay feeling betrayed and confused. Rather than hold him accountable, she blamed her mother for being cold and distant and ultimately driving him to have an affair.

Mary Kay threw herself into her studies. While at Arizona State University, she met fellow student Steve Letourneau. The two began dating, and Mary Kay quickly became pregnant. Despite Mary Kay acknowledging that she was not (and had never been) in love with Steve, the two married. It was not until later that Mary Kay admitted she'd married him because her parents had encouraged it.

Mary Kay and Steve moved their family from Arizona to Alaska and ultimately to Seattle, where Steve found work as a baggage handler for an airline. Despite not being happy in her marriage, Mary Kay gave birth to three more children. The Letourneaus struggled financially, and the strain took a toll on their marriage. Each of them engaged in multiple extramarital affairs, and Steve allegedly became physically and emotionally abusive, causing Mary Kay to file police reports and seek emergency medical care.

As the marriage further deteriorated, it was her work as a teacher that gave Mary Kay solace. She first met 8-year-old Samoan

American Vili Fualaau in her second-grade class at Shorewood Elementary. At the time, he was a sweet little boy who was taken by her blonde hair and smile; with his childlike innocence, he likened her to a movie star.

Mary Kay next encountered Vili several years later when he was assigned to her sixth-grade class. The year was 1996. Mary Kay was 34 years old and Vili was 12—one year older than her eldest son. Mary Kay noticed that Vili didn't quite fit in with the rest of the students in her class. He came from a strained background. His father was incarcerated and his mother was rarely home because she was working long hours to support the household; he was vulnerable. Mary Kay began spending more time with him under the pretense of helping to bring out what she called his unique gift— his artistic ability. The two saw one another alone and outside the classroom. He even visited Mary Kay's home and became friendly with her son. Their "friendship" developed into what Mary Kay later labeled a flirtation.

In a 2004 interview with Barbara Walters, Mary Kay recalled that it was Vili who initially expressed romantic feelings when he asked if she would ever consider having an affair. At the time, Mary Kay's marriage was crumbling, and although she was aware of her feelings toward him, she claimed that she had not planned to act on them (ABC News, 2004). Then, one night, the two kissed and the relationship quickly turned sexual; by the end of the summer of 1996, Mary Kay was pregnant with Vili's child.

In February of 1997, Steve Letourneau discovered love letters between his wife and Vili and began to suspect that he had not fathered the child Mary Kay was carrying; he turned the letters over to police, which sparked an investigation. A media firestorm ensued and Mary Kay was arrested. She gave birth to Vili's first daughter while out on bail in May of 1997 and was immediately forced to relinquish custody to Vili's mother.

Had she gone to trial, Mary Kay could have been facing more than 7 years in prison, so in August of 1997 she pled guilty to child rape in exchange for 3 months in jail plus probation. Her plea agreement was accepted with the stipulation that she have no further contact with the victim. However, within weeks of being released from jail in January of 1998, she was rearrested when police found her having sex with Vili in the backseat of a car. Also in the vehicle were cash, baby clothes, and Mary Kay's passport, leading authorities to speculate that the two were attempting to flee the country.

Mary Kay again went before the judge, who referred to her actions as egregious. Her suspended sentence was revoked and she was remanded to a custodial term of 7 years. The couple's second daughter, who was conceived during Mary Kay's brief period of freedom between bouts of incarceration, was born behind bars in October of 1998.

The prison strictly enforced the no contact order between Mary Kay and Vili; Vili was not permitted to visit, nor were the two allowed to phone or exchange letters. However, they devised another plan so that they could communicate. Because Mary Kay was granted visitation with her children, the couple used their daughters to send messages back and forth. In fact, on one occasion, the girls visited their mother and sang to her in Samoan to let her know that Vili would be proposing marriage upon her release.

From inside the prison walls, Mary Kay fantasized about a future with Vili, but others weren't so quick to forget the damage she'd done. In 1999, she and Steve Letourneau divorced, with Steve openly citing his disbelief that his wife had destroyed their family by behaving in such a reprehensible manner; he was awarded sole custody of all four of the Letourneau children. Then, in 2002, the Fualaau family sued the Highline School District for negligence for its failure to recognize the damaging and ongoing sexual relationship between Mary Kay and Vili. Under oath, Vili was forced to describe his interactions with Mary Kay, which reflected her grooming process. Specifically, he told the court that for each answer he got right on a test, Mary Kay would remove a piece of clothing. Mary Kay's attorney argued that the confused and well-meaning teacher had viewed her affair with Vili as something beautiful, not deviant. Despite Vili's testimony, the family's claim for damages was rejected (Cohn, 2015).

When Mary Kay's sentence expired in 2004, Vili petitioned the court to lift the no contact order. The motion was granted a few days later and on May 20, 2005, the couple wed in a 250-guest ceremony at a winery in Washington State.

After celebrating her 12th wedding anniversary in May of 2017, the 55-year-old Mary Kay downplayed her marriage to 36-year-old Vili as a not your average boy-meets-girl story. She does not view herself as a predator. When she describes her first exchanges with Vili, she gushes like a schoolgirl with a crush. Her distortions and lack of emotional maturation are apparent in her saccharine presentation. In fact, during an interview with *20/20* she noted, "There's a story of us that has a life of its own. But it's not our story. I don't know if enough time will pass where it will take away what the media did to our story. Because it was so big, and they ran with it so fast" (Walters, 2015).

The couple's daughters are now teenagers who have normalized their parents' relationship. They have never been told the underlying details surrounding Mary Kay's offense; they had to learn those through Google and gossip, and they have been exposed to a tremendous amount of gossip, as they attend the same school district where their parents met and are taught by the same teachers who were once Mary Kay's colleagues.

As for the victim himself, he minimizes his now-wife's crime, but does acknowledge that the whole ordeal had a significant impact on him. In an emotional interview with ABC, Vili opened up about his struggle with depression and disclosed, "I'm surprised I'm still alive today. I went through a really dark time" (Joseph et al., 2015). When Mary Kay became pregnant with his child, he, as a child himself, naturally lacked the financial and psychological resources to support himself and the baby, which he felt was his responsibility; he began to suffer emotional collapse. Although Vili does not view himself as a true victim, he does recognize that when his sexual encounters with Mary Kay began, he was vulnerable and lacked the support he needed at home. Mary Kay became his confidante, and when her pregnancy was uncovered and the court forbade the two of them from having contact, Vili once again had nowhere to turn; the loss of that relationship—regardless of its inappropriate and damaging nature—meant further isolation for Vili and sent him spiraling into depression. Despite everything, Vili does not appear to hold Mary Kay responsible.

In November of 2017, Vili filed for legal separation from Mary Kay. However, according to multiple media outlets, the two still reside in the same home and his reasoning may have been related to his desire to obtain a license to legally sell marijuana, which being married to someone with a criminal history could prevent.

Sex Trafficking

One class of sex crimes that is often overlooked, especially when talking about female-perpetrated offenses, is sex trafficking. Sex trafficking is modern-day slavery, which employs the use of force, threat, fraud, or coercion to engender a person into the commercial sex trade. Trafficking dens are covert operations, and victims rarely seek out help from law enforcement due to self-blame or fear of reprisal from their trafficker.

Sex trafficking traverses all demographics and locations; it is both a local and global issue, and traffickers have extensive resources to move their victims not only across state lines, but across international borders. While anyone can be a sex trafficking victim, vulnerable individuals, such as runaways, homeless individuals, and those who have survived trauma (e.g., domestic violence, sexual assault, military conflict, social discrimination) are actively targeted and exploited by traffickers (National Human Trafficking Resource Center, 2007).

Pathways to Trafficking

As discussed in Chapter 2, a significant link exists between a female's own victimization and subsequent offending. Therefore, before looking at a woman's entrée into the illicit realm of trafficking, it is critical to first evaluate her pathway to being victimized herself. Women who traffic other women typically fall into one of three categories. First, there are those who deliberately and willingly submit to sex work, knowing that the conditions will be both exploitative and humiliating. They are often from impoverished backgrounds and see this work as a viable option to make ends meet. In Southeast Asia, for example, underage females are encouraged by their families to enter the sex trade to work off debts incurred by relatives. While these girls find this scenario unattractive, they do not view themselves as victims but rather as contributing family members. These girls are victims not only of sex trafficking but also of socioeconomic conditions, familial expectations, and discriminatory biopolitics (Kienast et al., 2014).

A second category of females with full agential capacity, who also choose sex work, do so as a means of socioeconomic advancement. Unlike the first group, these individuals are not asked to pay off a debt. Rather, they are looking to leave behind an undesirable, frequently disadvantaged environment. They often have their sights set on an unrealistic image of the "glamorous West" and believe (or are told) that sex work is an adventurous and lucrative way of achieving social and financial advancement. Underscoring this misguided notion is these women's desperate desire for migration and globalization, which is further compounded by Western civilization's propensity for glorifying sex (Kienast et al., 2014). Consider sexuality with regard to advertisements, television, webcasts, and major Hollywood movies over the past several decades. What emerges is a superficially bedazzled image of women who have been objectified by an entire industry and global economy and who, despite this fact (or perhaps because of it), have achieved fame and fortune. That idea of "If I have sex or allow myself to be sexualized, I'll get fast money, social status, and luxury" resonates with women who want to get out of their current situation; sadly, they often find themselves shackled and then turned out.

Deception plays a key role in the third pathway to victimization. The women in this group are enticed with promises of high-paying nondegrading jobs at beauty salons, massage parlors, and modeling agencies or are offered opportunities to travel abroad for educational purposes. Unlike the individuals in the previous two categories, these women do not enter into sex work of their own volition. However, once they reach their final destination, they are enslaved and forced into prostitution. A disturbing element of the victimization of these particular women is that the people who lure them to these so-called "good" opportunities are often friends, relatives, or other women—all individuals whom they feel that they can trust (Kienast et al., 2014).

Whether a particular victim evolves into a perpetrator is influenced by numerous and varied factors. Typically, the individuals who *do* make this transition follow one of two trajectories. The first involves family dynamics, which play a key role in the development of one's moral and psychological capacity and, as such, can either hinder or increase one's likelihood of engaging in criminal behavior. The women who follow this path typically hail from a troubled family background and commonly have a male relative with ties to the criminal underworld. They have often been exposed to physical and/or sexual abuse, emotional torment, addiction, or neglect. Such childhood trauma commonly manifests behaviorally at a later age. Additionally, many of them have also had caregivers who were negligent and did not provide for their basic needs (food, clean clothes), which thus began a chain reaction; they were made to feel embarrassed, causing them to skip school, have strained peer relationships, etc. Ultimately, they sought refuge on the street, due to the shame they felt because of their neglectful and abusive home life.

It is a domino effect. In order to escape an intolerable home life, these (often young) girls turn to the streets, where they encounter a range of people from petty criminals to pimps and traffickers ready to exploit them. They are captivated by the attention these individuals lavish upon them, as they've been starved for it their entire lives. They quickly become not only emotionally but also materially dependent on the trafficker, who offers them love, acceptance, shelter, and financial support. However, it's not that simple, and here's where the relationship becomes exceedingly more complex.

These women (and girls) find the superficial charm and "loving" attention shown to them by their traffickers appealing—they almost feel as though these individuals have rescued them in some way. However, due to their intense vulnerabilities, they may themselves eventually become interested in cooperating or actually *participating* in the trafficking business and making it their livelihood—and sole means of survival. Thus, the line between victim and perpetrator is not only slightly blurred; it is crossed. While many of these women initially engage in illegal trafficking-related activities unwillingly or under physical, emotional, or economic pressure, they eventually become interested in perpetrating the crime themselves. Still others, however, become interested purely from an egoistic standpoint; they see trafficking other women as a viable means of earning an income. They are financially driven. As women are considered to be both biologically predisposed to and socialized to be nurturing, this seems counterintuitive. However, given their own trauma histories, the women who follow this pathway to trafficking often fail to develop empathic concern for their victims (Kienast et al., 2014).

The second pathway for women to become sex traffickers is referred to as "climbing the ladder." Many female perpetrators have themselves been former sex workers or victims who were forced into the sex trade by a (frequently male) relative or partner. As a means of avoiding further humiliation, degradation, or abuse, they slowly move toward the organizational side of the trafficking ring. To outsiders, this may seem like an unreasonable course of action; after all, if they were trying to escape continued victimization, wouldn't they just leave? However, aside from the coercion inherent in trafficking, the victims lack prospects for social and financial support, and thus their hope of reintegration is severely limited. They become stigmatized and dependent on the very system that has enslaved them. Thus, lacking a hopeful course for egress and resources, and being well versed with regard to the "intrigues" of the industry, they willingly or unwillingly start to fill in the gaps between traffickers and victims (or potential victims) by enticing and coercing other women. By contributing to the operations of the business, they gradually begin to shift their position within the organizational hierarchy; they put aside natural and "feminine" empathetic and emotional responses. Having themselves been subjected to the same abuse that they are now instrumental in inflicting on others, they adopt a "better her than me" mentality—it is survivalist. Soon, this survivalist strategy may even become viewed as a convenient way of making a living—and a good one at that (Kienast et al., 2014).

In a disturbing article about women trafficking other women, writer Julie Bindel spoke to an Albanian woman, who she called Elda (a pseudonym used to shield the victim's actual identity). Elda explained that the only way for her to escape the abuse of her trafficker, who had held her captive in a brothel in London, was to promise to return home and bring back new girls. She told Bindel (2013):

> I had to go to my town and tell the girls there that I knew from school that there were great opportunities in the UK for them, you know, as waitresses and even as dancers. They were poor and desperate like me, so they wanted to get away. I felt like I had stuck a knife in my own stomach, knowing what I was taking them to, but I could not stand one more day [in the brothel].

Sadly, Elda's story is becoming more and more common as the role of women in trafficking expands. Women are not only being sexually exploited themselves, but are also being used to sexually exploit other women because the social and societal narrative dictates that women are innocent, sensitive, and nurturing; They are more likely to be victimized than to victimize. Traffickers use these collective and sometimes subconscious biases to their advantage. Women have easier access to other women, and females are more likely to trust another female, rather than be seduced by or trust a male recruiter. Women are frequently forced or coerced into the recruiting process and typically work as prostitutes while trying to recruit other girls. Their hope is often to move entirely to the business side of the organization by offering the trafficker a "replacement" victim. They then move from recruiting to financial management and sometimes to overseeing the entire trafficking ring.

The Profile of a Madam

When people envision sex traffickers, they almost always think of pimps—of men prostituting women against their will. However, according to the United Nations Office on Drugs and Crime (2009), women make up the largest proportion of these offenders in approximately a third of certain countries. This perhaps lends credence to the concept of the victim-turned-perpetrator. One certainty is that women who are involved in trafficking are some of the most vulnerable victims, and in some regions of the world women trafficking other women is the norm, not the anomaly.

Due in part to the fact that sex trafficking is a global issue, there is no one-size-fits-all profile of a female sex trafficker or madam. The profile must adjust by region to account for cultural specificity. In Nigeria, for example, where madams garner respect, women recruiting and trafficking other women is an "ideal" approach. Madams often wear fine clothes and expensive jewelry to show outward signs of wealth to attract new girls. Madams are most frequently sex workers who have exhibited loyalty and are promoted from within the ranks of the trafficking den itself. They are revered as role models by their protégés who hope to achieve similar wealth and success. The madams promise to find jobs for their recruits, some of whom are told that they will be hired as beauticians in other countries, and others of whom are aware that they will work as prostitutes. Regardless, the madam's promises are a godsend—a chance for the recruits to have a better future and to be less of a financial burden on their families. Many of the girls aspire to be madams someday, as they see this type of promotion as an indication of "Western-associated" success (Kienast et al., 2014).

In Europe, on the other hand, women often remain in mid-ranking roles in trafficking enterprises and are only advanced to the very top of these organizations when the male leader, usually their husband or another male relative, has been arrested and is therefore unable to continue his criminal duties. However, there is much variation in this process throughout Europe, and so generalizations cannot be made (Kienast et al., 2014).

For example, the trend in Eastern Europe is that female traffickers tend to be businesswomen with no familial link to the prostitutes that they pimp out. An Italian study found that 60% of those prosecuted for trafficking offenses in the Ukraine are female (Denisova,

2001; Siegel & de Blanc, 2010). These women are educated and have superior communication skills that enhance their ability to secure their victims' confidence during recruitment. Many Eastern European madams do inform recruits as to the nature of the work they will be performing. However, they are not upfront with regard to the reality of the working conditions. Once a recruit is under the madam's control, she takes the girl's identification documentation away and, with it, her autonomy (Kienast et al., 2014).

Traditionally, these madams were partners in such crimes. However, they have been working independently more often—so much so that they have acquired a unique skill set in a rather evolutionary manner. Similarly, Russian prostitutes have developed proficiencies involving negotiation, seduction, and business acuity. They often work under the tutelage of colleagues and/or former prostitutes (Kienast et al., 2014).

In Thailand, sex trafficking is illegal, yet it continues to be a widespread problem. Sexual tourism draws money into the region and is a major source of revenue for the country's economy. Local families are financially dependent on the income earned by sex workers. *Mama-sans* (Thai madams) typically partner with their husbands or other (male) family members and are sometimes part of a larger crime network or mafia. They use social media and their knowledge of the language, culture, and domestic landscape to help recruit victims, who are usually young females from impoverished rural areas. These girls are then sold to sexual tourists and sent to other countries where they are forced into prostitution. The victims are often kept under surveillance, threatened, and physically abused by the mama-sans (Kienast et al., 2014).

Trafficking in Our Own Backyard

In a far-too-common scenario, 23-year-old Araceli Mendoza Alvarez was arrested alongside 35-year-old ringleader Ariel Guizar in conjunction with a California-based trafficking operation in March of 2016. She was Guizar's so-called "bottom girl," or his highest-ranking prostitute, meaning that while she herself was still being victimized, she was also involved in the "enforcement" part of the business with regard to the other (often newer) girls. At the time of her arrest, Araceli was accused of teaching a 15-year-old girl the ropes so that Guizar could turn her out. She was also accused of drugging the victim prior to an alleged sexual assault by Guizar, which involved both rape and sodomy. The extreme and disturbing behaviors for which Araceli was arrested provide a jarring illustration of the convergence of desperation and the desire to escape abuse at any cost.

Guizar's 20-year-old girlfriend, Jocelyn Contreres Alvarez (of no relation to Araceli), was also arrested for her involvement in this case. She was charged with conspiracy, criminal threats, human trafficking of a minor, pandering a minor, pimping a prostitute younger than 16, and child abuse. Authorities believe that she may have used deception to recruit new trafficking victims and that her baby daughter, whom Guizar had fathered, was present during both drug use and prostitution-related activities (City News Service, 2016).

Guizar, or "Shy" as he was known, was a tattoo artist who was popular on Instagram. He used social media to attract new victims and often preyed on isolated, lonely, or insecure girls from unhappy backgrounds. He frequently targeted children in foster care and struck up conversations with young girls who wanted tattoos. According to statements ascribed to prior victims, the chats quickly moved from "liking" pictures on social media to messaging, to friendship, to sexting, to meeting in person, to rape, to forced prostitution (O'Donnell, 2016).

In contrast to the male-run California operation, 68-year-old Hortencia Medeles-Arguello (aka Raquel Medeles Garcia), known as "Tencha," was the mastermind behind a Houston-based sex trafficking ring, which she ran out of her East End cantina called Las Palmas II. On April 24, 2015, she was convicted of conspiracy to commit sex trafficking, conspiracy to harbor aliens, aiding and abetting to commit money laundering, and conspiracy to commit money laundering. In an unprecedented move, 12 victims came forward at trial and testified about how they were lured from their home countries by promises of a better life only to be imprisoned and forced into sex work. Upon their arrival in Houston, Texas, pimps lured them to the 17-room brothel above the Las Palmas II bar, where they were brutally beaten and raped; many of the girls were as young as 14 at the time. In all, there were 40 people prosecuted in association with the case, and officials believe that the bordello attracted over 64,000 johns in the nearly 20 months that it was in operation. It is said to have netted Tencha over $1.6 million before it was shut down in 2013 (Salinger, 2016).

Tencha was sentenced to life in prison. Her brother, two of her sisters, and even her daughter pleaded guilty to helping her run the trafficking ring in various locations over the course of more than a decade. According to the U.S. Office of Public Affairs (2016), these convictions put an end to one family's reign of terror and brought down an international sex trafficking scheme that was significant in both scope and magnitude.

Conclusion

Gender stereotypes often prevent women from being considered capable of sexual violence. Female sex offenders are commonly regarded not only by society but also by the criminal justice system as less deviant than their male counterparts. In reality, some women, ranging from teacher/lover assailants to adult-target rapists to sex traffickers, familiarize themselves with existing social paradigms to lure their victims into a false sense of security. They later use these same constructs to their advantage to mislead law enforcement. With sexual offenses being the number one underreported crime due largely to victim reluctance to come forward for fear of being shamed or not being believed, misconceptions predicated on gender stereotypes put victims of female sex crimes at a dangerous disadvantage.

Chapter 8

Team Killers

The Craigslist Killer

In the early morning hours of November 12, 2013, residents of Sunbury, Pennsylvania, discovered the body of 42-year-old Troy LaFerrera in an alleyway behind a neighborhood home. He had been strangled and stabbed multiple times.

Within days, newlyweds Miranda (age 19) and Elytte Barbour (age 22) were arrested for the murder. According to statements ascribed to Miranda, she and her husband of only 3 weeks had plotted to kill together—for the sheer thrill of it. To put their plan into action, the twosome had placed a personal ad on Craigslist promising female "companionship" in exchange for money. Miranda claimed that she and Elytte intended to use these ads as ethical tests to protect young girls from would-be sexual predators by murdering the men who answered them; LaFerrera responded.

On the night of the murder, Miranda lured LaFerrera into the front seat of her car before telling him that she'd lied about her age in the online ad and was really only 16. She later told police that this was an ethical barometer of sorts; when LaFerrera wanted to proceed with the sexual encounter, he sealed his own fate. As LaFerrera began to slide his hand up Miranda's thigh, she asked, "Did you see the stars tonight?" The seemingly benign and almost flirtatious question was actually a prearranged signal between Miranda and Elytte, who was hiding beneath a blanket in the back seat. Upon hearing that, Elytte was to blitz LaFerrera from behind, wrap a cord around his neck, and strangle him. However, when Elytte didn't respond quickly enough, Miranda grabbed the knife she'd hidden in the driver's side door pocket and stabbed him. Elytte eventually joined in and ultimately choked LaFerrera to death.

After they'd disposed of the body, the couple bought cleaning supplies with which to wipe down their vehicle. They then went to a strip club to celebrate the emotional and physical high they felt following their kill. The homicide commemorated their 3-week wedding anniversary (Lysiak, 2014).

In a statement to police, Miranda, who quickly became dubbed the Pennsylvania Craigslist Killer, disclosed that LaFerrera was not her first victim. She claimed to have slaughtered dozens more in a 6-year-long satanic killing spree spanning multiple states. She had reportedly joined a cult at the age of 13 and warned police that they wouldn't find a trail of buried corpses, but rather would only "find body parts" (Murphy, 2014). Regarding her claims of serial murder, Miranda's family expressed doubt and characterized her as a manipulative liar. To date, there has been no evidence to corroborate any of the cult murders for which Miranda claimed responsibility (Lysiak, 2014).

Miranda is currently serving life for the brutal slaying of LaFerrera. She pled guilty to second-degree murder, a plea bargain that ensured the death penalty was taken off the table at sentencing. She has no regrets, and maintains that she loves her husband, and believes that her victim deserved to die. She has told authorities, "If I were to be released, I would do this again" (Draznin et al., 2014).

Perhaps even more jarring than her apparent lack of empathy is the fact that Miranda Barbour stated during a jailhouse interview, "I knew we were going to do this since the day we met" (Murphy, 2014). This statement begs the question, how does one know whether a potential mate is primed for murder? Certainly first-date conversation doesn't consist of "What do you like to do for fun? I enjoy killing people." How then, do killer couples come together? At what point do they cross the threshold from learning one another's boundaries to becoming co-conspirators? What are the dynamics underlying their attraction?

Serial Killing Teams

Psychologically speaking, Miranda and Elytte Barbour were on the path to becoming a serial killer couple. Although in the nascent stages of their homicidal career at the time of their apprehension, their intent was never to commit only one murder. They cast a wide net, as evidenced by their use of the Internet to lure potential victims. Additionally, their motive was akin to that of the mission-oriented serial killer who seeks to rid the world of a particular type of individual, in this case, sexual predators.

Serial murder is estimated to comprise less than 1% of all homicides annually (Federal Bureau of Investigation [FBI], 2005), with 13% of such crimes being committed by teams. Of these, 56% involve two killers, while the remaining 44% involve three or more offenders working in tandem. Male–male pairs account for the largest proportion of two-person killing teams (30%), and male–female duos rank second, comprising 25% of such partnerships (Newton, 2008).

When women commit serial murder, they are more likely to do so as part of a team than they are to act alone. In fact, some analyses indicate that close to one-third of all female serial killers have never committed a solo homicide and have killed only within the context of a team's endeavors. A female team killer is defined as a woman who kills or partakes in the systematic murder of multiple victims in conjunction with one or more accomplices. A woman is classified as a team killer, even if she does not physically commit the murders herself, as long as she participates in the homicidal activities of the team (Kelleher & Kelleher, 1998). For example, if she lures or restrains individuals who are then killed by her partner(s), she is considered to be a team killer.

Kelleher and Kelleher (1998) have distinguished three types of killing teams involving female serial killers (FSKs): (1) male–female teams, (2) all-female teams, and (3) family teams (see Table 8.1 on the next page). A team's overarching characteristics are determined by a host of factors, including the individual activities of the dominant team member, the number of participants, the group's gender makeup, and the relationship among team members. Given these differences, it stands to reason that each type of team enacts its crimes in a slightly different fashion.

TABLE 8.1 A Comparison of Serial Killing Teams and the Women Who Join Them

Male–Female Teams	All-Female Teams	Family Teams
One male and one female	Exclusively women (two or more)	Three or more persons of both sexes; not necessarily biologically related
Active period of 1 year	Active for 1 to 2 years	Active for 1 year or less
Sexual relationship between members	Sometimes involve sexual relationships; various motives (profit, crime, compassion, etc.)	Nonsexual relationships; members share a love of murder and mayhem or a compulsion to kill
Serial sexual homicide, maintained by the synergy of the pair's own sexual relationship	Target victims who are old, young, vulnerable, or otherwise incapacitated	Teams may go on crime sprees involving multiple felonies, commit serial sexual homicide, or both
Crimes involve sexual torture	MO mimics that of a solo female serial killer (poison, suffocation)	Kills are extremely violent
Various motives for female partner (transfer of sadism, psychopathy, domestic abuse)		Women involved tend to be young, submissive, and loyal to the group leader

Source: Adapted from Kelleher and Kelleher (1998).

Male–Female Teams

The male–female team is the most common of the three serial killing units, especially in the United States. It is composed of one male and one female who are usually sexually involved with one another. Serial sexual homicide is their primary criminal activity. The male partner is often a sexual predator and serial killer in his own right, while the female partner is easily dominated and manipulated by him; in a sense, she may be characterized as one of his victims. That said, there are also cases in which the female is an active and engaged killer who exhibits a level of sexual psychopathy that rivals that of her male counterpart (Kelleher & Kelleher, 1998).

The team's focus on serial sexual murder is maintained by the synergy of their ongoing sexual relationship with one another in addition to their pathological obsession with sexual domination and control; in other words, they are aroused by their murders. Such teams commit horrifically brutal crimes, commonly torturing their victims before killing them. They tend to target children and adolescents, and their offenses often garner a great deal of media attention before they are caught (Kelleher & Kelleher, 1998).

One of the key features of sexually driven serial homicide is the element of fantasy. As the male partner is often the dominant team member, it is typically his sadistic fantasies that become the blueprint for the team's activities. These deviant thoughts are the manifestation of years of his maladaptive response to adverse emotions such as fear, anxiety, and powerlessness, resulting from an abusive or otherwise traumatic past (Morton & Hilts, 2008). In other words, eroticizing violence is his escape from negative emotionality.

When women kill with a male partner, their motives often become commingled with those of their accomplice. In some cases, these women may be both vulnerable due to their own abuse history as well as impressionable. They may therefore be coerced or easily influenced by their male partner to sexualize violence. However, because many of them are significantly younger than their male counterparts and have had no trouble with the law prior to meeting their accomplice, it seems logical to assume that they are actually victims of sadistic, manipulative men under whose spell they've

172 • When Women Offend

fallen. However, this conclusion fails to recognize the fact that women such as Charlene Gallego, who murdered 10 victims in Sacramento, California, alongside her husband, and Karla Homolka, who, along with her partner Paul Bernardo, was responsible for the deaths of at least three teenage girls in Canada, quickly transformed into fully participating partners in crime; they not only recruited victims, but became complicit in torture and sexual assault and in some cases acted out their own violent fantasies. Therefore, one school of thought is that these women may have *always* had the potential to act out their rage and despair on others. The question, however, is whether they would have if they had never met their (male) partners (Johnston, 2012b).

Male–Female Dynamics

Serial killer couples forge an intense and nearly instantaneous connection and exhibit complex relational dynamics. It would be remiss not to discuss the application of attachment theory within this context given its relevance to the interactional styles, criminal patterns, and developmental trajectories of not just serial killer couples, but serial sexual homicide offenders in general. Attachment during one's formative years, whether secure or insecure, impacts many critical facets of adult life, including agential capacity (or the person's concept thereof), approach to trauma, self-image, response to impulsivity, ability to build trust, and, of course, the pattern and health of future relationships. Thus, it seems particularly apropos to examine attachment with respect to the bonds that the partners entrenched in serial killer couples form with one another.

Healthy relationships are established over time, with each person sharing increasingly more personal details about themselves; this lays the foundation for trust and emotional intimacy. In the rapid and sexual unions created by male–female serial killer teammates, the partners become too familiar too fast; they fail to respect or recognize both physical and emotional boundaries and offer too much personal information upfront, often expecting (or demanding) the same in return; these couples also frequently engage in sexual activity almost immediately upon meeting. As the male is usually the dominant team member, it is not uncommon for him to coerce the often dependent or vulnerable female into entering the relationship full-throttle. The female partner commonly loses her individual identity in lieu of her status as a member of the killing team.

Research reveals that romantic partners involved in these two-somes share some analogous traits; rather than developing a stable bond built on trust and respect, these commonalities prime them to forge a compelling, if combustible, kinship built on emotional insta-bility, deviance, and maladjustment. For example, in addition to disrupted attachment, many such partners (both male and female) experienced horrific childhood trauma, including physical abuse, neglect, exposure to criminal sexual behavior, and parental mental illness. Together, these factors laid the foundation for their dysfunc-tional adult relationships. For instance, serial killer Debra Brown was severely abused by her father, who reportedly suffered from psychiatric issues. Debra's boyfriend-accomplice Alton Coleman was neglected by his mother, who was a prostitute and frequently had sex with johns in front of him. Similarly, serial killer spouses Rose and Fred West were both raised in families where incest and deviant sexuality ran rampant (Johnston, 2012b).

It is not uncommon for both teammates to romanticize their relationship as well as their crimes. However, while the male is often the psychopathic and/or sadistic leader, the female, who is his follower and the facilitator of his crimes, may in fact participate because doing so transfers some of his sadistic tendencies onto a target *other than herself.* By the same token, some women join in the killing because it is their way of usurping some of their part-ner's strength, thus affording them a brief feeling of control in an otherwise chaotic situation.

Several notorious female serial killers have cited this notion of the transfer of sadism as fundamental to their crimes and have cast themselves as reluctant accomplices in the crimes of their abusive male partners. They have publicly spoken of fearing for their lives, of having been controlled, and of having to choose between saving themselves or killing someone else. While no one truly knows how they would respond if forced to choose between killing or being killed, it is difficult to reconcile such killers' presentations of themselves as victims with the facts of their cases.

As previously mentioned, women such as Karla Homolka and Charlene Gallego were not unwilling participants or even passives ones. Rather, they demonstrated extreme cruelty of their own accord, often when their male partners weren't present. They suggested new ways to abduct victims and even sought the best camera angles to creatively capture their rape-murders on film. As incongruent with "feminine nature" as these facts are, when the collective histories of spouses of sexual sadists are examined, domestic violence is a common thread. These women are often abused by their spouses and come to regard them with a combination of love and fear, which leaves the criminal justice system struggling to determine whether they should be treated as victims or accomplices once caught (Johnston, 2012e).

The period of homicidal activity for a male–female team tends to be relatively short (approximately 1 year), in part because these teams are often poorly organized. Additionally, due to the vicious and very public nature of their kills, they do not remain at large for long. Because the crimes perpetrated by these pairs are undertaken in a cooperative way, the level of criminal organization largely depends on each individual team member's capacity for organization as well as the degree of collaboration between the two. In some cases, the murders become opportunistic, reckless, and disorganized, leading to quicker apprehension. In others, however, well-organized male–female teams have been able to remain at large for several years (Kelleher & Kelleher, 1998).

Karla Homolka and Paul Bernardo

"[Karla Homolka] remains something of a diagnostic mystery. Despite her ability to present herself very well, there is a moral vacuity in her which is difficult, if not impossible, to explain."

—Dr. Angus McDonald (Kilty & Frigon, 2016)

Karla Homolka was arrested on February 19, 1993, after she and her husband Paul Bernardo raped and murdered three teenage girls in Ontario, Canada. The couple's first victim was Karla's younger sister Tammy.

When Karla was 17, she met 23-year-old Paul Bernardo. Within 2 months, the couple was engaged. Paul began spending much of his time with the Homolka family and soon developed an obsession with 15-year-old Tammy Homolka. He would peep through her window and sneak into her room to masturbate while she slept. Karla helped him by breaking the blinds in her sister's room so that he could get a better look.

In December of 1990, Bernardo convinced Karla to offer him Tammy's virginity as a Christmas present, as he was disappointed that he was not Karla's first sexual partner. With her parents asleep in the upstairs bedroom, Karla drugged her sister. She and Bernardo then stripped Tammy and proceeded to videotape themselves sexually assaulting her while she was unconscious. During the course of the attack, Tammy choked to death on her own vomit. Tammy's death was officially ruled accidental.

Six months later, on the morning of June 15, 1991, the couple took their second victim. Bernardo was driving through Burlington, Vermont, halfway between Toronto and St. Catharines, when he came upon 14-year-old Leslie Mahaffy. She was locked out of her house after having missed her curfew. He led her to his car where he forced her into the back seat and blindfolded her.

Once home, Karla and Bernardo proceeded to videotape themselves torturing and raping Leslie over the course of the next several hours. When the recordings were presented at Bernardo's trial, he could be heard threatening Leslie, telling her that her behavior would determine whether she lived. As the tapes progressed, the sexual torture escalated and Leslie cried out in pain. Bernardo could be seen sodomizing her with her hands bound with twine.

According to Bernardo's testimony, the day after the video was taken, Karla administered a fatal dose of Halcion to Leslie. However, Karla claimed that it was Bernardo who killed Leslie by means of strangulation. Whichever the case, the couple subsequently dismembered the body and put each piece into a different cement block before disposing of them in nearby Lake Gibson.

Nearly a year later, Karla and Bernardo claimed a third victim, Kristen French. On the afternoon before Good Friday, the couple was actively cruising for victims in the vicinity of Holy Cross Secondary School when they came upon the 15-year-old walking home. They pulled into the parking lot of a nearby church and Karla got out of the car, pretending to need directions; Bernardo then grabbed Kristen from behind. Once he'd forced her into the car, Karla restrained Kristen.

During the course of the 3-day Easter holiday, Karla and Bernardo recorded themselves torturing, raping, and sodomizing Kristen. They forced her to drink toxic amounts of alcohol and to be sexually submissive to Bernardo. Unlike Leslie, Kristen was never blindfolded, so one might assume that they always intended to kill her.

Kristen was murdered on Easter Sunday, 1992. Again, however, Karla and Bernardo's stories about the specifics of her death were in conflict. Bernardo reported that Karla had beaten Kristen after she'd tried to escape and then ultimately strangled her with a noose that she'd secured to a hope chest. He noted that immediately afterward, Karla had gone to fix her hair for Easter dinner. Karla, on the other hand, later testified that it was Bernardo who strangled Kristen. She indicated that he did so while she watched. That evening, the couple ate Easter dinner with Karla's family; they dumped Kristen's nude body in a ditch the next day.

Karla and Bernardo were arrested in 1993. In 1995, Bernardo was convicted of the murders of Leslie Mahaffy and Kristen French. He was sentenced to life in prison with a dangerous offender designation, the maximum penalty permitted under Canadian law. Throughout the course of the investigation, Karla told detectives that Bernardo had abused her and that she'd been a reluctant accomplice to the murders. As a result, the prosecution agreed to make a deal; Karla pled guilty to the reduced charge of manslaughter in exchange for serving a 12-year custodial sentence.

After the plea bargain had been accepted, graphic and unambiguous videotapes of the crimes surfaced, proving that Karla was a far more active participant than she'd led the court to believe. According to Bernardo's attorney, the tapes revealed Karla sexually assaulting *four* victims, engaging in sexual activity with a female prostitute in Atlantic City, New Jersey, and drugging an unconscious victim. As a result, the Canadian Press dubbed the deal she'd made with prosecutors the "Deal with the Devil."

Before being sent to prison, Karla was evaluated by a plethora of psychologists, psychiatrists, and court officials, and one thing struck them all—how radically different she presented herself to each audience. Research reveals that the masks worn by psychopathic female serial killers are a means of manipulating others to achieve the outcome that best suits them at any given moment. Thus, various emotional and psychological presentations are displayed in different settings and to different individuals, as such offenders' motivations are opportunistic in nature (Perri & Lichtenwald, 2008, 2010). In fact, according to an interview with Karla's former friend and colleague Wendy Lutczyn, she now believes that Karla is a psychopath, and not an abused woman as she had once claimed (Cairns & Fenlon, 2005).

As a result of the plea bargain, the central tenet of which was her assertion of having been abused at the hands of Bernardo, Karla was released from prison in 2005. Karla clearly played the gender card masterfully and relied on social and cultural scripts about the victimization of women and women's incapacity for heinous violence to minimize her culpability. Her psychopathic personality fostered her ability to manipulate not only the court system but the general public; she presented herself as a victim of gender violence, which, in turn, *forced* her to victimize other females. However, it is imperative to note that since Karla's release from prison she has led a relatively normal life. She is married and has children of her own. Can her previous serial violence therefore be characterized as a sort of dormant trait brought out by the dynamics of her relationship with Paul Bernardo? In other words, does the fact that she has lived without recidivating (something that is unlikely for both serial offenders and criminal psychopaths) highlight the impact or strength of her (specific) male partner's influence? Had she never met Paul Bernardo, would Karla Homolka have realized her own homicidal fantasies? These questions emphasize some of the enigmatic differences between FSKs who work alone and those who work with a male romantic partner.

Thrill Kills

Most people can at least rationalize the act of killing under duress from an abusive partner or can even understand the sexualization of violence as a maladaptive coping response to trauma. But what about killing for the sheer excitement of it? Dr. Joni Johnston (2014) tested three hypotheses for how murder teams form when two people kill for sport:

- A dominant, murder-minded individual coerces a good-hearted person.
- A dominant individual convinces someone who seems to be a good person, but who harbors murderous tendencies.
- Two homicidal yet cowardly people come together; their dysfunctional relationship gives them the courage to act on their dark fantasies.

Although these scenarios can be applied to both opposite-sex and same-sex couples, gender implications are embedded in the social dynamic. As the male partner is often the leader in a male–female team, the gender inequity and inherent power imbalance that is part of the larger cultural narrative is reflected in these pairs when a female kills (another female!) at the behest of her male partner.

Dr. Johnston's research did not support the concept that morally upright individuals are corrupted by partners with murderous intent. However, she did find striking examples of weak-minded dependent persons who were extremely malleable; their dominant partners were able to quickly and easily transform them into whatever they wanted—and needed—them to be. Myra Hindley is one such exemplar.

Myra Hindley and Ian Brady

Myra Hindley was a mousy, unremarkable woman, with a seemingly low chance of becoming a serial killer—until she met Ian Brady. Myra quickly became sexually intoxicated by Brady's commanding presence, and he knew it. Brady repeatedly tested Myra's loyalty, roping her further and further into his aberrant ruses.

Myra became adept at luring victims, many of whom she knew, and many of whom may not have fallen prey to the pair had she not been the one to entice them into the couple's car. Having a woman present changed their perception of the situation and ultimately their perception of their own safety, and Brady knew that, too. The victims felt safe with Myra; they trusted her.

Between July of 1963 and October of 1965, the couple sexually assaulted and brutally murdered five victims ranging in age from 10 to 17. They then buried the bodies on Saddleworth Moore in Britain. After she was apprehended, Myra admitted that despite knowing right from wrong and never having had a violent urge of her own, she not only willingly participated in the killings, but she also came to enjoy them.

As with Myra and Brady, thrill-kill duos typically have one member who drives the murder. However, this doesn't mean that the other partner is idle. Most of these teams consist of a dominant person who partners with an equally enthusiastic accomplice or someone who, due to an absence of intestinal fortitude or a substantial lack in their own character, is easy to bring on board (Johnston, 2014).

All-Female Killing Teams

All-female killing teams are the second largest group of team killers that involve FSKs. That said, these teams are exceptionally rare, even by the standards of obscurity set forth by the phenomenon of the FSK. As the name indicates, these units are made up of two or more women who work in tandem to commit serial murder. While the majority of such teams typically have only two members, there may be multiple perpetrators who are jointly active in the perpetration of the crimes. Similar to their male–female counterparts, these teams typically have one dominant member who orchestrates the killings and one or more submissive members who are easily manipulated and/or controlled. In such scenarios, the dominant woman may take on the role of active killer, or she may step back and assume the responsibility of primary organizer without ever committing an actual murder. Regardless of the particular dynamics and modus operandi, these teams are surprisingly prolific and often target victims who are very old, very young, vulnerable, or otherwise incapacitated (Kelleher & Kelleher, 1998).

In some cases, a sexual relationship exists between (or among) team members. However, exclusively female teams also form for a multitude of other reasons. Unlike male–female teams, which are principally driven by sexual sadism, the murders of all-female killing teams are spurred by a wide variety of underlying reasons, which may encompass an array of motivational categories, such as profit, crime, or angel of death (Kelleher & Kelleher, 1998).

The average age of the women involved in exclusively female killing teams is higher than that of female members of male–female teams. The typical member of an all-female killing team makes her first kill in her mid-20s. Moreover, female killing teams remain active for approximately 2 years before they are apprehended or the murders otherwise cease; this is an active period twice as long as that of the average male–female killing duo (Kelleher & Kelleher, 1998). There are other dissimilarities as well. Whereas the murders committed by the typical male–female serial killing team involve a variety of weapons or killing styles and are commonly gruesome, the murders committed by female killing teams tend to mirror those committed by solo FSKs. Therefore, "tidier" tactics such as poison and suffocation are the preferred methods.

Amelia Sach and Annie Walters

The first known case of a female killing team occurred in England just after the turn of the 20th century. Amelia Sach and Annie Walters established a private residence in London, from which they offered lodging and adoption services to unwed pregnant women. Playing on the stereotypes of the time, they advertised their services in newspapers, promising young women confidential assistance with guaranteed anonymity devoid of record keeping—pain- and stigma-free relinquishment of their babies. They soon had a healthy clientele.

When expectant mothers—of which there was a steady stream—entered the establishment, they were charged a fee. After they gave birth, Amelia would take the baby from them, and then hand the child over to Annie. Annie, who lacked the capacity to plan such an operation, had no difficulty following her dominant partner's instructions; she dutifully murdered the babies using chlorodyne before disposing of their tiny bodies in the Thames. Amelia would then return to the mothers and say that the baby had been adopted, offering no further details due to confidentiality restrictions. She would then demand further payment to cover miscellaneous expenses. The two women were arrested for their "baby farming" operation, which they'd undertaken solely for profit; they were ultimately sentenced to death.

The Murder District

A decade following the execution of Amelia Sach and Annie Walters, another female killing team was active in Europe, this time in Nagyrev, Hungary. This team, headed by Mrs. Julia Fazekas, was composed of several black widows. The group became known as "The Angel Makers" and is estimated to have killed approximately 50 men.

In Hungary at the time, the family of a teenage bride was tasked with choosing her future husband, and the girl had no choice but to accept her family's selection. Divorce was not socially acceptable, even in cases of an alcoholic or abusive husband. During World War I, able-bodied men were sent to war to fight on behalf of Austria-Hungary, and rural Nagyrev was designated as a holding camp for Allied POWs. The POWs were afforded limited freedom to move about the village, giving them the ability to interact with many of the young women in town—many of whom were glad to be temporarily rid of the husbands who'd been forced on them by their families. Thus, many women began sexual relationships with one or more of the foreign prisoners. However, when their husbands returned, they forbade these affairs and wanted things to return to their prewar status quo.

Mrs. Fazekas, the town midwife, presented a solution: eliminate the problematic husbands. She persuaded the unhappy wives to dispatch their husbands with arsenic made by boiling flypaper and skimming off the poisonous residue. As more and more women came forward with the same problem, Fazekas organized a murderous group that targeted husbands and later problematic parents and other bothersome relatives for the women of Nagyrev. Nagyrev eventually became known as the Murder District.

The network of black widows was shut down when one of the targets survived the dose of arsenic slipped into his red wine by a woman with whom he had only a passing acquaintance. His story launched an investigation into several women in the town, one of whom confessed to having poisoned seven victims under the direction of Mrs. Fazekas. When authorities went to arrest Mrs. Fazekas, she committed suicide before she could be placed under arrest.

Alpine Manor and Lainz General Hospital

In more recent years, two cases of serial murder committed by female teams have attracted media attention due to their extreme viciousness. Both cases occurred in the 1980s and involved the murder of patients in medical facilities, one at a large general hospital and the other at a nursing home. In both instances, a single dominant individual controlled the actions of the team and made life-or-death decisions about the patients under their care. The pathological need for control played a vital role in these killings.

In 1986, Catherine May Wood was the timid 24-year-old nursing aid supervisor at Alpine Manor Nursing Home in Walker, Michigan. By all accounts, she was depressed; she was dangerously overweight (reaching 450 pounds at her heaviest point) and had recently ended her 7-year marriage. That same year, Gwendolyn Graham moved to Michigan and was hired at Alpine Manor. Although Catherine was her supervisor, it was Gwendolyn who took the lead in their personal relationship, which developed quickly.

Gwendolyn was a staunch and demanding woman who exacted control over Catherine. Their relationship brought new meaning to Catherine's life, and she began to diet and take pride in her appearance. The two began a sexual relationship, which included casual sex with other women. Gwendolyn had a penchant for extreme sex, so their encounters often involved rough play and choking behaviors. As Catherine was intent on pleasing her new partner, she remained compliant.

It was in October of 1986 that Gwendolyn first approached Catherine with the idea of committing murder as a way of intensifying their sexual stimulation. At first, Catherine dismissed the comment as a nefarious joke. However, the couple took their first life within 3 months of that conversation (Kelleher & Kelleher, 1998).

Gwendolyn's initial plan was to select six victims whose first letters of their last names would spell out M-U-R-D-E-R. However, the scheme proved too elaborate, as she hadn't anticipated the tenacity of several of the would-be victims. She shifted gears and began targeting only the frailest patients. Between January and April of 1987, the pair attacked a total of 10 nursing home residents, resulting in the deaths of five. Each time, their MO was the same: Catherine was the lookout while Gwendolyn smothered the victims with a damp washcloth. On some occasions, the duo had sex immediately following their kill, as a way of reliving and often heightening the perverse thrill. Akin to many male–female teams, Gwendolyn and Catherine's crimes were sexually motivated, as their sole purpose was to increase the couple's level of arousal; murder became an integral and climactic part of their sexual discourse.

Unlike the Alpine Manor murders, the slayings at Lainz General Hospital in Vienna, Austria, did not involve a sexual relationship among the killers. This all-female killing team involved four perpetrators, who acted under the leadership of Waltraud Wagner between 1983 and 1989. Waltraud recruited other nurses to help her dispatch patients whom she found irritating. In short order, the team had its killing routine down to a science—administering a morphine overdose or pinching the patient's nostrils closed and forcing water into their mouth until they drowned. The team ultimately confessed to 49 murders after they were overheard bragging about their latest kill at a local tavern (Newton, 2006).

Family Killing Teams

The third category of serial homicide teams in which women play an integral part is the family killing team, which is composed of three or more individuals of both sexes. The members may be related by blood or affinity, or they may be unrelated persons who have come together to form a family-like unit for the sole purpose of conducting criminal activities. Typically, the dominant member of such teams is a male (Kelleher & Kelleher, 1998).

Family serial killing teams share many common characteristics with male–female teams. For instance, family teams may engage in crime sprees or commit serial sexual homicide or both. These teams can range from highly organized to very disorganized. However, regardless of their ability to coordinate their murders, family teams tend to be extremely violent and their crimes very public. Therefore, their period of murderous activity is often relatively short, about a year. The female team members are typically young and submissive, similar to the female members of the male–female teams (Kelleher & Kelleher, 1998).

When these teams are composed of individuals primarily drawn together by their mutual attraction to murder and mayhem, the team predictably engages in an extended crime spree that includes a host of felonies, not just murder. For example, the notorious Karpis–Barker gang, led by Ma Barker, was motivated primarily by profit, not murder, and their crimes included extortion, theft, and armed robbery (Kelleher & Kelleher, 1998).

However, in cases of (often not biologically related) family teams where the common denominator among members is the compulsion to kill, the sheer purpose of forming the team is to commit serial murder. In these cases, the killers will be controlled by an often charismatic figurehead who is a committed and sometimes experienced serial killer in his or her own right; while this person will direct the murders, he or she may or may not actively participate in the family's homicidal ventures. The leader, who is typically an aggressive or abusive male, demands extreme loyalty from the other members of the team. Such teams are exceedingly rare and fall within the scope of cult activity, with the Manson clan offering a notorious example.

Conclusion

Women who commit serial homicide with a partner or partners tend to exhibit a universal set of characteristics: (1) an average age between 20 and 25 at the time of their first kill; (2) a total number of known victims ranging between 9 and 15; and (3) an active period that lasts from 1 to 2 years (Kelleher & Kelleher, 1998).

The three types of serial killing teams in which FSKs become involved are male–female teams, all-female teams, and family teams. While the idea of women participating in any type of overt violence, let alone serial murder, is in conflict with gender conventions, it is the dynamics inherent in the male–female killing teams that most clearly highlight the explicit gender commentary germane to the operation of these partnerships. In such instances, some women initially become involved in the killing duo as a means of escaping domestic abuse by the male partner, while others lack strong character and demonstrate dependent personality features, making them likely to give in to their dominant partner's attempts to mold them despite the fact that they know the difference between right and wrong. Still other women have a need for power and control and/or a penchant for or fascination with murder, live a rich fantasy life in which violence and sexuality are fused, or display psychopathic tendencies. The murders committed by male–female teams are almost always sexually motivated and thus often increase the intensity of the couple's own sexual chemistry.

When women form all-female killing teams, their motives vary widely, ranging from profit to compassion, and their methods are reflective of those of solo FSKs (e.g., poison and suffocation). Comparatively, women who become members of family killing teams seem to have more in common with women in male–female partnerships due to the gender inequity resulting from the (usually) male domination of both teams. Whatever the specific combination of internal and external events that leads a woman to participate, whether passively or actively, in the serial elimination of others, it is a rare occurrence by any standard and one that is continually viewed by society as in violation of gender norms.

Chapter 9

Women and Psychopathy

Karla Homolka: The Aftermath

Chapter 8 examined women who kill as part of a team, and it took an especially close look at those who do so with a male partner. While some female team killers are compliant and easily overpowered by their accomplices, others are equally engaged in the act of killing; it is these women who tend to partner with sexually predacious men and who exhibit psychopathic traits to rival those of their male counterparts (Kelleher & Kelleher, 1998). A prime example of such a woman is Karla Homolka, who was adept at donning different masks in order to manipulate others to her advantage; such chameleon-like skills are common among psychopaths.

While the brutality of Karla's crimes certainly implies psychopathy, it is her behavior after the murders that clearly reflects a gendered and holistic manifestation of the disorder. In accordance with her plea agreement, Karla gave several statements under oath to law enforcement wherein she delineated the details of her crimes; these were to be used as evidence against her ex-husband and accomplice, Paul Bernardo. The tapes of these dialogues were subsequently released to the media, and they unequivocally highlighted her psychopathic tendencies.

It is interesting to note that these conversations were not handled like interrogations or other police interviews with known serial killers. Rather than questioning Karla in a dank police department or jail cell, authorities did so in a comfortable hotel room in Ontario. Investigators barely challenged or even interrupted her narrative, and Karla was therefore free to color her account of events sans interference.

As Karla recounted the sexual homicides of Leslie Mahaffy, Kristen French, and her own sister, Tammy Homolka, she cast herself as another victim of her controlling and abusive husband. She spoke in a sweet and steady "little girl" voice and presented the information in a matter-of-fact tone. Her affect was flat and grossly incongruent with the topic, a fact that further underscored her moral vacuity. As she attempted to convince investigators that she was victim-adjacent or at least more victim than she was perpetrator, she used phrases such as "That freaked me out," "I was really mad," and "He held knives to my throat," in reference to her interactions with Bernardo during the crimes. However, she did so without even a slight elevation in pitch or change in intonation.

In one particularly illuminating disclosure, Karla claimed that her greatest upset came after she and Bernardo had abducted Leslie Mahaffy. She reported that she became angry when she found Bernardo and Leslie drinking champagne from expensive flutes that the couple reserved for special occasions. This slip offered a glimpse into Karla's psyche; she made no mention of her own struggle against Bernardo's supposed domestic abuse or the guilt she felt when witnessing other women's suffering. Karla did not even broach the topic that her husband had sexually assaulted other women or that sadistic murders were being committed in her home. Instead, she cited Leslie and Bernardo's use of fancy glassware as the thing that upset her most throughout the entire ordeal. This statement revealed not only her utter lack of remorse, which is a key feature of psychopathy, but also that she felt threatened by this scenario as it likely indicated to her that her hostage had achieved an elevated status within the household—and in Bernardo's eyes.

During the course of her ongoing discussions with law enforcement, Karla walked investigators through the house that had served as the crime scene for the murders. In a blatant manipulation tactic, which further emphasized her psychopathic personality, she dressed as a schoolgirl for this endeavor. While in the basement where one of the victims had been dismembered, Karla stopped to ask police if she could remove belongings from the scene, specifically the cellar, or whether they needed to remain logged into evidence. She also expressed concern about whether her furniture had been damaged during the investigation. At no time did she exhibit empathic concern for any of her victims.

Karla did, however, claim that she had become emotionally involved with the victims and had even befriended them. Once again engaging in impression management, she characterized her interactions with her rape and murder victims as "girl talk" and stated that she had developed an attachment to them. Unsurprisingly, the persona that Karla presented of a scared, caring, and unwilling accomplice was later unequivocally proven false when her statements were compared with video footage of the actual murders that she and Bernardo had taken.

While not all female psychopaths are team killers, or even killers at all, they do all exhibit the personality features that Karla exemplified: absence of conscience resulting in a stunning lack of remorse, shallow affect/blunted emotions, manipulation, impression management, inability to accept responsibility, pathological lying, etc. When engaged in conversation, they often play the victim or the hero and will use anything at their disposal to gain the upper hand. In Karla's case, she relied heavily on gender expectations about domestic violence and women's capacity to commit serial murder; she further exploited these conventions by acting and dressing like a young (read: innocent) girl during her interviews. It was a brilliant, if evil, choice.

What Is Psychopathy?

Psychopathy is a cluster of maladaptive affective, interpersonal, and behavioral characteristics (Scott-Snyder, 2016). It is classified as a personality disorder in that it is pervasive; its characteristics begin early in life and are enduring. The key symptoms of the illness can be divided into two categories: emotional/interpersonal and social deviance. Emotional/interpersonal factors include glib and superficial charm, egocentricity/grandiosity, remorselessness, lack of empathy, manipulation, and poverty of emotion. The features that comprise social deviance are impulsivity, poor behavioral controls, need for excitement, irresponsibility, early behavior problems, and (adult) antisocial behavior. It is important to clarify that nonpsychopathic persons may exhibit one or more of these traits. For example, many people are impulsive or unfeeling. However, that alone does not qualify them as psychopaths. Psychopathy is a syndrome, and thus it is denoted by the presence of a multitude of associated symptoms (Hare, 1994).

Psychopaths are social predators marked by their striking lack of conscience. They engage in a persistent pattern of violating the rights of others to meet their own needs. They often present as charismatic and even likable, which allows them to more easily achieve self-gratification at the expense of others. By their very nature, they are users who implement a wide array of tools (e.g., charm, manipulation, intimidation, and violence) to achieve their goals—and all without a shred of remorse. They are cold-blooded and wreak havoc on the lives of those around them, frequently leaving a trail of despair, disappointment, and betrayal in their wake (Hare, 1994).

It may be surprising to learn that everyone has likely come across a psychopath or has dealt with the repercussions of such a person's actions. While it stands to reason that many psychopathic individuals are criminals due to their flagrant disrespect for others, there are some who remain in society, calculatingly and *legally* exploiting those with whom they come into contact (Hare, 1994).

Prevalence of Psychopathy

For years, research has underscored the assumption that most psychopaths are male. To date, the majority of studies conducted on psychopaths have utilized samples from men's prisons. While these studies yield useful information, it is key to remember that the subjects of such inquiries are behind bars. Thus, it is nearly impossible to accurately extrapolate from this data the *exact* prevalence of male (and especially female) criminal psychopaths at large in society or the proportion of noncriminal psychopaths of either gender. That said, Hare (2006) estimates that approximately 1% of the general population is psychopathic with much higher levels of psychopathy present in the prison population.

Warren and colleagues (2003) found psychopathy occurrence rates of approximately 17% among female prisoners—significantly lower than the 25% to 30% estimated occurrence rate for psychopathy among male inmates (Hare, 1985, 1991). Similarly, Salekin et al. (1997) found an overall psychopathy rate of nearly 16% in female offenders in a jail setting. Given these findings, the question remains whether there are really drastically fewer female psychopaths than there are male psychopaths. Is it possible that some psychopathic women go unnoticed because they are able to get away with antisocial and criminal behavior due to society's gendered expectations? The answer is most likely yes. In fact, the number of female psychopaths may potentially be much higher than reported (Meyers, 2015).

Measuring Psychopathy

The Psychopathy Checklist–Revised (PCL-R; Hare, 2003) has long been regarded as the universal method for diagnosing psychopathy in adults. It is a diagnostic tool based on a rich profile of psychopathy developed by pioneer researcher Robert Hare. On this 20-item rating scale, individuals are scored between 0 and 2 points depending on how well each item fits them. Achieving the maximum score of 40 is extremely rare, and 30 is the generally accepted threshold for determining psychopathy (Hare et al., 1991).

The PCL-R items have traditionally been divided into two categories: factor 1 and factor 2 (see Table 9.1 on the next page). Factor 1 traits refer to the individual's psychological and emotional composition, and are correlated with an inability to benefit from treatment (Seto & Barbaree, 1999). These characteristics have also been associated with premeditated predatory violence. Factor 2 traits appear to be related to spontaneous and impulsive violence (Hart & Dempster, 1997). Factor 2 traits such as impulsivity, poor planning, and extreme need for stimulation are linked to sustaining

TABLE 9.1 Psychopathic Features as Measured by the PCL-R

Factor 1 Items	Factor 2 Items
• Glib/superficial charm • Grandiose sense of self • Pathological lying • Manipulativeness • Shallow (or flat) affect • Lack of remorse • Promiscuous sexual behavior • Failure to accept responsibility	• Proneness to boredom/stimulation seeking • Poor behavior controls • Lack of realistic goals • Impulsivity • Irresponsibility • Juvenile delinquency • Many short-term (sexual) relationships • Parasitic lifestyle • Revocation of conditional release (e.g., parole) • Criminally versatile

Source: Adapted from Hare, Harpur, Hakstian, Forth, Hart, and Newman (1990).

a deviant and parasitic lifestyle. While factor 1 is a better overall indicator of psychopathy, factor 2 is a stronger predictor of general and violent recidivism (Scott-Snyder, 2016; Walters, 2003).

Although this instrument has been validated for use with women, gender disparities have been observed in the factor structure and the way in which items load (Dolan & Vollm, 2009). Because this measure was normed on men, the aforementioned two-factor model is more relevant to male populations (Hare et al., 1990; Harpur et al., 1989). Salekin and colleagues (1997) discovered a different two-factor model that proved more applicable to female offenders, in which women fell into two broad categories. The hallmark features of the first group (F1) included a lack of empathic concern or guilt, interpersonal deception, sensation seeking, and proneness to boredom. The second category (F2) was defined by early behavior problems, promiscuity, and adult antisocial or criminal (although not necessarily violent) behavior.

More recent research has explored the use of three- and four-factor models with female populations. In their three-factor model,

Cooke and Michie (2001) removed the original F2 items pertaining to antisocial behavior on the premise that psychopathy is a function of personality and that antisocial behavior is a consequence, or side effect, of the disorder rather than a central facet of it. They divided the remaining items into three factors: (1) arrogant and deceitful interpersonal style, (2) deficient affective experience, and (3) impulsive and irresponsible behavioral style. Hare and Neumann (2008) critiqued the removal of the antisocial features, and the data now support a four-factor model in which the PCL-R items are categorized along the following domains: interpersonal, affective, lifestyle, and overt antisocial behavior (Neumann et al., 2007).

What Causes Psychopathy?

The etiology of psychopathy has historically been poorly understood. Various theories exist, some favoring biological origins (nature) and others focusing on social environment (nurture). According to Quay (1965), a key biological aspect of the disorder is that psychopaths have an underaroused cerebral cortex, meaning that they are consistently understimulated (or "half in the bag"). Therefore, to feel satisfied, they must engage in more frequent, varied, and extreme forms of stimulation than the average person (Scott-Snyder, 2016).

Robert Hare favors the position that the disorder develops from a complex interaction between nature and nurture. That is, genetic influences contribute to the biological bases of brain function and personality composition, which, in turn, impact how a person responds to and interacts with his or her environment and social experiences. In essence, the critical elements needed for the emergence of psychopathy—such as the profound inability to feel a full range of emotions, including empathy—are at least partially provided by nature. Consequently, the capacity for developing internal controls, conscience, and the ability to forge emotional connections with others is significantly reduced (Hare, 1994).

Kent Kiehl, who was mentored by Hare, offers a different theory. According to Kiehl, psychopaths have a brain dysfunction that not only causes them to think differently, but that could also be classified as a severe form of mental illness. This deficit is associated with attention, self-regulation, and emotion (Scott-Snyder, 2016). Research conducted by Kiehl and his colleagues supports the hypothesis that issues with the paralimbic system (i.e., the system which includes the temporal and frontal lobes) underlie these neural processes and are correlated with psychopathy (Kiehl et al., 2006). Kiehl (2015) explains, "I liken it (psychopathy) to an emotional disorder with an adjunctive impulsivity problem. With those two facets, in conjunction with the right environment, psychopaths develop an unstable lifestyle that often leads to criminal behavior." Thus, expecting psychopaths to control their (harmful) behaviors and then experience remorse afterward is akin to asking those with narcolepsy to control when they fall asleep (Ramsland, 2014; Scott-Snyder, 2016).

Gender Differences in the Development and Expression of Psychopathy

Research reveals that the developmental trajectory of psychopathy may differ between males and females. According to research conducted by Robins (1966), girls who were later diagnosed with psychopathy were less likely to have been seen at a child guidance clinic for behavioral problems than were boys who later received the same diagnosis. Specifically, only 12% of girls with early behavior problems later met criteria for psychopathy, as compared with 50% of boys. Other studies have found similar results.

Background and lifestyle characteristics of individuals with both psychopathic traits and antisocial personality also appear to be influenced by gender. For example, antisocial women are more likely to be chronically unemployed, have high rates of marital separation, and be reliant on subsistence from welfare and other need-based social services than are antisocial men. Moreover, these women tend to break the law at lower rates than their male counterparts but are more likely to have relationship difficulties and to tell lies (Mulder et al., 1994). Other gender differences regarding the presentation of psychopathy include a later onset of childhood behavioral problems and more frequent sexual misbehavior in girls (Robins, 1966).

Evidence indicates that the behavioral patterns of female psychopaths also differ from those of male psychopaths (Hare, 1991). Mulder and colleagues (1994) found that psychopathic females are less aggressive and commit fewer acts of violence than do their male counterparts, thus suggesting a gender-based expression of psychopathy. While psychopathic men are more likely to engage in physical violence, females more commonly commit acts of relational aggression (Carroll et al., 2010; Crick, 1995). Relational aggression, also known as covert aggression, is purposeful and harmful behavior done to damage someone's relationship(s) or social status. It is inherently manipulative and is subtler than physical aggression, which is how males typically express such urges (Crick & Grotpeter, 1996). For example, a woman may spread rumors, talk behind someone's back, or launch an attack via social media (Scott-Snyder, 2016), while a man may engage in a fistfight.

According to Verona and Vitale (2006), relational aggression often presents as jealousy, verbal antagonism, manipulation, or self-harm in young women who are later diagnosed with psychopathy. Thus, while many male psychopaths act in a conventionally (i.e., physically) aggressive manner, which eventually leads them down the road to incarceration and to ultimately being assessed for psychopathy, female psychopaths' behaviors are more nuanced; they act in less overtly aggressive ways, despite their actions producing equally destructive results.

Notwithstanding that distinction, female psychopaths can and *do* have the ability to perpetrate callous and excessive physical violence. According to Hare (2003), "the variety and severity of criminal acts performed by these women, as well as their capacity for cold-blooded violence, are similar to those committed by their male counterparts" (p. 102).

As with the behavioral indicators of psychopathy, underlying motivations are largely influenced by gender. For instance, manipulation frequently takes the shape of flirting in women, while in men it translates to the commission of fraud. Unlike in men, where the interpersonal markers of psychopathy are characterized by charm and a grandiose sense of self (Rogstad & Rogers, 2008), promiscuity in psychopathic women may reflect an attempt to gain financial wealth or social status (Thornton & Blud, 2007). Such distinctions are underscored by a larger gender-based social and cultural narrative. Moreover, while neither male nor female psychopaths are able to process human emotional information, recent findings suggest that the brains of female psychopaths process moral judgment data differently than do the brains of male psychopaths (Harenski et al., 2014).

According to Hare, the bottom line is that women have the same capacity for psychopathy as men. The hallmark features of the disorder—an unnerving disconnection from emotion, a complete lack of conscience, superficial charm, and a distorted sense of pride when violating laws and/or social mores—are present in women and often go unnoticed at work, at the gym, or even at the local "Mommy and Me" group.

Differentiating Psychopathy

It can be difficult to distinguish psychopathy, as its presentation can appear similar to that of other personality disorders. As a result of its gender-based expression, women are more likely to be diagnosed with borderline or narcissistic personality disorder, even sometimes by skilled clinicians, than they are to be properly identified as psychopathic.

Data indicate that the interpersonal-affective and impulsive-antisocial features present in psychopathy may be associated with borderline personality disorder (BPD) in women (Coid, 1993; Hicks et al., 2010). However, empirical evidence specifically examining the gendered relationship between BPD and these features of psychopathy is largely lacking. Research by Sprague et al. (2012) found a correlation between high interpersonal-affective and impulsive-antisocial psychopathy features and BPD, thus suggesting an overlap of these disorders (at least insofar as they are measured by current instruments) in females. However, it is uncertain whether and to what extent psychopathic traits may manifest differently in women than in men. Some experts theorize that psychopathy represents a female phenotypic expression of BPD.

It is no mystery that female psychopaths are often misdiagnosed as narcissists. Even professionals are not immune to impervious gender and social bias. That is, when a male and female both exhibit a pattern of core psychopathic traits (e.g., grandiosity, egocentricity, manipulativeness, deceitfulness, shallow emotionality, lack of remorse, callousness, etc.), a clinician is more likely to diagnose the male with psychopathy and the female with BPD or narcissistic personality disorder because the clinical impression is influenced by conscious or unconscious expectations about how a psychopath *should* behave; that is, the clinician expects psychopaths to act tough and aggressive. Therefore, when a woman does not project these features, she is not thought to be a psychopath. Rather, the clinician should be mindful of how psychopathy is expressed differently between genders due to sex-role stereotyping.

That said, it is easy to see how the similarities between psychopathy and narcissism can cause confusion. Both diagnoses involve impression management, whereby the individual does or says things in an attempt to control other people's opinions of her. Also common to both ailments are a grandiose sense of self, exploitation, manipulation, and a lack of empathic concern, although to differing degrees. Afflicted persons thrive on admiration and feeling as though they are smarter than those around them. Narcissists and psychopaths appear "normal" and don't tend to fit any specific profile; they know whom to target and how to portray themselves in a positive light to achieve their goals (Stein, 2016).

Research has also found some overlap between histrionic personality disorder and psychopathy in women, which underscores the notion that the difference in psychopathy between the genders is not the existence of key traits but rather the expression of them. A woman who desperately needs to be the center of attention is likely to be labeled histrionic; she is not generally who one would imagine as a "typical" psychopath. However, she may be just as devoid of empathy and as capable of callous unemotional manipulation as the violent psychopathic male (Johnston, 2012c).

Types of Crimes Committed by Female Psychopaths

Female psychopaths engage in an array of criminal behaviors, including robbery, fraud, cyberbullying, assault, and homicide. As opposed to their nonpsychopathic counterparts, their offenses are cold-blooded in that they are more likely to be motivated by power or personal gain than they are to be driven by interpersonal factors and hot-blooded emotion; psychopaths are also more likely to reoffend. In a study of 75 female offenders, Zaparniuk and Paris (1995) found that within 1 year, approximately 60% of those who met criteria for psychopathy as measured by the PCL-R had recidivated, while only 25% of nonpsychopathic women had done so.

Society has come to view female-perpetrated violence as anomalous and deviant. It is therefore often assumed that particularly heinous crimes are rooted in psychopathy.

According to Vaughn et al. (2008), the presence of psychopathy in women is specifically predictive of both violent offending and fraud. However, it is not associated with substance abuse. This is because the combination of callous indifference, narcissism, and impulsivity are relevant to both violent crime and fraud, whereas drug use is often a way of self-medicating untreated mental illness or of escaping from painful feelings; psychopaths have blunted emotions. Research conducted by Weizmann-Henelius et al. (2004) found that when nonpsychopathic females commit murder, they are more apt to kill people close to them, unlike psychopathic women, who more frequently victimize strangers and acquaintances. However, Meyers (2015) hypothesizes that women who kill their own children may be an exception to this finding—at least under certain circumstances.

When a woman kills her child, the word *psychopath* is often used to describe her. However, women who kill their offspring may be motivated by a variety of reasons that are unrelated to psychopathy, such as psychosis or other psychiatric disorders, which preclude them from performing the complex responsibilities of parenting. These ailments are a far cry from disposing of a child simply because they never wanted the child in the first place or because they have determined that parenting interferes with their carefree lifestyle. Due to the dearth of research in this arena, one can only conjecture that the portion of women who murder their children without conscience exhibit psychopathic tendencies (Meyers, 2015).

Another type of offense often associated with psychopathy is school shootings. Because many offenders involved in such crimes kill themselves at the scene, it is often impossible to administer the PCL-R and properly evaluate them for psychopathy. However, anecdotal information indicates that many school shooters, both male and female, exhibit a significant number of psychopathic traits (Meyers, 2015). When these offenders are female, their profiles are consistent with characteristics of psychopathic female offenders: They engage in extreme violence and they target strangers. Their crimes are callous and cold-blooded as opposed to being the result of an emotional response to a heated argument or "bad trip."

Brenda Spencer

On the morning of January 29, 1979, 16-year-old Brenda Spencer crouched in her parents' San Diego home armed with a .22 caliber rifle. As the children lined up outside the Grover Cleveland Elementary School across the street, Brenda opened fire on the playground. The principal, as well as the custodian who ran to his aid, were killed. Nine others, including children and a responding police officer, were also wounded.

Amidst the chaos, reporters phoned homeowners in the vicinity of the school to ask what they had witnessed. One journalist inadvertently reached Brenda, who eagerly accepted responsibility. In a widely publicized statement she said, "I don't like Mondays. This livens up the day." She also declared that she'd shot a "pig" and wanted to shoot more. She further referred to the school children as "easy pickings" and reported having enjoyed watching them "squirm" after they'd been hit.

Unlike many school shooters, Brenda did not commit suicide at the scene but rather surrendered to law enforcement after having barricaded herself in her parents' home for nearly 7 hours. Following her apprehension, she underwent pretrial psychological testing, which revealed that she had previously incurred damage to her temporal lobe, which was attributed to a bicycle accident (Dower, 2006). Brenda was tried as an adult and convicted of two counts of murder and assault with a deadly weapon. She received a custodial sentence of 25 years to life and was remanded to the California Institution for Women where she was diagnosed with epilepsy and treated for depression (Bockler et al., 2012).

In 1993, Brenda was granted her first parole hearing. She claimed that she was under the influence of drugs at the time of the shootings, but toxicology reports proved otherwise. Brenda argued that the tests must have been falsified; she was denied early release. At a 2001 hearing, Brenda attempted to gain the sympathy of the parole board when she characterized her father as an alcoholic who had sexually abused her. Her father denied the allegations, and the chairman of the board confirmed through collateral information that Brenda had never reported these accusations to any prison staff and that he therefore doubted their veracity. Brenda was once again denied parole. During a subsequent hearing in 2005, Brenda apologized, but reported that she could not remember her crime. She exhibited no insight into her offense. This, coupled with the fact that she'd self-mutilated following a breakup with a fellow inmate, illustrated her inability to cope with negativity. She was once again denied parole.

During Brenda's most recent parole hearing in 2009, she insisted that she had not tried to shoot or kill anyone. Instead, her articulated motive was to cause a disturbance serious enough to summon the police in order to commit "suicide-by-cop." However, she was confronted with a series of facts, including her statement to the police negotiator that she'd shot and killed the custodian because he'd gone to the aid of the others; he had gotten in the way of her hurting more children. Under questioning, Brenda admitted to having been a good shot, and it was suggested by the district attorney's representative that she was telling the board a series of lies to manipulate them (Daly, 2014).

The son of shooting victim "Mr. Mike," as the school custodian was affectionately known, delivered a victim-impact statement during the proceedings. He noted that on the day of the attack everyone in the area scrambled about to find loved ones and/or to rush to the hospital. However, Brenda was seen undisturbed and apparently remorseless, singing as she tended to her parents' garden. He concluded his emotional testimony with the question, "Will there be another boring Monday for her?" (Daly, 2014). Brenda was denied parole and will not become eligible again until 2019.

From this account, several psychopathic traits become evident: pathological lying; manipulation; lack of remorse; callous lack of empathy; failure to accept responsibility for her own actions, as evidenced by Brenda's attempt to minimize her culpability by blaming her actions on (unsubstantiated) claims of sexual assault and then later stating that she didn't remember committing the offense; proneness to boredom/stimulation seeking; poor behavioral controls; impulsivity; early behavioral problems; shallow affect; and juvenile delinquency (on a grand scale). When considering additional evidence, such as a dysfunction in Brenda's temporal lobe, possible trauma history, and collateral information consisting of statements from classmates noting that they feared Brenda, that she dreamed of becoming a professional sniper, and that she had taken trips into the woods to practice her marksmanship—during which she shot and killed small animals (lizards and squirrels), and during which she almost never missed—(Bockler et al., 2012), a more complete picture begins to develop.

Psychopathy and Serial Homicide

Lack of empathy and stimulation seeking are two of the key traits associated with psychopathy that make this disorder common among serial killers regardless of gender. Psychopathic serial murderers display extreme indifference toward human life and do not experience remorse for their (often brutal) crimes. They have an absolute disregard for the rights of others as well as for the laws and standards of society. Reid Meloy (1992) describes psychopathic serial killers as "emotionally disconnected from their actions and, therefore, indifferent to the suffering of their victims. Their ability to dissociate themselves emotionally from their actions and their denial of responsibility effectively neutralizes any guilt or remorse that other people would feel in similar circumstances." It is important to note that psychopaths know the difference between right and wrong; they know that murder is not only in violation of the criminal code but also is an egregious violation of their victims' rights at the most basic level (Bonn, 2017). Additionally, with each kill they develop a sort of tolerance to the (frequently sadistic) violence. Their viciousness escalates, often into torture, as these killers require increasingly more stimulation to feel satiated. Despite assertions that it is the sexual component of serial murder that creates the gender divide (Hornberger, 2002; Pearson, 1997), psychopathic female serial killers, whether acting alone or in concert with a partner, have perpetrated kills that were both sexually aggressive and sadistic.

Another quality that predisposes psychopaths to serial murder is their inability to learn from experience. Psychopaths are capable of regret, but only when a situation negatively impacts them. This is a self-focused emotional response and does not inform their future choices, even when learning from it would ensure future success. Ongoing research is exploring how psychopaths process punishment and reward information to better understand why this disconnect occurs. Moreover, psychopaths are cortically under-aroused, and therefore they do not experience anxiety. Thus, legal ramifications or the threat of incarceration—even for a second time when their first time was difficult—do not trigger fear or anxiety; therefore, such things are not deterrents, as psychopaths do not fear these repercussions.

Aileen Wuornos

Aileen Wuornos was convicted of murdering seven men, for which she was executed on October 9, 2002, at the Broward Correctional Institution in Florida. She is often considered to be the first predatory female serial killer to be identified as such (Ahern, 2001).

Aileen's childhood was not a happy one. Born in Michigan in 1956, she was raised believing that her maternal grandparents were actually her parents. It was not until she was 11 years old that Aileen learned the truth. After Aileen was abandoned by her biological mother, her grandparents had adopted her and her brother Keith;

she'd always felt as though they were treated differently than their grandparents' other children.

There was frequent abuse in the familial household—and Aileen claimed to have borne the brunt of it. On one occasion, she was forced to lay naked while her grandfather beat her with a belt (Ahern, 2001). She further reported having been sexually abused by him. Moreover, her brother's friends recalled having witnessed incest between Aileen and Keith (Scott-Snyder, 2016).

By adolescence, Aileen's temper was volatile. Angry and violent outbursts were frequent, unprovoked, and wildly unpredictable. She had difficulty socializing with her peers and often traded sex for money and cigarettes. She began to detach and learned to disassociate herself; as a means of self-protection, she eventually became adept at shutting off her emotions entirely (Russell, 1992).

With adulthood came an increase in aggression, especially toward men. At age 20, Aileen wed a man 50 years her senior. During the course of their 1-month marriage, Aileen drank heavily, stayed out all night, and spent excessive amounts of money. Following a physical assault during which she attacked her husband with his own cane, he obtained a restraining order and subsequently filed for divorce (Russell, 1992). After the dissolution of her marriage, Aileen's criminal versatility became evident as she accrued a string of arrests for assault and battery, disorderly conduct, and driving under the influence, in addition to a multitude of weapons offenses (Ahern, 2001). She eventually went to prison for the armed robbery of a convenience store. It wasn't long after her release that she was arrested again, this time for forging checks and driving a stolen car. Aileen also began prostituting herself—sometimes as many as 25 times per day.

It was also around this time that Aileen met Tyria (Ty) Moore, and the two women became sexually involved. During their intense relationship, Aileen's life was chaotic and regularly involved violence, prostitution, transience, drinking, and grandiose, if unrealistic, plans. The couple remained together throughout the period of Aileen's homicidal activity (Arrigo & Griffin, 2004).

Aileen committed her first murder when she was in her 30s, and all of her kills followed a similar pattern. She would stand by the roadside, waiting for a man to offer her a ride. Once inside the car, she openly admitted to being a prostitute in need of money and offered up her services. Once her target had agreed, the two drove to a secluded area and Aileen convinced the john to undress. She then engaged in minimal sexual activity before getting out of the car and shooting him. She often yelled, "I knew you were going to rape me" as she did so (Russell, 1992, p. 149). Sometimes Aileen fired multiple times before ultimately watching her victim die. She often robbed the deceased prior to leaving the scene and heading home to have a beer with Tyria (Arrigo & Griffin, 2004).

When she was arrested, Aileen provided investigators with various accounts of her crimes. However, prior to her execution, she acknowledged having "killed those seven men in first-degree murder and robbery. As they said, they had it right. Serial killer." She described her motives as robbery and the elimination of witnesses. She further stated, "I pretty much had them (the victims) selected that they were gonna die" (Broomfield & Churchill, 2003).

Myers et al. (2005) evaluated Aileen Wuornos for psychopathy shortly before she was put to death. They determined that she evidenced a psychopathic personality with a PCL-R score of 32. She also met DSM-IV-TR diagnostic criteria for antisocial personality disorder and BPD. Despite her articulated motives, ambiguous evidence suggests that Aileen's crimes may have been sexually motivated and/or gratifying on some level. The convergence of childhood attachment disturbances, psychopathy, and personality disorders in combination with her severe trauma history clearly contributed to Aileen's propensity to commit serial murder.

It is important to acknowledge that Aileen's murders straddle the gender barrier. Often categorized as serial sexual homicide, her kills have been given a label typically associated with vicious and predacious male perpetrators. While Aileen, along with her male counterparts, can certainly be described as callous and ruthless, she used gender as the catalyst to manipulate her interpersonal interactions with her victims. Such relational aggression is reflective of the borderline-adjacent expression of female psychopathy. Specifically, Aileen used her gender to her advantage and exploited social conventions to lure her victims; gender therefore became a central feature on which her crimes were predicated. For example, she targeted johns and then yelled "rape" as she killed them in an effort to characterize herself as a victim of sexual violence, thus undermining every woman who has ever endured sexual abuse.

Conclusion

As illustrated by the stories of Aileen Wuornos and Brenda Spencer, the female psychopath can be just as deadly as her male counterpart, perhaps even more so. Although she appears different at first glance because her behaviors are often more nuanced, make no mistake: She is just as capable of the same conscience-free, cold-blooded, manipulative, and violent acts as is the male psychopath. She is the socially adept predator who uses her gender—and her victims' lack of awareness about her very existence—to create an exploitative climate in which she is in control. Due to gendered expectations and social conventions, society is much less likely to see her coming, making the female psychopath perhaps the most dangerous yet inconspicuous of offenders.

Chapter 10

Mafia Godmothers and Drug Queenpins

The Rise of the Madrina

Among "connected" women, Maria Licciardi was referred to as "The Princess." She was respected for her charismatic yet cold style, and her fabled ruthlessness earned her the respect necessary to rise to power as the godmother, or "madrina," of the Camorra, the Naples-based counterpart of the Sicilian Mafia. By the time that the 50-year-old matriarch was arrested in June of 2001, she had climbed high enough on the criminal ladder to warrant being placed on Italy's list of the 30 most-wanted criminals—a designation given to few females (Jacinto, 2017).

* * *

Maria Licciardi was born in 1951 in the Neapolitan suburb of Secondigliano. Like many others in the region, she was raised in the culture of the Camorra. Her father was a well-known local mob boss, and thus Maria was entrenched in organized crime circles and taught their values from a young age. The Licciardi family was heavily involved in weapons, cigarette, and drug-smuggling operations, and never hesitated to employ violence as a means of enforcement.

From the time that she was a child, Maria was exposed to the mob's patriarchal structure, and therefore was likely expected to assume a supporting role in its ranks when she matured. Steeped in tradition, the organizational hierarchy dictated that women were to fill secondary and outwardly submissive positions, publicly offering assistance to male relatives despite frequently advising them on strategy behind closed doors. Maria's expectant role was to be loyal and tight-lipped, and to conquer midlevel criminal responsibilities, such as cutting and packaging heroin, often while simultaneously cooking for the family. As women were also tasked with childrearing, she would have also groomed the younger generation by doling out trivial payments to neighborhood children who acted as lookouts. While her efforts would have contributed to the organization, she would not have been a shot-caller, nor would anyone have expected her to be. Women were to be devoted wives, sisters, and daughters who tended to the domestic responsibilities and assisted with the illicit activities, as directed by the men in charge, and Maria's anticipated path was no different. It was not until her brothers were imprisoned and her husband and nephew were murdered as the result of a vendetta that she became arguably the most influential boss in the history of the Camorra (Jacinto, 2017).

Maria was a shrewd and focused businesswoman, who used her gender and diminutive stature to her advantage. She spoke with the leaders of rival Camorra clans and convinced them that bloodshed over territory disputes had to stop; turf wars meant lost income. She advised the clans to set borders, pool their resources, and work together to increase the reach of their smuggling and racketeering enterprises. The local bosses conceded. Maria's relational skills led her to effectively form a coalition of several Camorra families to expand control over the city's most lucrative rackets.

Perhaps Maria's most unique contribution to the Camorra was that she involved them in the business of prostitution. Previously, the mob had refused to engage in it despite its financial implications because it violated their moral code; women's bodies were not to be bought and sold. At Maria's behest, however, the Camorra bought girls, many of whom were underage, from the Albanian mafia. Upon delivery, the Camorra drugged the girls into compliance. When they became too old to be profitable, they were killed to prevent them from running away or snitching.

Despite her unprecedented achievements, Maria, unlike her male predecessors, was not drawn to the spotlight, nor was she motivated by bravado. Under her control, the Camorra functioned surreptitiously; the gunfights in the street ceased, and violence—at least that which was public knowledge—was at an all-time low. The Camorra was elusive to police, as many of the people living in the suburbs of Naples came to support the organization. Most of these people were from modest backgrounds and needed work; as the mob was a major employer, the townspeople felt obliged to protect them. Many people became involved in low-level drug trafficking for the Camorra. Additionally, the Camorra put money back into the community, and therefore many people felt a sense of loyalty to them. Thus, whether out of fear of arrest, fear of reprisal, or fear of poverty, the public created a protective barrier between the police and the Camorra, making it difficult for law enforcement to infiltrate and take down high-ranking members, such as Maria Licciardi.

Maria's coalition began to disintegrate when a feud erupted with the Lo Russo family over a drug deal gone bad. In the spring of 1999, Maria received a shipment of uncut heroin that she'd bought on consignment from Turkey. Realizing that it was too pure for distribution, she ordered that it be returned for fear that it would potentially kill users, thereby decreasing the Camorra's clientele. Maria was also aware that a rash of drug-related deaths could trigger unwanted attention from law enforcement. However, the Lo Russo clan, who had always resented her leadership, disobeyed Maria's mandate, and within 1 month's time, 11 people had died from using the lethal packets of heroin. Widespread police crackdowns targeting the Camorra drug trade followed, and many Camorristi were arrested.

The Lo Russo clan eventually seceded from the alliance, and Maria's sovereignty began to crumble. An all-out war among the individual Camorra clans ensued. There were car bombings, shootings in the street, and attempts to overthrow one another's business endeavors. When four of Maria's clan members were murdered in her stronghold of Secondigliano, she had to retaliate. Casualties began to climb as Maria Licciardi fought to regain control of the Neapolitan underworld.

With over 100 casualties attributed to the gang war, Maria was on law enforcement's radar and was forced to go into hiding. While on the run, she remained the undisputed boss of the Licciardi family and was rumored to have ordered hits on several of her rivals. As the authorities closed in on the Licciardis, Maria's security network atrophied. Afraid that her whereabouts would be compromised, she sent a message to senior prosecutor Luigi Bobbio. In January of 2001, she orchestrated the bombing of his office in the hope that no more of her clan members would be prosecuted. Although Bobbio continued his work with the help of police protection, the Licciardi clan members remained loyal to Maria, due in large part to the "culture of silence." They quietly accepted their sentences and refused to make deals with the prosecution, wherein they would give up information about Maria in exchange for less prison time. According to Camorra tradition, those who "snitched" on the clan could expect deadly repercussions.

After 2 years of changing her appearance and moving from one location to another, Maria Licciardi was apprehended without incident. Even from her cell today, she continues to wield power, as prison walls are not considered a barrier for the Camorra (Zaccaria as cited by D'Emilio, 2009).

* * *

The ingress of women to the upper ranks of the mafia has been a highly publicized topic. Does this rise in so-called "girl power" among mob syndicates reflect a gender revolution? Are women effectively shattering the glass ceiling of one of the world's most male-dominated social structures? Or, are they filling a "power vacuum" created by men? (Jacinto, 2017).

Maria Licciardi, for example, took control of the Camorra only after her father, brothers, husband, and nephew were all unable to attend to their duties. Having been raised in the business, she had the requisite knowledge to step into the vacancy created by her male predecessors. Thus, her case underscores the assumption that it is not that women are making their way to the highest levels of the mob based purely on tenacity and skill, nor are they being *chosen* as leaders. Rather, their power is contingent on their relation to male bosses. When those men are arrested or executed, the women closest to them are then, and only then, able to fill those positions. They inherit their power by default, and said power only exists in relation to these male relative(s) (Jacinto, 2017).

The mafia uses gender expectations to its advantage. In Italy, Mafia wives, daughters, and sisters are thought to suffer in silence, unaware of the offenses of their male relatives. Crime is considered to be men's work and this façade is meant to protect women from the harsh penalties of the law while ensuring the privacy of mob secrets. However, women have long played varying roles in organized crime, such as keeping the books, negotiating drug deals, and even ordering executions. In her book *The Antimafia* (1999), Allison Jamieson differentiates between what she calls the "enterprise syndicate" and the "power syndicate." According to her, women have not yet broken into the power syndicate, which entails physically exacting violence. "In the Mafia, power rests on the actual execution of violence." According to officials, Maria Licciardi ordered executions with the utmost poise. However, some argue that the lack of hands-on violence is a hindrance to obtaining "true" power and remands women, including the likes of Maria Licciardi, to the enterprise syndicate.

Regardless of how a madrina's power is measured, questions still remain regarding how she is viewed by society. People often find it difficult to believe that women can be not only compliant but also complicit in organized crime; to think of a female giving kill orders seems incongruent with social mores. While some cultural narratives dictate that it is understandable for mafia wives to stand by their men as they break the law, others imply that women are expected to rally against a life of crime. However, according to Clare Longrigg's *Mafia Women*, "Instead of leading the tide of righteous citizens against crime, women turned out to be even more entrenched in mafia values than men" (Jacinto, 2017).

What Is Organized Crime?

Organized crime is illegal activity conducted by self-perpetuating associations or syndicates that operate irrespective of geography, meaning that they are often transcontinental, or, in the case of the Licciardi clan, can operate without regard for incarceration. While there is no single configuration under which criminal organizations function, as they can range from hierarchies to networks to cells, to be defined as a criminal enterprise the group must have a hierarchical or similar structure; such groups typically have extensive supporting networks. These organizations are often insular and protect their activities through the use of corruption, violence, and complex communication technologies as well as an organizational composition that exploits national and international borders (Federal Bureau of Investigation [FBI], n.d.-b).

With rare exceptions, these groups are primarily motivated by power and financial gain, and they utilize a host of legal and illegal tactics to generate profit. Drug, human, and weapons trafficking, migrant smuggling, money laundering, extortion, dealing counterfeit goods, smuggling antiquities, and illegal gambling are some of the cornerstones of organized crime (FBI, n.d.-b).

Although this chapter focuses mainly on two factions of organized crime, the Italian Mafia and the Mexican and South American drug trade, it is important to understand that criminal enterprises can operate from anywhere and may include individuals with far-reaching ethnic, cultural, and/or financial ties. These groups, in turn, have the ability to target victims and execute their crimes anywhere in the world; thus, the extent of their presence in any one given area does not accurately reflect the extent of their network or the actual threat that they pose (FBI, n.d.-b).

The History of Organized Crime

According to the FBI (n.d.-b), Italian crime syndicates, more commonly known as the Mafia, began to emerge in Sicily in the 1800s. Initially, these groups formed as secret societies, the purpose of which was to combat oppressive authorities and to exact frontier vigilante justice. Those who joined relied on blood ties for safety and survival in the midst of a turbulent political climate.

In Sicily, the word *mafia* means "manly," and members were viewed as men of honor; they were respected and admired because they protected their family and friends and remained silent about the organization's activities until death. At its inception, the Mafia was unconcerned with whether it profited from its actions because they came at the expense of a tyrannical establishment. However, over the course of multiple periods of invasion and exploitation, these enterprises evolved from a group of honorable Sicilian men into an organized criminal unit in the 1920s (FBI, n.d.-b).

The Mafia's criminal influence has spread beyond Italy's borders, and they are now considered to be one of the most widespread organized crime consortiums, having impacted the financial and social atmosphere of multiple nations. They currently have four main groups operating in the United States: the Sicilian Mafia (La Cosa Nostra), the Camorra, the 'Ndrangheta, and the Sacra Corona Unita. According to the FBI, these four groups have approximately 25,000 members and 250,000 affiliates operating in Canada, Australia, South America, and Europe. These entities also pool resources with other organized crime syndicates around the world (FBI, n.d.-b).

Sicilian Mafia and La Cosa Nostra

Since the early 1900s, the Sicilian Mafia has evolved into an international criminal enterprise. Some experts estimate that it is the second largest organization in Italy. Based in Sicily, it specializes in trafficking heroin and military arms in addition to political corruption; it is also known to engage in arson, counterfeiting, fraud, and other racketeering crimes. The group is infamous for its hostile assaults on law enforcement and has been responsible for the assassinations of prominent officials, including police commissioners, judges, and members of the Italian parliament (FBI, n.d.-b).

In the United States alone, the Mafia has over 3,000 members. While its most significant presence is centralized in the metropolitan area of New York City, New Jersey, and Philadelphia, there are also affiliates in California, the Midwest, and the South. The main threats posed to American society by these groups are money laundering and drug trafficking, specifically heroin. However, these syndicates are also involved in kidnapping, fraud, murder, bombings, illegal gambling rings, extortion, and weapons trafficking (FBI, n.d.-b).

La Cosa Nostra (LCN) developed from the original Sicilian Mafia and is one of the principal organized threats in the United States. It is a nationwide criminal alliance comprised of different geographically arranged "families." They are committed to protecting their own at all costs, and their illegal activities run the gamut. They are involved in murder, extortion, labor racketeering, loan sharking, drug trafficking, prostitution, illegal gambling, etc. While the LCN has its roots in Italian organized crime, it has been a separate entity for a number of years and remains cooperative with various criminal enterprises headquartered in Italy (FBI, n.d.-b).

'Ndrangheta (Calabrian Mafia)

The 'Ndrangheta formed in the 1860s, when a group of Sicilians was banished by the Italian government and settled in Calabria. They went on to form small criminal assemblies. There are approximately 160 'Ndrangheta cells and about 6,000 members. These cells are loosely connected family groups based on blood, affinity, or marriage. Their areas of criminal focus are kidnapping and political corruption, but they also engage in drug trafficking, bombings, counterfeiting, illegal gambling, murder, fraud, and labor racketeering. It is believed that there are between 100 and 200 members and associates operating out of New York and Florida (FBI, n.d.-b).

Camorra (Neapolitan Mafia)

The Camorra first came into existence in the mid-1800s in Naples, Italy. Initially a prison gang, the members formed clans in cities and continued to grow in power once released from incarceration. The Camorra has more than 100 clans of approximately 7,000 members, making it the largest of the Italian criminal enterprises.

The Camorra's focus is on cigarette smuggling, and they receive a payoff from other criminal groups for any cigarette traffic through Italy. They additionally partake in other smuggling ventures, money laundering, robbery, blackmail, kidnapping, political corruption, and counterfeiting. The FBI (n.d.-b) estimates that nearly 200 Camorra affiliates reside in the United States.

Sacra Corona Unita

The Sacra Corona Unita, or "United Sacred Crown," came to the attention of law enforcement in the late 1980s. Similar to the Camorra, it began as a prison gang. Upon release, its members settled in the Puglia region of Italy and continued to forge connections with other mafia groups.

The Sacra Corona Unita has approximately 50 clans and 2,000 members. While they mainly concentrate on smuggling operations (cigarettes, drugs, weapons, and people), they are also involved in extortion, money laundering, and political corruption. As they have laid claim to the southeast coast of Italy, they collect payment from other criminal groups that wish to utilize this passageway for smuggling their own products to and from countries such as Croatia, Albania, and the former Yugoslavia. Very few members of the Sacra Corona Unita have been identified in the United States, although they have a small presence in New York, Florida, and Illinois (FBI, n.d.-b).

Overview of Women in Organized Crime

Over the course of the past 20 years, research has revealed that women play key and diverse roles in organized crime. While this is not a new phenomenon, the recent focus on this topic highlights women's involvement in the criminal underworld throughout various points in history and casts doubt on the notion of women's "sudden rise" to power in these enterprises (Siegel, 2014).

Traditionally, women have been regarded as invisible and rather insignificant members of organized crime. In the Italian Mafia, their roles were previously limited to cooking, cleaning, and raising the children. They were similarly pigeonholed based on gender in the Russian mob, as their bejeweled appearances were a reflection of their man's wealth and power. In either case, women were never thought to be directly involved in violent operations and were in fact assumed to lack any true grasp of the inner workings of the enterprise's criminal activities. However, the rise of female bosses within organized crime circles has led to these ideals being questioned as the result of perceptions predicated on archaic and gendered stereotyping (Siegel, 2014).

Wives and sisters of Mafiosi were expected to assume supporting roles in the home; not only were they to raise the children, but they were to instill in them the values pertaining to mob culture (Longrigg, 1998; Paoli, 2003). According to Longrigg (1998), the woman's job was to be "the moral reference point for children . . . passing down these morals and values" (p. 42). Although a fictionalized account of mob life, *The Godfather* correctly portrayed the value of "family" as being of the utmost importance.

Mafia women have a history of being deeply rooted in organized crime values, and therefore it is not surprising that marriages between different clans have provided women with another important yet auxiliary role. In becoming the bride of a man from another family, a woman creates or strengthens a criminal alliance, thereby increasing the ability for both families to profit. However, she herself is not seen as having made a powerful move. Instead, she is seen as "a showcase for displaying her husband's wealth, status and power; a valuable piece of property; a loyal helpmate; a good cook; a showy and ego-boosting mistress" (Gage, 1971, p. 95). Thus, while a powerful association is being created *because* of her, she is viewed as a bargaining chip or a pawn—an inanimate object to be controlled by the men around her.

By marrying women from within their own circles, these men not only ensure better business practices through the creation of strategic alliances, but they also guarantee the preservation of mob traditions. Because their wives were themselves raised in organized crime, disputes over whether or not to teach children the values and traditions inherent to mob culture are prevented; important conventions, such as the culture of secrecy, wherein mobsters refuse to turn state's evidence if captured, are perpetuated without disagreement (Fabj, 1998).

Unlike the portrait of the passive mafia women depicted in *The Godfather*, several biographies and media projects focusing on mob bosses and their spouses have indicated that women were not only aware of their husbands' activities but also emotionally and financially invested in them. For instance, in 19th-century Sicily, many women took an active part in advising their husbands, while others assisted in the roles of "postina" (mailwoman) or "messaggera" (messenger) (Fiandaca, 2007). Additionally, they frequently used their relational skills to assist in mediation efforts with rival families (Siegel, 2005). For some women, marrying a Mafioso was a means of escape from poverty, and thus their interest in their husband's illicit business dealings was survivalist and led them not only to counsel their partners on financial matters, but also to encourage them to defend the family's honor—violently if necessary. These wives came to enjoy the wealth, authority, and status that resulted from these power plays (Siebert, 1996). Historical evidence indicates that for some women, their participation in criminal activities extended far beyond knowledge and support of illegal dealings to critical and leading positions in major criminal networks (Siegel, 2014).

While women's ascent to power is seemingly progressive given the patriarchal nature of organized crime, female mob bosses are caught in a complex and confusing matrix somewhere between modernity and sexist tradition. Madrinas, unlike their male counterparts, are subject to arcane rules. They are empowered to order hits in the absence of their husband or male relatives but are dissuaded from taking a lover or leaving their husband. They can decide how to invest the syndicate's money or make business decisions but are prohibited from wearing makeup while their spouse is incarcerated, as that would be akin to infidelity because it is viewed as symbolic of their desire to be unfaithful. These women are bound by inseverable family ties, and with rare exception their power exists only in relation to their men.

Theoretical Perspectives

In recent years, arrests of women in positions of authority within various criminal syndicates have become increasingly common. A socially pervasive assumption is that women have inexplicably transitioned from passive to active roles in criminal enterprises. However, it is more accurate to say that they have evolved from secondary and subservient posts, dictated in large part by chauvinistic ideologies, to decision-making and oftentimes power-wielding capacities. However, even these more authoritative roles are not unmarred by gender bias.

Much of the criminological theory surrounding this issue converges on the idea of increased opportunity for women. This approach views their function within organized crime as previously limited to domestic responsibilities. Women were tasked with caring for the household and being obedient to male family members. Mob wives focused on supporting their husbands, raising the children, and taking care of the house, all the while promoting the image of the male family members as "men of honor." Although essential, they were background players whose primary purpose was to highlight their husband's attributes and encourage his endeavors; they were not sought after for their knowledge or ability. As women began to gain more opportunities in society at large (e.g., education, jobs, etc.), they developed a broader skill set, and their opportunities within organized crime circles expanded in parallel. Carroll (2009) suggests that "the rise of mafia women in Italy is connected to women's increased participation in universities and the labor market, as women are gaining equality in all institutions from which they were previously excluded" (p. 11).

Is there a direct correlation between better opportunities for women and greater equality or more even distribution of power within the mob? According to Beare (2010), the answer is not that clear-cut. Following a meta-analysis, she determined that women's involvement in organized crime is attributable to family and gender role divisions (Daly & Chesney-Lind, 1988; Datesman & Scarpitti, 1980; Millet, 1970) or the specific structure of criminal organizations (Hagan et al., 1987). This stance corresponds with the idea of the power vacuum, in which women in the Mafia are only considered with relation to and as a result of their connections to male criminals. In other words, their influence is an offshoot of their male relatives, without whom they would not rise to power in these infrastructures.

So, what does this have to do with opportunity theory? It is likely that as the broad spectrum of educational and professional opportunities increase for women and gender barriers are broken down,

Mafia-affiliated men become more accepting when a woman *does* step into the powerful role vacated by her husband. The men with whom she interacts inside the mob are aware of the capabilities and achievements of women outside these circles; thus, her position becomes more palatable despite the fraternity-like environment of the Mafia. However, according to Miller (1978), "It is important to strike a balance between recognizing the significance of gender and gender inequality but not to reduce everything to gender" (p. 43).

Therefore, while feminist perspectives such as opportunity theory offer significant insight into this topic, these models alone do not suffice to explain the role of women in organized crime. Many people are taken aback by the thought of a woman—a caregiver—ordering hits, prostituting other women, or orchestrating the trafficking of large quantities of drugs. From a psychodynamic standpoint, one should consider superego morality and the impact of being raised in mob culture. The internalization of the same-sex parent's values specifically impacts little girls who grow up surrounded by organized crime because it is the mothers and mother figures (e.g., aunts, grandmothers, sisters, etc.) who are tasked with laying the moral foundation for children and who serve as moral tethers. One could argue that this, combined with global emancipation, sets the stage for a subsequent rise to power for some female mob bosses.

Consider Maria Licciardi, whose female relatives were deeply devoted to the organized crime lifestyle and whose responsibility it was to pass mob culture along to the younger generation. Maria would have received the message that the behaviors perpetrated by her male relatives, the ones for whom she ultimately took over, were not only acceptable and not to be judged as immoral, but were rather to be revered. Therefore, it follows that she would have found no reason *not* to engage in those criminal behaviors herself.

The cognitive perspective, on the other hand, indicates that women with a desire to rise to power, potentially those who got a taste for emancipation, have learned the specific codes and values from having been reared in mob tradition. Because of their involvement in this lifestyle, they themselves are lower in moral judgment and therefore resort to breaking the law as a means of problem solving.

Their cognitive scripts involve harmful and illegal ways of making money and obtaining power; these are paths that were prescribed to them throughout their lives and which they have come to understand and internalize as viable options. Thus, it appears that the theoretical underpinnings of why and how women become mob bosses may lie in a combination of feminist-driven and classical perspectives.

Narco-Trafficking as Organized Crime

While the term "organized crime" typically conjures images of Mafiosi and the New York underworld, these stereotypes fail to recognize a segment of organized criminal activity that is not only lucrative, but global: drug trafficking. According to the FBI (n.d.-b), narco-trafficking has become an immensely profitable form of transnational organized crime. Many groups, known as cartels, have hierarchical leadership and transport illicit substances across borders to where the demand for the drugs is highest.

The FBI primarily breaks down the areas of trafficking activity into three critical domains: (1) the source zone (where the illegal activity originates), (2) the transit zone (the areas through which the activity moves), and (3) the retail zone (the activity's destination). Source zones include countries such as Colombia, Peru, and Bolivia where narcotics are produced. The transit zone includes Mexico, in addition to the Central American nations of Panama, Nicaragua, Honduras, and El Salvador, with Mexico being the largest producer of heroin, methamphetamine, and marijuana in the Western Hemisphere. Due to the increasing amount of attention paid to transnational criminal threats by Mexican law enforcement, Central American drug flow has increased dramatically over the course of the past 10 years. This has resulted in the displacement of criminal activity and associated violence from Mexico to other countries in the transit zone. Finally, the retail zone consists mainly of Canada and the United States, with the United States providing the largest drug consumption market in the Western Hemisphere (FBI, n.d.-b).

While the FBI classifies these transnational drug trafficking rings as organized crime, Calderon (2015) makes a slight but important distinction. In an article in the *Harvard International Review*, Calderon states that drug trafficking "clearly refers to the smuggling of illegal substances from producing regions in Latin America to the consumer market, mainly in the U.S. Organized crime, in contrast, can be defined as the criminal activity that, through violence or threatening people, seeks to extract illegal or legal rents from the community" (pp. 52-53). In other words, drug trafficking and organized crime are correlated, but not all drug smuggling qualifies as organized crime; a significant shift has occurred in Mexico and Central America, which now qualify cartels as criminal enterprises (Calderon, 2015).

Drug trafficking has long been a foundational source of income for organized crime, gangs, and other groups alike. However, the transition from "mere drug trafficking" to organized crime occurred when groups began attempting to control territory and using violence to do so. Additionally, within the constructs of these organizations, there is a tiered structure of individuals who carry out said violence versus those who are responsible for delivery of goods, etc. Thus, many cartels become strictly and violently managed commercial enterprises, which women are more frequently commanding.

Drug Queenpins

Until recently, Hollywood has excluded powerful women from its portrayals of Latin American cartels. Instead, women have been placed in roles only within the context of their involvement with men. For example, they have been portrayed as pawns, sex objects, and gold diggers who have sought money and status from the men involved in the black-market industry of narco-trafficking. However, while drug trafficking organizations (DTOs) have been chiefly controlled by men, women have been active, albeit supporting, players in these groups since the 1920s. Many have acted as drug mules and some have subsequently become bosses (Council on Hemispheric Affairs [COHA], 2011).

According to Arturo Santamaria, author of *Female Bosses of Narco-Traffic* (as cited in Duerson, 2012), more and more women are playing key roles in Mexico's drug underworld due in large part to the fact that violence has claimed many of the drug war's men. Violence on the streets is escalating. For instance, a leader connected with the Zetas cartel was arrested in association with the murders of nearly 50 people whose bodies were decapitated—a not-unheard-of intimidation tactic (Duerson, 2012). It is exactly this type of coercive and statement-making violence, carried out by specific individuals at different levels of the cartel's ranks, which places these groups beneath the umbrella of organized crime.

Similar to mafia women who step into the power vacuum, one woman in Santamaria's book revealed that she took over cartel operations after her father and brother became casualties of the cocaine wars. Such losses are common in the drug trade. In fact, according to the *Daily News*, between 2006 and 2012, nearly 50,000 people were killed. As a result, the widows, fiancées, daughters, sisters, and girlfriends of men involved in DTOs have stepped into increasingly powerful posts; they have transitioned from transporting drugs to laundering money to so-called narco-diplomacy. The female bosses in the highest-ranking positions are known as "Queenpins" (Duerson, 2012).

"Kingpin Strategy," a tactic that, if employed correctly, forces the creation of a power vacuum, is at least partially responsible for the rise of Queenpins. Based on this approach, law enforcement targets cartel kingpins, leaving the "lieutenants" or second-highest ranking (male) members of the DTOs to fight amongst themselves for control of the organization. In so doing, the lieutenants call attention to themselves, thus allowing police to then target them. As authorities take out the upper ranks, the male leaders' wives assume control. These women are aware of their husbands' operations and are able to carry on the cartel's work almost seamlessly.

However, not all women who become involved in narco-trafficking do so as a result of vacancies left by their male partners. Many are recruited into lower-level positions within the cartels' ranks. They are assured that smuggling will be quick and easy money and are often blind to the consequences. Some have drugs hidden in their breast implants, while others are instructed to swallow pellets containing the drugs; these capsules result in a lethal overdose if the "swallower" does not arrive at her destination in a timely fashion to pass the material (Abadinsky, 2003).

Because women are thought to be able to use their appearance and feminine charm to bypass (male) security/TSA agents, cartel associates conduct some of their recruiting efforts at beauty pageants. For several young contestants, the high income potential is alluring, while others are compelled to engage in smuggling operations because of dire economic situations. For some, attracting a trafficker and undertaking dangerous missions may be their only way out of poverty; for others, it can afford them access to luxury and financial comfort that they perhaps would not otherwise have. Undoubtedly, there is also a small portion of women who are simply drawn to the excitement and power associated with narco-trafficking (Campbell, 2008).

Queen of the Pacific

Sandra Ávila Beltrán witnessed her first shootout at the age of 13. Dubbed the "Queen of the Pacific" for having orchestrated the movement of 10 tons of cocaine from Mexico's Pacific Coast to the United States aboard small fishing boats, she keeps a candlelit altar in her home, which serves as a shrine to her first husband who was gunned down, her second husband who was fatally stabbed, and her brother who was tortured to death; all were casualties of Mexico's cocaine wars, in which Sandra played a leading role.

***

In an interview following her release from prison in 2015, Sandra revealed that despite the lives claimed by cartel violence—including her own personal losses—she feels no responsibility and no remorse. She refused to criticize the world of narco-trafficking and noted that illicit drug use is a consumer choice that comes with the well-known consequence of violence, which she believes results from either Mexican government-sponsored terrorism or prohibition policies. Sandra likened herself to those who sold alcohol during prohibition; they were considered immoral at the time, but once alcohol became legal, their professional positions were not only deemed respectable, but became sought after (Franklin, 2016).

Despite the well-documented and undeniable barbarity employed by the cartels, Sandra insisted that her conscience was clean, as the drug war bloodshed was due to black-market competition and political assassination tactics: "The government at times has to kill people because it is not convenient to imprison witnesses who could testify against them" (Franklin, 2016). Although her distortions appear deeply rooted, it has been previously noted by Drug Enforcement Agency (DEA) agents that Sandra herself never shied away from utilizing the most violent of enforcement tactics (Contreras, 2007).

Sandra Ávila Beltrán was born into cartel culture. The daughter of Alfonso Ávila Quintero, a relative of the founder of the Guadalajara cartel, Sandra lived an extravagant lifestyle as a child with private school, music and dance lessons, and frequent vacations. She was a third-generation trafficker, with the "family business" dating back to her great uncle Juan José Quinetero Pyán. Her uncle Miguel Ángel Félix Gallardo gained notoriety for having murdered DEA Agent Enrique Camarena in 1984. On her mother's side (the Beltráns), Sandra also had several relatives who were involved in heroin smuggling.

Although many of Sandra's friends rose to become leaders of the Sinaloa cartel, she chose to explore other avenues. At age 17, she enrolled in journalism classes at the Universidad Autónoma de Guadalajara, but a few years into her coursework a jealous boyfriend with ties to the cartels kidnapped her. Within months of the ordeal, Sandra left town and abandoned her dream of becoming an investigative reporter. Instead, she entered the drug underworld with the goal of becoming the Queen of Cocaine.

With her mindset having shifted, Sandra was acutely aware of her gender and of how women were viewed by male cartel members. She was beautiful and used her looks to her advantage while simultaneously being careful never to let her guard down. Having been previously victimized by her boyfriend, she refused to allow herself to be in a position that would place her male counterparts at a greater advantage than their sex already gave them. For that reason, Sandra never used cocaine herself because she had come to realize that the women who did were viewed as weak and disposable by the men involved in the world of trafficking.

Sandra was acutely aware that she was a woman trying to climb the ranks in a man's world. The men in the drug trade objectified women and often surrounded themselves with a harem of females whom they used and abandoned without so much as a second thought. However, none of these women were respected as intelligent or capable individuals. For Sandra, commanding respect was of the utmost importance.

Everything she did was a calculated move intended to take her one step closer to becoming a queenpin—including dating men in the upper echelons of the cartels. Throughout her younger years, Sandra was romantically linked to multiple drug barons. She was twice married, both times to former law enforcement officials who had subsequently become involved in trafficking operations. Sandra's far-reaching power is largely attributed to her romantic relationship with Juan Diego Espinoza Ramírez, an influential figurehead in the Colombian cartel known as Norte del Valle.

In 2002, Sandra's reign was interrupted when her son was kidnapped and a $5 million ransom was demanded. Although her son was returned safely, the incident raised suspicion and authorities began to scrutinize her. She was forced to go on the run, constantly changing location and appearance. Although she relinquished her "normal" life and was exhausted, she later admitted that she had become addicted to the adrenaline of wondering whether or not she would be caught.

It took more than 4 years and a team of federal agents, but in September of 2007 Sandra was arrested without incident. She served 7 years behind bars, 2 of which were in isolation.

***

Sandra's case highlights several key elements pertinent to female-perpetrated violence. Similar to the mob wives discussed previously in this chapter, she was raised in a criminal culture, which encouraged her to internalize violence and to develop a moral code that would permit such actions. As evidenced by the distortions exhibited during her postincarceration interview, her cognitive script did not find fault with the savagery that she and others perpetrated as part of the cocaine wars.

Additionally, one cannot overlook the fact that Sandra herself was victimized on various levels. At age 13 (and likely several times thereafter) she experienced vicarious trauma when she witnessed a shooting. Such incidents can create lasting distress, especially for young people with malleable and developing identities, even when they don't know how to express or conceptualize the emotions surrounding the experience. Then, after deciding to extricate herself from cartel life, Sandra was kidnapped by a boyfriend. This form of gendered violence only compounded the subtle, or perhaps not-so-subtle, misogynistic cues that she'd been receiving her entire life from men in narco-trafficking: Women are objects, women are disposable, and women are to be used. Sandra clearly didn't want to be a victim; she wanted—no, needed—to be respected. She was clearly motivated by profit, but more than that, she was driven by power envy. Sandra had the desire to attain the same level of power and control that the men around her had, and had wielded over her and other women her entire life—and she succeeded. Additionally, never having dealt with the emotional scars of her own victimization, it is likely that Sandra's feelings turned to anger, which allowed her to perpetrate violent drug war retaliations without remorse.

Griselda Blanco

On September 3, 2012, outside a butcher shop in the suburban neighborhood of Medellín, Colombia, witnesses heard the roar of motorcycles followed by gunshots. By the time authorities arrived, Griselda Blanco was dead, her body surrounded by a pool of blood in the middle of the street. She was 69 years old and had been dubbed the "Queen of Cocaine."

* * *

Griselda Blanco Restrepo was a native of Cartagena, Colombia. Born in 1943 to an abusive mother, she began engaging in criminal activity, including prostitution, at an early age. She eventually became involved with the Medellín cartel and began trafficking cocaine throughout the United States, to New York City, Miami, and Southern California. Griselda designed special undergarments to be worn by drug mules, which allowed them to smuggle large quantities of cocaine across the border undetected; this invention advanced her trafficking career. Griselda also had street smarts and a ruthlessness about her, which helped propel her to the top ranks of the Medellín cartel.

In the mid-1970s, Griselda relocated from Colombia to New York. She was heading a major narcotics ring at the time, and her standing in the drug trade could have rivaled Pablo Escobar's. From New York, she was forced to flee back to Colombia to avoid apprehension by the DEA, but she ultimately returned to the United States and settled in Miami.

During her time in the United States, Griselda continued to be heavily immersed in the Colombian drug trade, which led to her involvement in multiple murders, including drive-by shootings and other killings driven by drugs, money, and power. By the late 1970s, investigators had connected Griselda to dozens of homicides, including the 1979 shooting of one of her rivals in a Miami liquor store. However, she managed to evade capture for several years.

After earning millions from narco-trafficking, Griselda was apprehended by the DEA in February of 1985. At her trial in New York, she was convicted of one count of conspiracy to manufacture, import, and distribute cocaine, and was sentenced to 15 years in prison. She was transported back to Miami in 1994 to face murder charges. However, the case was unexpectedly thrown out as the key witness, a former hit man employed by Griselda, was reportedly caught paying secretaries in the Dade County Prosecutor's Office for phone sex (Latham, 2000). This caused prosecutors to question his credibility if put on the stand. Some suspected that he had thrown the case on purpose for fear that he would be killed by members of Griselda's cartel if he testified against her (Iannelli, 2018). Ultimately, Griselda pleaded guilty to three counts of murder. In concordance with a plea agreement, she received a 10-year sentence, after which she was deported back to Colombia (Biography.com, 2017).

The media has had a near-infatuation with Griselda Blanco. For example, Lifetime Television recently announced that Catherine Zeta Jones will portray her in an upcoming biopic entitled *Cocaine Godmother*. What accounts for this interest in Griselda's life? Likely, it is her gender-bending penchant for excessive violence. She had a reputation for viciously killing her enemies, often indiscriminately; if someone crossed her, they ended up dead. She showed little regard for who they were. For instance, Griselda was accused of orchestrating hits on 40 people spanning from New York to Miami, including a 2-year-old boy who was killed in a drive-by shooting on South Dixie Highway in Miami. She also had a propensity for killing her own husbands and slaughtering anyone who harmed her children (Iannelli, 2018).

One theory for her sheer brutality is that Griselda was motivated by power envy and wanted to show that she was as capable of exacting violence as her male counterparts. Having been abused as a child and used as a prostitute, she did not want to be seen as weak and, similar to Sandra Ávila, wanted to ensure that she would be powerful and respected—and perhaps feared. Also like Sandra, Griselda lacked remorse. According to a federal informant, she was reportedly glad that she had murdered the 2-year-old boy because it upset the child's father (Iannelli, 2018). Consider for a moment the requisite level of sadism needed to rejoice in the murder of a child because of the resultant emotional suffering of his father. However, unlike Sandra, who explained away drug wars and placed the blame for such violence elsewhere, Griselda Blanco owned up to her role in the cocaine killings and was proud of it; she was not afraid to be cruel and she made that fact public knowledge.

The further that we dig, we see that Griselda's background is riddled with red flags. She was raised in poverty, which is a predisposing sociological risk factor for criminality, and one that makes sense in light of profit as a motivating factor. It also paved the way for her to work as an underage prostitute, during which time she undoubtedly endured even more abuse than that which she received at home. Little surprise that she committed her first murder at the age of 11. Those close to Griselda described her as a nurturing, caring woman to those in her inner circle so long as they remained loyal. As with many violent women portrayed in this book, she suffered attachment difficulties stemming from the abusive relationship with her mother. These expanded into a tenuous ability to trust those around her, and therefore Griselda required complete allegiance to feel secure. Once disrupted, she had extreme difficulty repairing the bond of trust. She felt the need to take violent action to assert herself and regain control if betrayed. These feelings underscore her abuse history and lack of support from her own mother.

Conclusion

Organized crime is one of the most socially patriarchal conventions in society. Historically, women's functions have been considered tributary or derivative at best. Within recent years, women have begun to assume positions of power within both the Italian Mafia and narco-trafficking empires. While it is tempting to view this seeming explosion of girl power as a feminist statement, it is imperative to understand that women's roles are expanding in a power vacuum; their power is measured by and often only exists in relation to their spouse or male relative(s) for whom they have taken over.

The parallel phenomena of madrinas and queenpins do not indicate a sudden climb to the top of male-dominated institutions as the media would seem to indicate. Rather, even while empowered, these women are still bound by gendered expectations and subjected to rubrics (spoken or otherwise) that are not imposed on male bosses. Additionally, the reasons why some women are interested in governing organized crime groups and others are willing to engage in dangerous missions at the behest of such syndicates are rooted in gender-based experiences such as abuse, marginalization, and misogyny, as well as traditionalist perspectives, including moral development, cognition, and learned behavior.

Gender and Terrorism

Chapter 11

The Erez Crossing

On January 14, 2004, Reem Riyashi approached the security terminal at the Erez Crossing, the checkpoint at the Israel–Gaza border. Pretending to be disabled, she told security personnel that she had metal plates in her leg that would trigger the alarm should she go through the metal detector, so she requested a private body screening instead. As a result, she was escorted to an area where soldiers and police were checking bags and was told to wait for a female officer to pat her down. Reem then detonated the 2-kilogram bomb that was strapped to her person in a suicide mission that killed four Israeli officials and injured a total of 11 other people, both Israelis and Palestinians (McGreal, 2004).

* * *

Twenty-two-year-old Reem Saleh Riyashi left behind two young children: a son, age 3, and a daughter, 18 months. Her attack was an apparent joint operation between Hamas and the Al-Aqsa Martyrs Brigade in response to weeks of Israeli incursions into West Bank cities that had resulted in the deaths of approximately 25 Palestinians (McGreal, 2004). The strike was the first time that Hamas had used a woman as a human bomb in a terrorist plot.

Unlike the majority of suicide bombers, Reem came from a wealthy family. She was the eighth Palestinian woman to carry out such an attack and only the second Palestinian mother to do so (McGreal, 2004).

Prior to her death, Reem composed a videotaped manifesto, in which she wore combat fatigues and held an automatic rifle; there was a rocket-propelled grenade in the foreground. She stated:

> It was always my wish to turn my body into deadly shrapnel against the Zionists. . . . I always wanted to be the first woman to carry out a martyrdom operation, where parts of my body can fly all over. . . . God has given me two children. I love them (with) a kind of love that only God knows, but my love to meet God is stronger still. (MacKinnon, 2004; McGreal, 2004)

Despite Reem's fervent dedication, her family denounced her actions and made known their commitment to peace. They further denied any prior knowledge of her plan or understanding of why she chose to carry out an act of terror. In fact, Reem's brother-in-law offered a statement that railed against her attack: "We don't accept women doing such things. She has two children. It is not right" (McGreal, 2004).

The media responses to Reem's operation, however, were mixed. Criticism among the Palestinian press was unprecedented (Intelligence and Terrorism Information Center, 2004). Hamas was widely condemned, even by some of its own supporters, for having deployed not only a woman but a mother as a suicide bomber and then for having published photos of her posing with her children alongside weapons (McGreal, 2004). Some argued that these images undermined the Palestinian cause, while Hamas responded by claiming that they gave a tragic face to the frustration and desperation of Palestinian women, thus bolstering their stance. Their hope was that Reem's example would lead more women to assume active terrorist roles (McGreal, 2004).

In the Arab world, on the other hand, Reem was hailed as a hero (MEMRI, 2004):

- Columnist Ahmad Mansour in the Egyptian weekly *Al-Usbou*: "Despite her strong motherly instincts . . . Reem Al-Riyashi had a heart that was bound to a greater emotion than her feelings towards her children, one that not every woman can bear and implement. . . . She looked at her place in paradise and at the long columns of children martyrs and their parents and decided not to falter, because after all she would be a source of pride for her own children."
- In *Al Usbou* regarding Reem's "female martyr" predecessors: "[T]hey were human souls walking among human beings and carrying within them the traits of angels and supreme human aspirations."
- Head of the Lebanese Progressive-Socialist party, Walid Jumblatt, stated: "Yesterday, the Palestinian mother Reem Al-Riyashi sacrificed herself, and by so doing joined the columns of the brave Jihad warriors. . . . She offered hope in a sea of complacency, indecisiveness and fear."

* * *

Five years after their mother's death, Reem's children were featured on an episode of the Palestinian children's show *Tomorrow's Pioneers*. A musical reenactment of Reem's preparation for the attack at the Erez Crossing was portrayed in an effort to explain that "her homeland [was more precious than] her own flesh and blood." The show's conclusion consisted of Reem's daughter vowing to follow in her mother's footsteps as a Jihadi martyr (Al-Sha'arawi, 2009).

Understanding Terrorism

Reem Riyashi's actions were immediately and unquestioningly recognized as terroristic. Terrorism is defined as the use of violence or intimidation tactics to further specific ideological agendas, usually political or religious in nature. Generally speaking, terrorist organizations are driven by a host of common motives, several of which can be identified in Reem's suicide bombing (Scott-Snyder, 2016):

- To instill fear
- To undermine the military capacity of a regime that they oppose
- To cause economic damage by discouraging trade, tourism, etc.
- To create doubt about a particular administration's ability to protect its citizens, thus damaging its ability to govern
- To obtain resources (e.g., money, weapons, etc.) to perpetrate future attacks
- To achieve vengeance
- To attain recognition for a cause

As Reem's attack was unexpected and largely unprecedented due to her gender, she was able to successfully play on stereotypes to dupe the security officers at the border crossing. She presented a vulnerable persona: Not only was she female, but she also claimed to be disabled. She convinced officers to forego the standard security screening and to take her to an area that afforded her the opportunity to target not just a greater number of victims, but specifically Israeli officials; in so doing, she disrupted any semblance of safety that those who used the passageway may have previously felt.

By targeting Israeli military, police, and security personnel, Reem's attack touched on several of the aforementioned motives. Her ability to skirt security measures in tandem with her premeditated victim selection undermined the image of the Israeli administration as capable of protecting its citizens and its border, while also casting doubt on the capacity of the Israeli security force. Because the Erez Crossing was used for trade, Reem's plot also had the potential to impact the flow of money and resources into Israel due to safety concerns.

Because of the rarity of female suicide bombers, especially mothers who carry out such missions, Reem's actions gained notoriety. She accrued followers to strengthen Hamas's cause and simultaneously gained revenge for Israel's actions against Palestine. As it was the first time that Hamas had used a woman to conduct a suicide mission, conventional views about terrorism were challenged. Reem's act was hailed as heroic by some, while others viewed it as controversial; either way, it garnered widespread press. Although it didn't result in money and weapons for Hamas, the attack did encourage women to emulate Reem and to ultimately consider embarking on a fundamentalist path.

Classifying Terrorism

According to the Federal Bureau of Investigation (FBI, n.d.-a), terrorism can be classified as either international or domestic. International terrorism involves violence, the aim of which is to intimidate civilians or influence governmental policy or conduct through threat, coercion, or extreme violence, such as mass murder, kidnapping, assassination, or catastrophic destruction. These offenses occur primarily outside the United States and cross national borders. Conversely, domestic terrorism consists of similar activity within U.S. jurisdiction.

Terrorist activity can be further classified based on the mode of attack. For instance, it can take the form of person-to-person violence, as is perpetrated by the Islamic State of Iraq and Syria (ISIS); nuclear terrorism, which utilizes weapons of mass destruction; bioterrorism, which weaponizes biological agents such as anthrax; cyberterrorism, in which attacks are conducted virtually; or eco-terrorism, the purpose of which is to financially destroy businesses that pose an environmental threat (Scott-Snyder, 2016).

Terrorism is not a new concept and can be traced back from the mass executions that occurred during the French Revolution's Reign of Terror to a host of 20th-century anarchist, fascist, nationalist, and socialist anticolonial movements (Tyan, 2012). However, the phrase "terrorist attack" took on new meaning and has been a topic in the forefront of the media since September 11, 2001, when Al-Qaeda hijackers flew two passenger jets into the World Trade Center in New York City, decimating the towers, and crashed a third plane into the Pentagon, killing nearly 3,000 in the name of inciting a holy war or jihad (Gunaratna, 2002). The events of September 11th are considered mass casualty/mass destruction and are labeled as international terrorism. Although they occurred on U.S. soil, the hijackers were foreign nationals who executed most of their planning and training efforts overseas, and thus the plot crossed international borders (Scott-Snyder, 2016).

What Is Jihad?

The term *jihad* is an Arabic word that literally translates to "struggling" or "striving," but it can take on various shades of meaning within an Islamic context. It can be interpreted as fighting against immoral proclivities, attempting to convert nonbelievers, or working to improve the moral fabric of society (Bowering & Crone, 2013; Esposito, 2014; Peters & Cook, 2014). However, it is most often associated with holy war (Jackson, 2014). Under classical Islamic law, jihad refers to armed conflict with nonbelievers (Peters & Cook, 2014) and has strict rules of engagement, such as not harming innocents, including women and children. Modernist scholars describe military jihad as defensive warfare, whereas some individuals have come to interpret it as an aggressive or, in some cases, a violent occurrence. In these instances, the bastardization of the concept is typically due to its having been hijacked by terrorist groups to promote their own political and/or religious agenda. This misuse of jihad to oppose the established Islamic order contradicts the very principles of Islam (Islamic Supreme Council of America, n.d.).

In the years since September 11th, other radicalized groups besides Al-Qaeda, such as ISIS, have been in the forefront of the media due to the commission of frequent, deadly, and religiously motivated attacks (Table 11.1). ISIS initially began as an Al-Qaeda splinter group and is known for implementing public executions, destroying antiquities, and claiming responsibility for attacks in public places around the world, such as marketplaces. With the goal of reinstating ancient fundamentalist practices in the areas under its control, ISIS has implemented Sharia law, which is based on 8th-century Islam. The group uses modern technologies, including social media, to spread its message to a wider audience. In 2015, ISIS reportedly took approximately 3,500 hostages, whom they kept as slaves, most of whom were women and children (CNN Library, 2017).

TABLE 11.1 Highly Publicized Terrorist Attacks Since September 11, 2001

Year	Number of Victims	Description	Responsible Party
2001	5 dead, 17 injured	Anthrax-laced letters sent to media and politicians.	Unknown
2001	None	Attempt to detonate a shoe bomb while aboard an airliner.	Al-Qaeda
2006	9 injured	SUV driven into a group of pedestrians at UNC-Chapel Hill in retaliation for Muslim deaths worldwide.	Mohammed Reza Taheri-azar
2009	1 dead, 1 injured	An Arkansas-based military recruiter was shot and killed and another injured in response to anger over the U.S. Army's actions in Iraq and Afghanistan.	Abdulhakim Jujahid Muhammad (Al-Qaeda)
2009	13 dead, 29 injured	Military psychiatrist Hasan opened fire at Fort Hood in a self-proclaimed act of jihad.	Nidal Malik Hasan
2009	None	Umar Farouk Abdulmutallab attempted to detonate plastic explosives sewn into his undergarments while aboard a plane.	Al Qaeda
2010	None	A car bomb failed to explode in Times Square. Shahzad had trained at a Pakistani terrorist training camp and wanted to kill Americans.	Faisal Shahzad
2013	5 dead, nearly 300 injured	Two bombs were detonated near the finish line of the Boston Marathon as revenge for U.S. actions against Muslims.	Dzokhar and Tamerlan Tsarnaev
2014	Hundreds dead	Videos were posted to social media of beheadings of journalists; mass executions were being conducted.	ISIS

(Continued)

TABLE 11.1 *(Continued)*

Year	Number of Victims	Description	Responsible Party
2015	1 dead	Video was released of a Jordanian pilot being burned alive in a cage.	ISIS
2015	Hundreds dead and injured	A series of coordinated attacks around Paris were launched on the same day. These consisted of suicide bombings and mass shootings.	ISIS
2015	14 dead, 25 injured	Mass shooting at the Inland Regional Center in San Bernardino, California, for which two "homegrown" terrorists were arrested. They were inspired by foreign terror organizations.	Rizwan Farook, Tashfeen Malik
2016	49 dead, 58 inured	Mass shooting at the Pulse nightclub in Orlando, Florida. The shooter claimed to be an Islamic soldier of God and pledged allegiance to ISIS.	Omar Mateen, influenced by ISIS
2017	22 dead	A bomb was detonated outside Britain's Manchester Arena after an Ariana Grande concert.	ISIS
2017	8 dead, 40+ injured	Three men drove a van into a group of pedestrians on London Bridge before stabbing customers at nearby Borough Market.	ISIS

Sources: Adapted from CNN Library (2017); Dalton et al. (2015); Hanna (2017).

The Psychology of Terrorism

Putting terrorist threats into context is impossible to do without an understanding of the psychological makeup of terrorists and the role of group dynamics. Understanding what makes someone decide to join a fundamentalist organization is critical. While studies indicate that most would-be terrorists do not present with severe psychopathology, they do share common cognitive distortions and experience pervasive negative emotionality. They are often angry as a result of feeling marginalized by society and believe that their current political and/or religious affiliation does not afford them enough ability with which to effect sweeping change. In essence, they feel powerless.

Moreover, the vast majority of individuals who are vulnerable to radicalization have a propensity for sympathizing with victims of the perceived (often political) injustice that they oppose; they also fail to view violence against those persons or regimes who oppose their cause as immoral. Additionally, these people often have close ties to individuals who identify with a terrorist cause and may believe that joining such a movement will provide them with social, psychological, and sometimes religious rewards in addition to camaraderie, power, and a higher purpose (DeAngelis, 2009; Scott-Snyder, 2016).

Terror Management Theory and Collectivism

Unlike many of the other criminal behaviors discussed in this book, the psychological dynamics of terrorism are strongly tied to individual as well as group dynamics. Several theoretical perspectives have been developed to describe this relationship. However, as terrorist activity was previously narrowly considered a male domain, these models have not adequately addressed gender differences between male and female terrorists.

For instance, terror management theory (Pyszczynski et al., 1997) states that people have a tendency to cling to religious and cultural values in an effort to protect themselves from a subconscious fear of death. Research has shown that when subjects are reminded of their mortality, in-group identity is strengthened, resulting in a propensity to condone violence against the out-group, who is viewed as a threat (DeAngelis, 2009).

More recent derivative studies have revealed that the relationship between mortality salience and risk-taking behavior in men and women is indeed different. According to Hirschberger and colleagues (2010), an awareness of the inevitability of death leads to an increased likelihood to engage in risky behaviors for men, but not women. However, this willingness is moderated by self-esteem, which has implications for participation (or lack thereof) in terror-related activities.

A collectivist mentality, best explained as a communally focused mindset (Scott-Snyder, 2016), is a related concept that imposes the belief that the group as a whole is more important than any one of its members. From this viewpoint, individuals are considered disposable, and those who subscribe to this framework are willing to sacrifice themselves for the greater good (i.e., the group's cause). As with terror management theory, in-group identity is fortified and cultural and/or religious tenets are stringently adhered to. This self-sacrificial line of thinking lays the groundwork for the pride experienced by suicide bombers who "martyr" themselves for a terrorist cause.

Studies reveal that persons who have achieved little in the way of personal success are more likely than those who have attained lofty personal goals to be ensnared by the promise of security and deeper meaning associated with collectivist terror organizations. Also related is the idea that terrorism can be conceptualized as reactive aggression to a deep fear of cultural extinction. In other words, terror attacks are a response to the belief that radicalized movements and the fundamentalist way of life are being attacked and may be permanently destroyed (DeAngelis, 2009; Scott-Snyder, 2016).

The Emergence of Female Terrorists

The concept of women carrying out terrorist activity often elicits a visceral response. It is unexpected and largely rejected by sociocultural norms. The juxtaposition of a woman, an iconic and stereotypical nurturer, with imagery of her committing uncharacteristically egregious violence undermines the victim's feeling of security. It also allows terror cells to succeed in inflicting psychological anguish.

Following the September 11th attacks, the Department of Homeland Security created a profile of the "typical" terrorist to improve the efficacy of visa screenings; it included only males. Because terrorists are adept at finding vulnerabilities in their enemies' countermeasures, this failure to consider and scrutinize women as potential terrorists created an obvious opening for Al-Qaeda and other similar organizations to manipulate gender conventions (Pape, 2003). For this reason, female-perpetrated suicide bombings have become a more commonly chosen weapon among terror groups. By using women as explosive devices, these attacks have successfully exploited the elements of surprise and accessibility to targets (Zedalis, 2004).

However, female suicide bombers are not a purely post-9/11 phenomenon. The modern concept of suicide bombing itself dates back to 1983 when the U.S. embassy and later the U.S. and French military barracks in Beirut, Lebanon, were attacked by trucks wired with explosives; the (female) drivers detonated the trucks once they reached their destination. Since then, multiple terrorist organizations have deployed women for similar missions across the globe, beginning with the Syrian Socialist Nationalist Party in 1985 (Speckhard, 2008).

In 1991, the Liberation Tigers of Tamil Eelam (LTTE) began using female suicide bombers to conduct attacks in Sri Lanka and India; the Kurdistan Workers Party (PKK) has been utilizing women bombers to target Turkey since 1996; women joined the ranks of Chechen rebel organizations in 2000; Palestinians began using female suicide bombers in 2002; women have been detonating themselves in Uzbekistan since 2004; and women from various countries have been undertaking suicide missions in Iraq and Somalia as part of Al-Qaeda missions since 2005 and 2006, respectively (Speckhard, 2008).

Although official statistics conflict, there have been more than 200 female suicide bombers between the years of 1985 and 2006, representing approximately 15% of completed suicide bombings as well as those intercepted in the final stages prior to detonation (Schweitzer, 2006). These figures have increased dramatically in the past decade, with women in certain organizations outnumbering men in the commission of these strikes.

In addition to acting as suicide bombers, women have undertaken many other, albeit not as highly publicized, roles in terrorist organizations. According to the French Interior Ministry, 40% of French citizens recruited by ISIS in 2015 were female and a documented 220 women left France to join the terror group that same year. Similarly, British authorities reported that a minimum of 60 women left the U.K. to join ISIS—and join forces with other female recruits from countries including Sweden, Canada, Belgium, and the United States (Zheng, 2017).

Once inside ISIS, women are responsible for promulgating the fundamentalist ideology. Mothers, wives, and sisters are successful in appealing to other women to join the jihad; they glorify the underlying cause of the war, while trivializing the violence. They scout for women through online forums and encourage those traveling to regions such as Syria to participate in the radicalized efforts. From within their own homes, the women's reach is global. They additionally lend critical logistical support, smuggling jihadists and weapons from place to place to coordinate attacks.

However, these functions lack an overarching fear factor and are therefore often not emphasized in the propaganda. Instead, it is the female suicide bombers, ISIS brides, and the all-female Al-Khansaa Brigade that dominate the headlines. ISIS brides often meet their jihadist warrior husbands on terror-focused websites. Some are then subjected to strict rules and gendered violence before they are threatened with torture and/or death should they attempt to escape. Others become enmeshed in the ideological terrorist culture and engage in recruitment efforts. Others become so entrenched in the radical cause that they choose to take up their spouse's work when and if he is killed. Moreover, the Al-Khansaa Brigade is a militaristic unit comprised solely of women meant to raise awareness of the Muslim religion among females and to act as "religious police," brutally punishing women who are noncompliant. They are known for their talented snipers and knowledge of IEDs (Pellegrini-Bettoli, 2017).

Profile of a Female Terrorist

When attempting to compile the portrait of a woman who engages in terrorist activity, it is helpful to identify those static and contextual risk factors that make her vulnerable to radicalization, thus increasing her likelihood of offending (Horgan, 2008). Theorists have put forth varying hypotheses, which underscore the stereotypes associated with female-perpetrated terrorism and which focus on interconnected demographic characteristics.

For instance, youth is often considered a predisposing risk, as it is associated with limited ability to self-regulate, the search for personal identity, and naivety, which opens the door to recruitment efforts (Shelley, 2008). According to research by George Washington University and the Belgrade Centre for Security and Policy, female jihadists in the United States and Europe are a heterogeneous group composed of individuals ranging in age from 15 to 40 years (Zheng, 2017). Pape (2005) posits that uneducated women represent a vulnerable demographic because their ignorance and susceptibility to indoctrination act alongside their belief that terrorism yields the only viable avenue toward earning respect. Additionally, a stunted education is correlated with poverty and unemployment. It is a chain reaction; insufficient education leads to unemployment, which, in turn, results in economic hardship. Women facing financial struggles may be more inclined to join terrorist movements as a means of support and survival (similar to those women who commit other offenses and are motivated by poverty and marginalization). Consequently, their social identity, which is usually stripped as a result of unemployment, is restored (Atran, 2003; Taylor & Lewis, 2004). Additionally, some reports indicate that the construct of social isolation is critical to terrorism (Jacques & Taylor, 2013). Some researchers believe that Muslim women residing in America and Europe tend to feel isolated due to the intensifying anti-Muslim sentiment and are therefore increasingly in search of camaraderie, which they often find among terrorists (Zheng, 2017).

Jacques and Taylor (2013) analyzed key components of the backgrounds of women involved in a range of terrorist conflicts to develop a sense of the validity of etiological hypotheses about female-perpetrated terrorism. They also utilized a control sample of male terrorists to tease out those characteristics with gender specificity. Their findings challenge some of the existing stereotypes surrounding female-perpetrated terrorism, including the conventional conceptualization of the female terrorist as an isolated individual who lacks attachment to a social group (Atran, 2003), education (Pape, 2005), and/or employment (Krueger & Maleckova, 2003).

Perhaps surprisingly, the data reflected a host of psychosocial circumstances, but not psychopathologies germane to terrorist involvement. In accord with the aforementioned hypotheses, the mean age of female terrorists at the time of their first involvement in terror activity was approximately 22 years of age. However, the majority of them completed secondary and tertiary education, with more female terrorists having gained a degree than their male counterparts. More than half of the women surveyed were employed or pursuing their education full-time while engaged in terroristic endeavors; employment rates for women were less than for men, in keeping with comparable available estimates of global employment (International Labour Office, 2011).

Moreover, the authors also found minimal occurrences of prior criminality among both female and male subjects. The absence of a link between criminal activity and terrorism contrasts starkly with the typical trajectory for other types of (violent) crime (Mullins, 2009). One possible explanation for this is that terrorists are unwilling to confess to other crimes and therefore this portion of the study is inaccurate. However, another and perhaps more insightful possibility is that the avoidance of criminal involvement is a methodological tactic; a previous criminal history attracts the undue attention of the authorities—something that is undesirable for would-be terrorists.

While the previously enumerated domains indicate similar patterns and parity between genders, the etiologies of male and female terrorists should not be viewed as equivalent. Other elements illustrate significant disparities between men and women, reinforcing the claim that terrorism must be understood in gender-specific terms. As compared with their male counterparts, females are less likely to be religious converts or to be immigrants. They are also less likely to be employed. Although female terrorists are just as apt to be single or married, they are more likely than men to be widowed or divorced. Collectively, these differences suggest an etiology for women that is more strongly tied to individual rather than group engagement, with revenge as a possible overriding factor. However, Jacques and Taylor (2013) also acknowledge that previous studies were correct in indicating that some, although not all, female terrorists are compelled to offend as a result of peer activism, as nearly one-third of the female terrorists in their sample had relatives who were associated with terror groups.

Gender and Pathways to Terrorism

While motivations vary for joining terrorist organizations, the literature suggests that women may have different ideas and expectations when doing so than do men. Women tend to be more idealistic and to hold onto their ideals longer. They are sometimes in pursuit of a better life for their children or are motivated by a seemingly righteous desire to stand up against an intransigent establishment, while men more commonly appear to be seeking power and admiration (Galvin, 1983).

For some women, their entrée into a life of terrorism has been through the prior involvement of family or close friends (Jacques & Taylor, 2013). Their personal relationships with people who embody terrorist paradigms allow them to become sympathetic to the cause. In cases where an antinationalist conflict has been ongoing, women are more likely to internalize a desire to join the effort. While men are more strongly influenced by group pressure, which can result from kinship association to terrorist organizations (Jacques & Taylor, 2008), these situations can result in revenge motives for women when someone they love is killed at the hands of the enemy. Women exhibit a stronger propensity than men to engage in terrorist activity when motivated by revenge (Jacques & Taylor, 2008).

Unlike males, females are less likely to be driven to join a terrorist organization for religious or nationalistic reasons. They are more often compelled by personal aims (Jacques & Taylor, 2008). Some women have been courted and subsequently lured into terror groups via various modes of recruitment, in which men and women are equally active (Jacques & Taylor, 2008). Despite not having a terroristic bent, some of these females have been targeted because they can provide specific operational support (Galvin, 1983).

A related pathway, and one that lacks understanding, is that of the terrorist bride/female lover accomplice. Women who enter terrorism via this route are not mere "camp followers." Instead, they have an actual desire to engage with a terror organization but do not always develop the same skill set or level of ability as their jihadi husbands. They are often considered ancillary members who are subordinate to the men in the group. These women assume peripheral roles in terror plots, such as transporting weapons and other miscellaneous courier activities; some of them are also utilized as decoys to mislead authorities. They may additionally be sexually exploited or assaulted by their husbands or other male associates (Galvin, 1983).

Recently, ISIS has begun supporting what French journalist Matthieu Suc termed "family jihad," wherein women are urged to travel to Syria, marry jihadist fighters, and subsequently bear and raise children who will support ISIS and its ideologies. This route to terrorism instills fundamentalist beliefs in youngsters and strengthens the radical cause through family ties. It seeks to recruit both male and female fighters and ensure that terrorism is a way of life carried on from generation to generation. ISIS also uses Al-Khansaa to attract young women by branding the recruits as resilient and independent women with "jihadi girl power," in stark contrast to the stereotype of the oppressed and subservient Muslim woman (Zheng, 2017).

From the perspective of most terrorist organizations, recruiting female operatives has considerable utility, as women have been proven to bolster the success of many undertakings by virtue of their gender. Terror groups exploit stereotypes surrounding gender and sexuality to advance their operational goals. For example, despite recent attacks and the increasing amount of research surrounding women's involvement in fundamentalist causes, the element of surprise is still attached to female-perpetrated terrorism. Women, especially those who appear particularly vulnerable (e.g., disabled, pregnant, ill, etc.), continue to evoke less suspicion than do men, and therefore are better positioned to carry out an array of terrorist activities such as smuggling arms, ambushing law enforcement, or detonating themselves amidst civilians in public places. Female terrorists play on gendered impressions of women as weak, nurturing, nonviolent, and easily victimized to more quickly pass scrutiny by security forces. Some of these women also trade on their attractiveness to distract (male) officers or targets, making them useful but deadly operatives.

The Portrayal of Female Terrorists in the Media

Although it has been proven time and again that female terrorists are just as lethal and ruthless as their male counterparts, the media continues to depict these women in patronizingly sexist ways. For instance, the following was the opening sentence of a news article which ran in April of 2002: "Her nails manicured and hair pulled back from her face, the Palestinian woman asks that she be called by an Arabic name for a faint star—Suha." The future suicide bomber "is barely 5 feet tall, fair-skinned and pretty, with a quick smile" (as cited in Nacos, 2005).

This piece, laden with frilly and "feminine" descriptors, falls into the "appearance trap"; it takes the focus off Suha's terroristic capabilities and places the emphasis on her looks, as the media so often does with women, regardless of their roles. The author plays into the rigid and gendered expectations that terrorist groups exploit, while somehow glossing over the brutality of the act Suha is contemplating and how it has the potential to be *more* psychologically destructive than if it were to be carried out by a man. *Her* victims will be caught more off-guard and be made to feel more psychologically vulnerable; their sense of cultural norms will be shattered—all because she is female.

The description of Suha was published only months after an article that correlated terrorism with male hormones: "Testosterone has always had a lot to do with terrorism, even among secular bombers and kidnappers" (Dickey & Kovach, 2002, p. 48). Whether the message is implicit, as in the first account, or explicit, as in the second, the meaning is clear: Men are terrorists and women are not.

To further illustrate the point, a report about the wave of "Palestinian women strapping explosives to their bodies and becoming martyrs" was posted on the website of the Christian Broadcasting Network with the headline "Lipstick Martyrs: A New Breed of Palestinian Terrorists" (CBN, 2003). A *New York Times* article, which highlighted the apparent likeness between a young terrorist and her teenage target, began: "The suicide bomber and her victim look strikingly similar. Two high school seniors in jeans with flowing black hair" (Greenberg, 2002, p. A1). The piece went on to tell how the would-be bomber failed to follow through with her plot and was remanded to an Israeli prison; she was later described as a "petite, dark 25-year-old with an engaging smile and an infectious giggle" who was "well-suited to her job arranging flowers for weddings in her village" (Nacos, 2005).

The attention paid to the appearance of female terrorists is nothing new. Over 30 years ago, Leila Khaled, member of the Popular Front for the Liberation of Palestine, was described as a "trim and dark-eyed beauty with sex appeal" (Nacos, 2005). She received extensive press coverage for her "pin-up" girl looks (Viner, 2001) and for being the "glamour girl of international terrorism" (Baum, n.d.).

The media fixation on the attractiveness of female terrorists strongly undermines the heinousness of their crimes and how they and their organizations exploit gender as an operational tool. In comparison to male terrorists, the news media concentrates much more heavily on women's physical attributes, only mentioning male terrorists' appearances when the need arises to explain a specific facet of their attack or when pertinent to an investigation (e.g., the hair color change of a fugitive) (Nacos, 2005). It is also worth noting the incessant use of the word "girl" to describe these female terrorists in the news; although they are often being sexualized, they are also being infantilized. These women are being objectified and their actions are not being portrayed as the grave threat to national security that they are.

Perhaps even more glaring than the gendered physicality lens is the equality frame that is applied to female terrorists. Freda Adler described female-perpetrated terrorism as a "deviant expression of feminist" (Klemesrud, 1979, p. A24). According to the *New York Times,* she noted that the publicity encompassing terrorism affords female terrorists "a platform to say, 'I am liberated from past stereotypes, I am accepted in the ultimate masculine roles'" (Klemesrud, 1979, p. A24). In her book *Sisters in Crime,* discussed earlier in this text, Adler (1975) wrote, "Despite their broad political pronouncements, what the new revolutionaries . . . wanted was not simply urban social gains, but sexual equality" (p. 20). In the late 1970s, European experts offered similar accounts for the considerable number of women joining terrorist organizations, suggesting that their activity was an "unwelcome consequence of the women's liberation movement" (Hofmann, 1977, p. 7).

More recent explanations have attributed female terrorist activity in customarily male-dominated locales to demonstrative expressions of gender equality. In 2002, when Wafa Idris, the first female suicide bomber to attack Israel during the Israel–Palestine conflict, detonated herself, the response of witnesses was reportedly not one of extreme surprise because Palestinian women were considered the most liberated females in Arab society (despite the male domination common in the Middle East) (Copeland, 2002). Many considered Wafa's attack to be of great cultural significance. Of the bombing, Abdel Hamuda, editor for an Egyptian weekly, wrote that it "shattered a glass ceiling" and "elevated the value of Arab women and, in one moment, and with enviable courage, put an end to the unending debate about equality between men and women" (Bennett, 2002, p. 8). In a commentary in the *Chicago Tribune*, a terrorism expert concluded that "these female suicide bombers are fighting for more than just national liberation; they are fighting for gender liberation" (Shemin, 2002, p. 23).

Sally Jones

She was known as the "White Widow." British-born punk rocker-turned-terrorist Sally Jones quickly became the face of ISIS. She recruited hundreds of women to join the jihad through her role as a propagandist.

In October of 2017, Sally was reported to have been the first woman killed after having been specifically targeted in a U.S. airstrike; as a result of her terrorist activity, Sally had been deemed a high priority for assassination by the U.S. military (Gadher, 2017).

* * *

By any account, Sally Jones had a difficult childhood. Following her parents' divorce, her father committed suicide. Sally was only 10.

Her strict Catholic upbringing conflicted with these two tragic familial experiences, yet Sally remained an active participant in Christian youth groups for several years before ultimately denouncing the faith and debasing all Christians everywhere. By the time she turned 16, she had dropped out of school to become a beautician (Humphries, 2017).

Throughout the 1990s, Sally sang and played guitar for an all-female punk band known as Krunch (Weaver, 2017). Prior to her immersion in radical Islam, she became reliant on subsistence from welfare and resided in public housing. She also developed an interest in alternative lifestyles, including witchcraft (Gadher, 2014, 2015).

In 1996, Sally gave birth to her first son with paramour Jonathan Wilkinson. Wilkinson died 3 years later from cirrhosis of the liver. Sally then birthed a second son, Joe, better known as Jojo, in 2004 with Darren Alfred Dixon. In 2013, Sally abandoned Dixon and converted to Islam. Via a host of social media exchanges with *Sunday Times* journalist Dipesh Gadher, she explained that she had met British jihadi fighter Junaid Hussain online and the two had begun a virtual romance. However, Sally continued to receive support from the food bank at the Church of the Good Shepherd in the U.K. even after she began to subscribe to the tenets of Islam. According to one of her neighbors, Sally disclosed, "It's so hard. I love a Muslim man and he's fighting jihad" (Gadher, 2015). Later that same year, Sally and Jojo traveled to Syria where she and Hussain were married and both became prominent members of an ISIS computer hacking group known as "TeaMp0isoN." Sally's articulated reason for conversion was the Iraq War (Gadher, 2014).

On August 25, 2015, Hussain was killed amidst a U.S. drone strike (Cronk, 2015). Sally was proud that her "husband was killed by the biggest enemy of Allah" (Whitehead, 2015) and vowed to never love anyone but him. She referred to Hussain as an excellent role model for her sons, the youngest of whom she'd chosen to raise as a child warrior. She adopted the name Umm Hussain al-Britani and quickly became an ISIS spokesperson. She urged Western women to join the Caliphate and used social media to propagandize. She further encouraged female sympathizers to initiate terror attacks throughout the U.K. during Ramadan of 2016 (Weaver, 2017) and gained further notoriety for having compiled and published dossiers that contained the names and addresses of American military members intended as targets for jihadi militants.

Due to Sally's active involvement in numerous terror plots, she became a prime target for American military strikes, and in October of 2017, it was reported that she and her son Jojo had been killed in a drone strike in Raqqa, Syria. One of only two women at the time to be considered by the U.S. State Department to be a foreign terrorist combatant, she was the first woman to be directly targeted in an airstrike (Weaver, 2017).

***

Sally Jones is most commonly classified as a terrorist bride. Like many women who wear this label, she appeared to have a genuine interest in joining ISIS. Although she noted that her motivation was related to the armed conflict in Iraq, her history hints at other compelling situational and potentially causative factors.

At the time that she joined ISIS, Sally was in her mid-40s, considerably older than the majority of female terrorists. Unlike many female jihadists, she had a stunted education. Sally also gave birth to two children by two different men. The combination of these things resulted in financial hardship and a potential survivalist mentality.

Sally additionally suffered multiple significant losses throughout her life, beginning with the dissolution of her parents' marriage. As (an only) child, she was forced to face her father's suicide. It is likely that she felt let down, neglected, or even confused by traditional measures of support such as family, religion, society, or education, which resulted in her exploration of alternative lifestyles. She was possibly searching for not only a lifestyle but also a sense of belonging and self. These all-too-familiar negative and uncomfortable feelings were potentially reinforced during adulthood when she lost the father of her firstborn son.

Like many female terrorists, Sally was eventually widowed by her jihadi husband. However, unlike many women who fall into the terrorist bride category and are content with taking a backseat to the male group members, Sally had been active in terror plots since the beginning. She continued the work in which she and Hussain had been engrossed and proudly became a leading recruiter for ISIS, directing various operations. She garnered the attention of both American and British authorities.

Unlike other female terrorists, Sally's relationship with the media was different. As exhibited in the last section of this chapter, other women have been pawns of the press. However, Sally used her social media expertise to manipulate not only reporters, but also a larger global audience. She used various digital platforms, such as Twitter, to post targeted threats as a form of psychological warfare. She also posted edited images of herself. One such photo, which pictured Sally dressed as a nun holding a firearm in one hand and a dog in the other, went viral. The image not only highlighted her attractiveness and race (Caucasian), but it also served to disrespect the Christian upbringing she had come to so vehemently oppose.

Through her use of social media, Sally named herself the #White-Widow and #MrsTerror and accrued a large number of followers. She recruited extremist converts via various terror-related websites and assumed a leading role in ISIS even while her husband was alive, a fact that she made sure to publicize. In essence, Sally, at the behest of ISIS, branded herself in such a powerful way that the mainstream media did not have the opportunity to constrict her with gendered labels.

According to Azedeh Moaveni, author of *Lipstick Jihad*, the images of Sally Jones on the web made her one of Islamic State's "most iconic recruiters." She further offered:

> Having [Jones] . . . was really important in terms of projecting the idea that ISIS could get into the very furthest reaches of British society. They could pluck up this woman who was a punk rocker, who was white, who was kind of attractive and they could put her up as their kind of poster woman. (as cited in Weaver, 2017)

Despite her far-reaching recruiting efforts, strategic propagandizing, and critical role in plotting deadly attacks, Amnesty International released a statement characterizing Sally's assassination as having been of "questionable legality" (Iaccino, 2017). Additionally, according to the International Committee of the Red Cross (ICRC), she may not have been a legitimate member of ISIS, and thus not an appropriate military strike target because she did not carry out a "continuous combat function" (Sari, 2017). This statement has been criticized by Department of Defense experts for its restrictive, not to mention gendered, nature, as organized terror groups such as ISIS continue to actively engage female members—and to exploit gendered stereotypes to their advantage—in combat and combat-supportive roles, including recruiting and intelligence missions.

Shortly before her death, Sally Jones changed her profile picture on Twitter to the Statue of Liberty—weeping. She posted the following quote from the Quran: "We shall cast terror into the hearts of those who disbelieve [3:151]."

Conclusion

Gender stereotypes persist in the mass media portrayal of female terrorists. Although women figure prominently in the history of terrorism, the female terrorist continues to be perceived as an exception to the rule. The media continues to place female terrorists in stereotyped boxes, and radicalized organizations continue to exploit these gender norms for operational gains; women are becoming a tool of terrorism.

Female terrorists are a heterogeneous population in that there are many reasons why women join fundamentalist causes and there is no specific profile of such females. However, research reflects significant and impactful sociocultural factors that may underlie women's decisions to engage in terrorist activity. Despite these varied influences, it remains a definitive fact that the female terrorist differs from her male counterpart and cannot be understood simply in terms of him. She remains a paradox, which inevitably increases the level of threat she poses.

Part III

In Her Own Words

Overview of Interviews

Due to the fact that until recently women comprised only a small portion of the prison population, the vast majority of criminological research has focused solely on male perpetrators. That, in combination with the socially pervasive and stereotypical

cal attitudes about women's ability, or lack thereof, to commit acts of violence, has made the idea of female offenders—especially recidivistic or violent ones—somewhat of a foreign concept. Women have long been regarded as nurturers and caretakers, incapable of brutality and cunning.

As previously discussed, female-perpetrated crime has been a widely ignored and minimized phenomenon, which has most often been conceptualized as an offshoot of male offending, and thus the motivating factors for such crimes have traditionally been overlooked or misunderstood. Because of

this, correctional programming for male offenders has historically been seen as a "one-size-fits-all" model and therefore been
applied to female offenders without regard for gender respon-
siveness and the importance of understanding the unique needs
of female offenders.

As gendered theories of crime have evolved, it has become evident that female offenders *do* in fact have different needs than
their male counterparts and also experience different risk factors.
Women begin to offend at different ages than do men; they have
different developmental trajectories toward crime, experience
social strains differently, and are more prone to certain psychological conditions than are men, with 32% of incarcerated women
estimated to be affected by a serious mental illness (e.g., schizophrenia, bipolar disorder, or major depression). Additionally, more
than 80% of jailed women have a history of substance abuse or
dependence, and nearly 80% are mothers (Swavola et al., 2016).

Despite the recent strides made in feminist-aligned theories, such
frameworks are by their very nature impersonal; they strive to be
objective and can seem intangible, especially when applied to the
concrete, palpable, and often emotional world that exists behind

bars. As of 2014, there were over 215,000 females incarcerated in the United States alone (Sentencing Project, 2015)—each with her own unique story to tell.

The Interviews

While the majority of women are incarcerated for nonviolent offenses, females can and do commit violent crimes—crimes that violate gender norms. When stories about women who abuse children, kill spouses, or have sex with minors make headlines, society vilifies them. Not only is the condemnation of these offenders evident in the subtext of the news media, but it also permeates society; it is in the blatant judgments of the public, which are based on the collective stereotypes of a patriarchal culture. There is no substitution for understanding these women's offenses and pathways to crime from their own perspectives.

The following are excerpts from interviews with justice-involved women. At the time of these conversations, some of the individuals were incarcerated in state prisons, while others were in county jails or under community supervision and thus facing significant reentry challenges. Some of the interviewees grappled with cognitive distortions, including denial and minimization, as well as

guilt and impression management. However, many of them spoke openly about the types of aggression in which they engaged and the stigma they faced as jailed women. They opened up about their past traumas, domestic violence, and drug abuse, as well as their experiences with racism, sexism, and mental health.

Supplemental information and analysis are included only as necessary to orient the reader to pertinent details in each case. The raw transcripts offer invaluable insight into the women's perceptions of their own unique experiences. In an effort to tell the women's stories in their entirety, readers can access the full audio through SoundCloud (https://soundcloud.com/user-798575661/sets/when-women-offend), Cognella Active Learning (https://active.cognella.com/courses/1846/modules), or their home Learning Management System.

"Terri," 56-Year-Old Caucasian Female, Murder

On her crime:

> TERRI: I was charged with first-degree murder. . . . I got 55 years. What happened was, um, I was livin' with this man for 6 years and . . . he was abusive . . . but not that bad. I mean it was bad, but like, he would pin me down and scream in my face for like

an hour, and he would like spit in my face and call me names and stuff. . . . He went like, from like real nice to being real mean.

On mental illness:

TERRI: I, like an idiot, moved to northwest Indiana with him, where we owned five acres of property and there was nowhere for me to go. I didn't have any family there, nothing. And he, um, just got extremely bad with me there. Every day I was a fat lazy bitch. I didn't know how to cook; I didn't know how to clean. . . . I was thinking, "It's me; it's me, cause I [also] have bipolar disorder." And then I started realizing it's him, you know? And uh, so anyway, that, so he started hitting me and he was just, you know, he beat and raped me a month before I shot him. And um, I um, I sat there; I didn't shower, I didn't do nothing for a month. I sat in a chair and I drank every single day. I got drunk, and plus I was taking my head meds, and um, so that day he pinned me down in the morning and screamed in my face . . . and it was just a big mess. And then, like after he pinned me down . . . he said something . . . and goes, "Your mother's a cunt and so are you," and I just—the gun was right there. I picked it up and I shot him.

On psychological abuse and its impact on her arrest:

TERRI: So I didn't mean to kill him, you know. It wasn't like I was planning it or anything, but it sounded like that because I . . . I made, uh, one or two phone calls. He was alive and then um, I called 9-1-1 to get him some help and um, I . . . I didn't know he was gonna die. So when the cops came, cause he always told me about like, hitting me and stuff, "No one will believe you." You know, so I had that in my head, and plus, I didn't wanna tell on him, which is evidently some kind of sickness when you don't wanna tell on the person that's abusing you. So when the cops came and they said, "Why did you shoot him?" and I didn't know what to say and I just go, "cause, because uh, I wanted to see how it felt to shoot, to shoot him, to shoot somebody" or something like that. And he's like, "What did you say?" And I repeated it . . . that looked really bad. I had been a drug addict and alcoholic for years, and I had calmed down on it a lot, but I wasn't taking street drugs anymore, for probably about 15 years I was going to counseling and receiving like, you know, head meds for bipolar and depression.

On addiction:

TERRI: Oh so, anyway, when they arrested me and put me in um, put me in lock, in this room, first of all they put me in . . . the chicken coop. . . . I was going through withdrawals. I mean, severe withdrawals 'cause I was on like 500 milligrams of Seroquel. I was on Cymbalta, Klonopin; I was on Vicodin for my arthritis. So, and plus alcohol, because I had been drinking like a fish. I went through Hell going through that detox. . . . I was a total mental friggin' mess. Total.

On domestic violence:

INTERVIEWER: At what point did you find that you were able to say the words that he was abusive without feeling guilty about saying it?

TERRI: Um . . . it was basically towards the end of my stay at um, at uh, [prison name redacted]. I mean I told some of the girls, but then I was trying to tell the lawyers, and by that time . . . I had just denied the fact that, you know, they just didn't believe anything I said. If I had told them right off the bat, the circumstances would've come out differently and I wouldn't have got 55 years. . . . Then when I went to court and the judge said, "Did he hit you?" I said, "No." I still wouldn't tell. I don't know what was wrong with me. And then my mom and my sisters were there [in court] and I had told the lawyers I didn't want them there. I didn't want to testify because I didn't want them there; I didn't want my mom there.

INTERVIEWER: How come?

TERRI: Because I didn't want her to know he raped me and stuff. [Crying] I just didn't want to say it and I didn't want her to hear all that—I didn't want her there. . . . Then it's like, [the victim] looked like he was this perfect angel and I looked like this crazy murderer. . . . I take medication but I've never been violent in my life. I'm not a violent person it's just not me. And he was—he treated me like shit. I moved out there and left everything I know and loved to be with him out there and he treated and did that to me. I couldn't do anything right in his eyes. He had me so down, I couldn't talk to my sisters. I couldn't see my family, nothing.

INTERVIEWER: So you were really isolated?

TERRI: Yeah, I was totally isolated out there. I didn't know anybody out there or nothing. . . . I knew I needed to be punished for what I did. I understood that, but the rest of it, like, the severity of it, 55 years? No, because he was wrong too. I don't deserve that. And people in this place, they get less; it's like they get less time for worse things. You know, now that I'm in prison I realize that. And I, and so the judge was like, well, it looked like I was this really bad, like, um, drug abuser and stuff like that. It made me—it just made my character look bad to the judge. And then, like, and then his sister was saying, "Well she was on, uh, food stamps and she was on Medicaid." Yeah, now I need that where I didn't before, and so that made me look like I'm this lazy drug addict . . . that does nothing but sit there and do drugs and ya know, take off the state.

On her feelings at the time of the murder:

TERRI: I shouldn't have been drinking at all. I mean I was a-an alcoholic—I-I'm an alcoholic, yeah. But I can like—I wasn't—it's—there's nothing that ever made me mean or shoot anybody. Ya know what I'm saying? I was an alcoholic, but I was functional. I worked my whole life.

INTERVIEWER: Can you describe what you were feeling in the moment that you reached for the gun that day?

TERRI: Hatred.

INTERVIEWER: Hatred?

TERRI: Yeah. Absolute hatred. It was like something I never felt before. And I just picked it up and shot him.

INTERVIEWER: So all this stuff had built up over time?

TERRI: Yeah. It did.

INTERVIEWER: And you just—snapped.

TERRI: I snapped. Exactly. I mean, I just absolutely snapped, because I didn't—I didn't think about it. I just did it. And when I was in court reading my statement, I said, "Well, I uh, me and [the victim] were arguing more than usual that day. Um, I meant to shoot him, but I did not mean to kill him." That's what I said. So, you know, I was trying to take—I was taking total blame for all of this. I wouldn't even tell what he did . . . but a lot of it's my own fault, because I wouldn't speak up about what he did to me.

INTERVIEWER: What advice would you give to a woman who's in an abusive relationship?

TERRI: Well, I've met quite a few of them since I've been in here and there's one . . . her baby daddy punched her in the face, or whatever—broke her, fractured her face, and she wants to marry him. First of all, when they do that, they don't quit, they keep on hitting you. It just doesn't get better, all it does is uh, it escalates, and next thing you know you might be shooting them and spending the rest of your life in prison. I mean, I just—I kinda wanna send that message. Like if you're feeling like it's all your fault and stuff, just get the f— away from them, for real, because it's just not worth it. It can ruin your life, like it did mine.

"Jackie," 25-Year-Old Caucasian Female, Theft by Extortion

According to the Department of Corrections, Jackie's commitment offense was "theft by extortion." However, during her interview she revealed that she was arrested for "robbery," which is categorized as a violent crime by the FBI. Robbery is considered to be theft coupled with physical harm or the threat of physical harm. This charge was likely reduced as a result of Jackie's plea bargain.

Although Jackie's account of events does not involve overt violence, it does highlight two key factors: the repetitive drug use (and associated criminal activity) common among female inmates, and the fact that substance use, abuse, and addiction affect individuals from various walks of life; privilege does not equal protection.

JACKIE: I grew up . . . in an upper-middle-class family. My parents were married for 30 years. They're in a process of getting divorced now. I've come from a really supportive family. There's no addiction in my family. I'm the first one to ever be incarcerated in prison or county jail.

INTERVIEWER: How old were you when you got arrested?

JACKIE: For this charge? Um. Twenty-two.

INTERVIEWER: Twenty-two? What was going on in your life at the time?

JACKIE: I had been using heroin for the past, I guess, 3 and a half years. And, um, I met a girl in rehab and I was, she was 10 years older than me. I met her in Florida and I came home and my parents, every time I would get high, [they] would kick me out. So I was staying with her and we got in an argument one night and she threw me out. And 2 days later I went back to get my stuff with two of my friends and was arrested for robbery.

INTERVIEWER: Okay, and did you rob her?

JACKIE: No.

INTERVIEWER: It was your stuff that you were taking?

JACKIE: Yeah I was gonna go back and get my stuff—um— because I was using. She was an addict too. We didn't know she was home and we were gonna take her drugs too, but she was home so—um—we left and she called the cops.

INTERVIEWER: Aside from her, at that time in your life, what were the significant relationships that you had?

JACKIE: I have friends who use. I have friends who don't use. My family is really supportive as long as I'm not getting high. Um, I don't think I was in—I wasn't in any type of, like, intimate relationship at the time.

INTERVIEWER: When's the last time that you were in an intimate relationship? Do you remember?

JACKIE: Like a year and a half ago.

INTERVIEWER: Mmm . . . hmm. And how did that end, or did it not end?

JACKIE: I—it was someone through—I met in NA, and I was getting high. He was clean and, it just—it just wasn't working.

INTERVIEWER: So correct me if I'm wrong, when you're in [a program] like that, you're not supposed to intermingle, right?

JACKIE: You're supposed to wait but I—he had been clean for a year. I was clean for 7 or 8 months, so they say a year.

INTERVIEWER: Okay.

JACKIE: So it wasn't like we were, like, both newly in recovery, but I think I was just looking—. First, I don't think we were compatible, it's just that he—I thought he was gonna help keep me clean 'cause he was—had a lot of time clean and was always at meetings. And I thought he would help me and he just wanted to save me. And I just didn't want any part of it.

INTERVIEWER: Do you remember the first time you picked up heroin?

JACKIE: Yeah.

INTERVIEWER: What was going on?

JACKIE: I had a relapse. I went to Montclair State University for graphic design and I was on academic suspension and I came home for a semester . . . and all my friends who'd never like left town were already getting high for the past 2 years and I kind of just fell into it. I fucked up school, I was back home, my other friends who made it to college were still away, and I was left with these people who've been using for the past couple years. And I just—I don't know—just felt like a failure because I failed school, was on academic suspension, failed out of college, and had to go to county college for a year. And I don't, I just kind of fell into it. I was really against it for years, 'cause my friends were doing it for 2, 3 years before me. I would like go to my best friend's house and like tell his parents that I thought he was gonna die, and I just—I just fell into it; I don't know.

INTERVIEWER: What happened that you were academically suspended?

JACKIE: I-I had to get my grades up. I was an art student and, you know, I was 17 years old. I didn't know what I wanted to do with the rest of my life. I had to stay up all night doing paintings and sculptures and it was just a lot at 17, then 18 years old, to keep up your first time away from home. And I hurt my arm too, my right arm, and I was an art student, so I just stopped going to class. I'm like, "I can't draw, so why am I gonna go to class?" And I failed a few classes and had to go home.

INTERVIEWER: Mmm hmm. Prior to your arrest, what were the values or beliefs in your life that were really core to who you are—really important?

JACKIE: I don't think I'm better than any other person who uses, but I've never robbed anyone; I could never do it. I—my family's really important to me. I-I've been sick withdrawing more times than I've been—done anything crazy to get drugs 'cause I like refuse to lose my family over—I've chosen drugs over them in some ways, but there're some things I just would never do. So my family is really important to me.

INTERVIEWER: Okay. How has it been for you to be in here [prison]?

JACKIE: Well, ah, it's—I related to some people, but most people, not gonna lie, like my values don't—I don't even speak my mind sometimes because I don't want to seem like I think I'm better than or anything. But usually one arrest doesn't land you in prison. I just—I was so naïve to the legal system that I didn't fight my charge and took my first offer, which was drug court or jail. I gave them a few dirty urines and they sent me to prison. But it's been all right. . . . I'm in a TC program. I'm in a rehab cottage. Um, but I never wanna come back. I'm leaving in 28 days.

INTERVIEWER: Congratulations.

JACKIE: Thanks.

INTERVIEWER: So what are your plans for when you get out?

JACKIE: I have to go to a halfway back for 90 days and then I'll be on parole for 2 years.

INTERVIEWER: Okay. And what plans do you have for progressing in your life while you're on parole?

JACKIE: I want to go back to school; I'm not sure for what. I have one more semester for an associate's, and then I don't know where I'll go after that. I'm not really sure what I want to do. Um, I just want to make up for lost time.

INTERVIEWER: What significant people or events in your life do you think led you on the path to being here today?

JACKIE: Um . . . the people that I used with are people I've been friends with for years. We all kind of like were friends before drugs, so it's hard to let them go 'cause I'm—I'm really loyal and probably like, if I love someone or been friends with them, it's for life no matter what they do. So . . . my parents are always like, "You have to get rid of these people," but I've been friends with them since I was 12/13 years old. It's hard to let them go.

INTERVIEWER: Are they males? Females? Both?

JACKIE: Mostly males. Some females. Most of the girls I was friends with growing up made it to college and graduated and kind of got past the party stage, where I didn't. I don't know. There's nothing—I-I can't complain about my life. I have a great life. I have a great family. There's nothing traumatic or anything that led me here. I just, you know, heroin's an epidemic in suburbia.

"Valencia," 49-Year-Old African American Female, Voluntary Manslaughter

VALENCIA: My name is Valencia. Um, my charge is voluntary manslaughter. I've been locked up since 2006. How I got to be locked up was, um, I was in a [turbulent] relationship—9-month relationship—with my boyfriend, and um it got to the point that we started having real bad problems: no communication, things started getting physical, very verbally abusive as well as a lot of physical abuse. A lot of spittin' on me and telling me I'm worthless and just things like that. So I stayed in the relationship because I never wanted to give up. I always wanted to try hard to win his love—keep winning his love. He always used to tell me . . . that's why he never wanted to be with a black woman before, because when he's with a white woman, they'll never tell the police on him; he'll never get locked up. So the times he would beat me a lot . . . I just never would tell . . . because I never wanted to be that woman—that black woman—to get him locked up.

On the dynamics of her relationship with the victim:

VALENCIA: Things spiraled out of control like, really fast. When I finally made up my mind that I'd had enough, I got the police involved. They came to my house at least three times. They put him out, but I played the back-and-forth game. I was done, but then when he come around, we'd talk a li'l bit; I'd let him back in. We'd fight a little bit more; I'd kick him back out. Back and forth, back and forth. That went on for about a month and a half. I just know when I was finally done, I said, "no," and no is what I meant.

After finding the victim in her apartment on the night of the murder:

VALENCIA: Well, I went home that night. . . . When I looked down the hallway, it was like a silhouette laying in my bed. . . . He jumped up, off the bed, out from under the cover and says, "I wanna talk to you for a minute." I says, "No, you not gonna talk to me for a minute. As a matter a fact, how'd you get into my house?" He says, "But I wanna talk. I say, "You know what? Don't even worry about it." So . . . I . . . turn my back to go call the police. I walk out the bedroom and turn my back, he jumped on me, grabbed me from the back, threw me down. We got to fighting . . . that's how I got my teeth knocked out.

On experiencing a flashback:

VALENCIA: At that point, I seen his eyes go into like, a rage. I seen a look in his face that I will just never forget it. . . . Well, the first thing my mind told me was run, run, run. But then

I became paralyzed; I couldn't move. I became paralyzed because I had a boyfriend previous to him that had shot me with a 9mm and paralyzed me from the waist down. I put a police report on him . . . and it did me no good. So all of that back abuse, all the things that happened to me in my past, all that was replaying in my mind. Just quick. I can't explain it to you. It just like, flashed.

On the murder:

VALENCIA: By the time I opened my eyes up, he was standing back in front of me. This time he had a big knife. I says, "What are you gonna do with that?" He says, "I hate you, fat bitch. I'm gonna kill you." And he just starts spitting. So I'm just like, you know what, I said, "You need to let me up out of here right now." He said, "Well, nobody's leaving. Somebody's gonna die tonight." . . . So at this point, I'm fearful. But he got me all backed up in the corner. . . . I'm in danger, and . . . there is nobody for me to call for help to. So now we're arguing back and forth but I'm still trying to stay strong. . . . If he smells fear, it's over for me.

So I say, "Well you know you can have everything in this house. Let me out of here right now. Please, just let me out of here." "Fat bitch, this and that." I say, "You know what? I don't care anymore; I just don't want you no more and this is why." He . . . just ran towards me . . . with that knife and as he leaped with that knife, I just grabbed the closest thing to me. . . . There was just one knife in the holder. . . . I just, plunged forward, my eyes was closed and I was just like, "Nooo!"

On remorse:

VALENCIA: So immediately I could tell you what I felt because still it bothers me today, 'cause it's like I could smell all the smells still today, fresh in my mind. I could hear the argument fresh in my mind, and I could still feel when the knife went in and when he tugged off.

Shortly after the stabbing, Valencia phoned her mother:

VALENCIA: I said, "Mom, this guy tried to kill me. This dude tried to kill me. You know, does anyone understand that?" She was like, "Baby, you got to come back because the police—" I said, "I'm not coming back. I'm not coming back." And I didn't. I just kept running. I just kept running and running for my life. I felt like everything was against me; everybody was against me. Then they told me that my boyfriend was dead, you know what I'm saying? And—and—it just happened so fast. I didn't try to hurt him—that was the last thing—he was trying to hurt me!

On trauma:

VALENCIA: I got raped before—prior to all this—years prior to all this. So the way I handle myself is different from how another woman who never got raped handle herself. When I sleep with a man, I never take my bra off because inside my bra is my keys, and my keys—door key, car key. [Crying] I know how to work my keys real fast because I got raped real bad.

On reentry:

VALENCIA: My biggest fear is going back into society and I don't want to fall in love again. I'm scared to move . . . on and love, because I don't want to kill nobody again. I don't want to be hurt. I don't want nobody to love me so much that they want to kill me.

"Talinqa," 35-Year-Old African American Female, Murder

TALINQA: I'm here for murder.

(Talinqa explained that a week prior to killing her 66-year-old male victim, whom she viewed as a father figure, she was "raped by some guys" who she had considered to be her friends. On the day of the crime, she went to her victim's home to seek solace. She wanted to drink and knew that she

usually drank to the point of passing out; she reported that she thought she'd be safe there. The interview picks up with Talinqa discussing her thought process on the day of the offense and her memory of the murder.)

On the crime:

TALINQA: I'm thinking I'd be safe and we start drinking again. I threw up and then he [the victim] start touching on me. I kept asking him to stop; he wouldn't. It was a hammer in front of me—that was the only thing in my reach. I picked it up and I hit him. And I kinda like blacked out and I hit him more. But when I snapped out of it, I just dropped the hammer, looked at him, and kept apologizing.

On childhood trauma and its impact on her offense:

TALINQA: It all started from when I was like, 8 years old. I was outside playing with some friends. My mother called me in and my mother used to drink real bad. And she called me in and had sex with me. But she told me I better not ever tell nobody because what happens in our house—in our roof, you know, stays up under here. When I was nine, my oldest brother was 6 years older than me; he molested me. And this just kept going on . . . then his friends started joining in.

And then one time, my other brother—he's 21 months older than me—me and him was playing. My mother made us come in, made us take our clothes off, and she made him get on top of me. We both cried the whole time, but she just sat there and laughed. It was funny to her. . . . So at the age of 10, one of my brother's friends had molested me and I was getting tired of it. So I grabbed my mother's sharpest knife . . . and stabbed him in his leg.

On her relationship with her mother and her own children:

TALINQA: My mother used to beat me all the time, just for no reason. . . . I had every abuse there is from my mother. . . . I'm the darkest one of her kids, she'd tell me . . . I'd never amount to be nothing, number one. She'd make fun of my color.

INTERVIEWER: How many kids do you have?

TALINQA: I have four. I have four now. My oldest son, I planned him. His father is my best friend, which is a drag queen. My, um, other daughter, I gave her up for adoption, though, but she's in my life now. She found me. She's 18. And I was mad at my girlfriend, so I went and slept with her friend and got pregnant [laughs]. It's just crazy . . . the last one was a rape baby.

On race:

TALINQA: I turned myself in.

INTERVIEWER: Why do you think you did that?

TALINQA: Conscience.

INTERVIEWER: Fair enough.

TALINQA: And then they was going after somebody else. I'm like, I'm not gonna let somebody go down for something that I done. I mean that's really not fair to the next person.

INTERVIEWER: Sure.

TALINQA: So . . .

INTERVIEWER: How much time did you get?

TALINQA: Fifty-five to 27 and a half. I've been down—April will be 15 years.

INTERVIEWER: Wow.

TALINQA: And then I try and be funny and throw the color in there, but . . . my victim was white. . . . And there was a sheriff . . . she came to my cell one time and was like . . . "I hate to tell you—you're gonna get sentenced on the color, not your crime." . . . This one girl . . . she killed this older black woman, stabbed her 37 times with a screwdriver. They only gave her 10 to 5.

On her mental health:

Talinqa informed the interviewer that she wished she'd had a psychological evaluation following her arrest.

INTERVIEWER: What do you think that an evaluation would show?

TALINQA: Basically, it would've showed that I was—I wasn't—I wasn't—right in the mind at that point in time. When I seen the um mental health here [in prison] and talked to her, she was . . . surprised I hadn't snapped a long time ago. She was like, "You finally hit your breaking point." So.

TERVIEWER: Mmm. You've been through a lot.

TALINQA: Mmm. It's a lot. It's a lot more, but yes . . . I mean, every relationship I'm with, I'm like, only thing I'm good for is sex—that's how I feel because that's what everybody wants. And if I don't do that, then it's a big old thing. . . . I just feel like shit.

"Amy W.," 36-Year-Old Caucasian Female, Multiple Charges

AMY W.: My name's Amy. My charges are aiding, inducing, or causing murder; aiding, inducing, or causing robbery; and conspiracy to commit robbery.

(Amy W. was arrested and charged following a 2003 incident during which she and multiple codefendants lured a man from a bar, robbed him, and beat him to death. Amy and her co-conspirators befriended the victim, and the interview picks up with her discussing her knowledge and expectation of, as well as involvement in, the night's events.)

AMY W.: There was five of us. Me and my girlfriend and her sister, were at a bar . . . we met up with two of her friends . . . drinking, having fun. This guy starts buying our drinks. Next thing I know, he's playing pool . . . while all of us girls are dancing on the dance floor. Having fun. Drunk. We'd already done other drugs that day. Um, I guess he flashed money at them—playing pool and stuff—making bets or whatever. There was a robbery planned. Um, I don't remember any of that because like I said, we were dancing on the floor. Somehow he [the victim] ended up with me in my car, and we followed the other people in their car into their backyard. We get out. Another guy jumps out from behind the garage, starts beating him up. And another guy or another girl starts also beating him up—takes his money; we leave; he ends up passing away.

INTERVIEWER: So you physically drove him there. . . .

AMY W.: Correct.

INTERVIEWER: And did you have any sense of what was going to happen to him there?

AMY W.: I thought we were using him for his money, but at no time did I think that this was gonna happen. Honestly, I don't think anybody intended to kill him. It was just to rob him, but he ended up bleeding to death of blunt-force trauma to the chest and head.

INTERVIEWER: What was he hit with?

AMY W.: Hands, feet, that's it.

INTERVIEWER: And how many people were beating on him?

AMY W.: Two.

INTERVIEWER: Two. Okay. So what did you do after? What happened? Was he alive when you all left?

AMY W.: I couldn't tell you. I think so, though.

INTERVIEWER: Okay.

AMY W.: So then we went back to my girlfriend's house and that's where they were cleaning up and getting rid of his wallet—things like that.

INTERVIEWER: Took the money out of the wallet first?

AMY W.: Correct.

INTERVIEWER: And what did you do?

AMY W.: They tried to distribute the money—split it up. I didn't want any of it, so I was freaking out.

INTERVIEWER: Okay. Did you not want any of it because you didn't want it to get traced to you? You thought it would get you in trouble, or . . . ?

AMY W.: I just didn't want a part of it. I had never seen that. I came from a good home. I had never even seen a fist fight. I was in shock, very much so.

INTERVIEWER: And what about your girlfriend? Had she seen things like that before?

AMY W.: Yeah. I had only been with her for like a week before this, so we had just started hooking up and I didn't know until afterwards that she had done the same thing with her brother before and put someone else in a coma . . . like this I guess was her thing.

INTERVIEWER: And if you had known that about her up front, do you think you would have been involved with her?

AMY W.: Um, I don't think so, but I don't know. But I don't think I would have.

"Mari," 44-Year-Old Hispanic Female, Human Trafficking

At the time of her interview, Mari was in jail awaiting trial. She had been charged with human trafficking, endangering the welfare of a child, and promoting prostitution. These charges resulted from accusations that she had pimped out her two minor daughters to her boyfriend. Mari allegedly sent her daughters to stay overnight with her boyfriend, where they served as sex slaves in exchange for money, food, clothing, and other provisions.

At Mari's request, a fellow inmate served as a Spanish-to-English translator for this interview. Although Mari had previously established a rapport with her while incarcerated, this was the first time that Mari made her story known to her friend.

MARI: My charges are trafficking [human] and prostitution.

INTERVIEWER: Promoting prostitution?

MARI: Promoting child prostitution.

INTERVIEWER: Okay, so what happened? What did you actually do?

MARI: Well . . . I did it. I needed the money. It wasn't . . . because I wanted to do that. I needed money for rent. . . . I'm a single mother. I don't have a husband. That's why I did that—by necessity. I repent for doing it.

INTERVIEWER: You had mentioned earlier, before we really started the interview, that it was your daughters [that were victimized]?

MARI: Yes, two daughters.

INTERVIEWER: And how old were they?

MARI: One 12; another one 14.

INTERVIEWER: And so, how did you get them to have sex with men?

MARI: It was just with one man.

INTERVIEWER: Okay.

MARI: Not many, just one man. I couldn't keep a job for a long period of time and they were very, very underpaid jobs. So I went to welfare. . . . They didn't help me. . . . They just gave me food stamps. They didn't help me for rent or for my children. . . . They knew I was a single mother—still they didn't help me. So then I [made] that decision. I had to give my daughters to my boyfriend so that he can give . . . money for rent, buy clothes, and the utensils for school.

INTERVIEWER: So the man in this case was your boyfriend?

MARI: Yes.

INTERVIEWER: Can you tell me about your relationship with him?

MARI: We were good friends. He's not rude. He's not mean. He never raped them. If my daughters wanted to have sex, it was okay; if they didn't want, it was okay. He will buy their stuff for them even if they didn't have sex.

INTERVIEWER: Did he ever hurt you?

MARI: No. Thank God.

INTERVIEWER: How did you feel about the fact that he wanted to have sex with your daughters?

MARI: I feel very bad. [Crying] I feel really bad, but he understood. I'm not going to touch them.

INTERVIEWER: Were you there in the room when this [the offense] happened?

MARI: Yes.

INTERVIEWER: Where is he now?

MARI: He's in jail.

INTERVIEWER: . . . Are you still in a relationship with him?

MARI: Yes, he still loves me and he still wants to be with me. He changed a lot.

TRANSLATOR ASIDE: [She said] He doesn't think of having sex with her daughters.

INTERVIEWER: Do you still love him?

MARI: A little bit, but it's not as it used to be.

INTERVIEWER: How old were you when you came here [to the United States]?

MARI: Nineteen.

INTERVIEWER: Okay. How old were you when you met your boyfriend?

MARI: All my kids are from my marriage. I was like 36 [when I met my boyfriend].

INTERVIEWER: The marriage that you had, [with] the father of your children, what was that relationship like?

MARI: Very bad. Ugly.

INTERVIEWER: Very bad. He hurt you?

MARI: Yes.

INTERVIEWER: Did you have relationships before that?

MARI: Yes. This last boyfriend helped me a lot in everything.

INTERVIEWING: With money?

MARI: Sometimes [yes]. Sometimes no. Because other guys just make fun of me. They just want to have sex and that's it.

INTERVIEWER: Why did they make fun of you?

MARI: Because I was easy, I guess. . . . They just wanted to have sex and that's it.

INTERVIEWER: That had to hurt you. . . .

MARI: Yes.

INTERVIEWER: What was your childhood in Mexico like?

MARI: Very hurtful. Very difficult. My mother prostituted me.

TRANSLATOR ASIDE: Oh my God! I'm sorry. I just never heard that. She said her mother gave [her] medications . . . to activate her sex—wanting to have sex?

INTERVIEWER: Hormones?

TRANSLATOR ASIDE: Hormones or something. Oh my God!

INTERVIEWER: And how old were you?

MARI: Twelve.

TRANSLATOR ASIDE: I'm sorry. I'm getting . . . [crying].

MARI: Then at 16 I got pregnant. When I was 4 months pregnant, my mother took me to have an abortion because it [the baby] was of her lover. . . . I think that's why it's been very bad in my marriages.

TRANSLATOR ASIDE: She [Mari's mother] used to call soldiers and they used to make a line to have sex with her [Mari].

INTERVIEWER: Oh my God.

MARI: That's why I don't want to go back to Mexico.

TRANSLATOR ASIDE: She applied for asylum.

(A few weeks following this interview, Mari pleaded guilty to two counts of human trafficking and was sentenced to 20 years by statute with parole ineligibility. Due to her immigration status, she will be immediately deported following her release from incarceration. Records reveal that the judge was unable to find any mitigating factors to justify a reduction in sentence.)

"Daniela," 44-Year-Old Hispanic Female, Child Endangerment, Fraud

Daniela reported that her criminal history comprised "one thing after another." At age 23, she endured a traumatic divorce followed closely by the devastating loss of her grandmother. She sought comfort in a sexual relationship with a 14-year-old boy whom she met at her Bible study group; this resulted in a charge of endangering the welfare of a child and a lifetime Megan's Law stipulation with Community Supervision for Life (parole). She violated the terms of her parole when she requested permission to travel out of the country to visit a man she'd met online, but was denied and chose to go anyway.

In the interview, Daniela discusses why, after having been through the revolving door of prison for various other charges, she made the decision to leave her children behind, jump parole, and travel to the Dominican Republic to be with a man she'd met via Instagram.

> DANIELA: I needed love at that time. I felt very lonely. . . . My ex-husband cheated on me and left me while I was in jail and that really destroyed me. And I was going through a divorce. And yeah . . . I really needed some, some love. I did have the love of my kids, but you know sometimes you just need something else and that's how I got with him. So I done give up my kids and everything—left them with their father because nobody had given me the attention and the love that he [my boyfriend] was giving me even through the phone. I left everything. Everything. . . . And I just left because I was being loved. That's it and I'm paying for that now.
>
> INTERVIEWER: So you're still with the guy in [the] Dominican Republic?

DANIELA: Well I haven't talked to him like for one month or two. . . . He wants to be with me so that's like a dream to me, you know, because that's been my dream even with my kids. You know, being with the person you love. Having a family. That's the main goal.

INTERVIEWER: Right.

DANIELA: . . . He said that he would fight for me. You know? That's why he wanted to come [to the United States]. . . . Nobody . . . never say that to me.

INTERVIEWER: How'd that make you feel hearing that?

DANIELA: That somebody is there, that never been there.

INTERVIEWER: Yeah.

DANIELA: Never. I never had nobody for me. I've been there for my kids and for whoever needs me, but I never had anybody for me. Not even as a little girl. I had to do everything on my own.

"Pam," 31-Year-Old Caucasian Female, Child Molestation

When she was 20 years old, Pam pled guilty to having molested a 12-year-old female who was asleep at the time of the offense. Now, 10 years later, Pam looks back on her offense differently.

PAM: They charged me with a Class C felony of child molestation. . . . I was 19 years old at the time and what happened was . . . I was celebrating my birthday and I invited a few people and they invited a couple of girls over. . . . One of them brought alcohol . . . and truth to be told she was 15. And what happened was we ended up kissing and she ended up telling her mom and her mom ended up turning me in to the cops. And that should've been a sexual misconduct with a minor charge, but . . . they kinda screwed me. . . . I've been in and out of here for the last 11 years of my life and dealing with the same stuff . . . you know, being charged with that first charge. It's stemmed off from parole violations to not registering and stuff like that, and. . . .

INTERVIEWER: So you have to register as a sex offender?

PAM: Yes. I do . . . for 10 years. . . .

On self-reflection and self-improvement:

PAM: I need to get myself together; there's a lot of things I need to work on.

INTERVIEWER: What do you think some of those things are?

PAM: My attitude for one. . . . I've been hurt a lot as a kid. So I have a defense mechanism. And like certain things . . . uh, that people say trigger that. And I uh, I step off on the wrong foot and then get defensive and take things the wrong way. Um,

I talk to mental health a lot here [in prison] so I can work on those problems, because as I was growing up I never had the therapy that I needed for being raped and molested as a child, and beat and stuff. . . . And I have really bad nightmares and I relive that in my sleep, so I try to get on the right medication to help that. . . . Right now I'm on uh, Depakote, which is a mood stabilizer, which helps me with night terrors and everything, so I haven't been having them. Thank God, because it takes a lot out of me. And then . . . there's times where I'll have flashbacks when I'm wide awake and there's nothing nobody can do about it. And that's the sad thing, because I end up flashing back to when I was a kid and then coming back and they're like, "Do you remember just doing that?" And I'm like, "No."

On growing up in the system:

PAM: I've been in and out of a facility since I was 17. I was in girls' school and then, I was only out like maybe a couple months and then I got locked up on that child molestation charge, and I've been in and out of here for the past 11 years. And . . . I'm going on 32 and they've known me since I was 19.

INTERVIEWER: So you really grew up in the system?

PAM: Yeah. And so like I—it's kinda hard. I hate to say this, but this is all I really know. Growing up, I've only spent my 26th birthday out and . . . my um, 29th, and I never um . . . every other birthday I've been locked up. And I'll be turning 32 next month and hopefully I'll be out for my 33rd birthday, so I don't have to see this place.

INTERVIEWER: Mmm. What are your plans [for] when you get out?

PAM: Um, well, right now, I can't really say I have some set in stone, but I do wanna go to school. I wanna go back to school. . . . I know that the community college has GED classes that I can take and then I wanna go to college after that. . . . I wanna become an EMT; that's one of my main things I wanna be—I like helping people. And, um, I was a volunteer firefighter . . . before I came here, and you know, just helping people randomly, whether it's . . . helping homeless people or . . . I'd help a lady that works at the mission, feed all the homeless . . . people during the night. She would go downtown and would feed all the homeless people and I'd help her out. And you know, or I'd help volunteer in nursing homes and stuff like that. Just little stuff. . . . But being in here, it's setting back a lot of stuff.

On responsibility:

INTERVIEWER: There was something in your paperwork that said . . . that your daughter had talked to the police or had testified against you? Did that happen?

PAM: Um, she um, talked to the cops yeah, but she was more on my side than anything. She was trying to keep me from going to prison.

INTERVIEWER: She didn't want to lose Mommy.

PAM: Yeah, she didn't.

INTERVIEWER: Yeah. Did she see anything? Was she there when your offense happened?

PAM: No. My mom and dad had her at the time. . . . I was at a totally different place. I'm glad she wasn't a part of that situation because . . . I wouldn't want my child taken away from me, and, um, I'm glad that, you know, she wasn't there because you know, that's traumatizing to a little child.

INTERVIEWER: Of course.

PAM: For anybody to see that at a young age . . . but um, you know, I should've listened to my parents. My mom and dad told me not to go. And, I should've listened and I didn't. And you know—I was at the wrong place at the wrong time. And, the girl . . . I personally don't know what happened, but somebody had to have messed with it for her to even think . . . you know, for her to blame me for that. She . . . passed out and we moved her . . . from the living room to a bedroom and somebody had to have messed with her in her sleep for her to even think of. . . .

INTERVIEWER: Right, 'cause that's what—what was in the police report, right? That's what she had said?

PAM: Yeah. Yeah. And then she told the cops; she's like, "I don't even know if she even did it." You know, for her to say that then, they should've been like, "Well, okay, maybe she didn't do it." And then, when she was supposed to come to court, her and her mom skipped state. So they, they fled and didn't even show up when they were supposed to, and that should've dropped the whole case.

INTERVIEWER: What you actually physically did to her, though, was you kissed her?

PAM: Yeah, that's it.

INTERVIEWER: Okay. Do you think that you should've gotten in trouble for that? Or no?

PAM: I mean I can understand if it was a sexual misconduct with a minor charge. It wouldn't have been as bad. But as a child molestation charge, I don't see . . . nothing molestation involved in that. I mean, yes, she lied about her age. She said she was 21 and come to find out she was 15. You know, if her mom had more control over her child—it was a school night, too. If you had more control over your child and had known where she was, this would've never even happened. You know, I think she, the mom, has part fault in this too because she had no—she had no control over her child. She should be more responsible over her child. You know, when I was 15, I wasn't able to do stuff like that. I wasn't able to go out—I was too focused on school and I had a job. . . .

INTERVIEWER: So you feel like a lot of different elements came together to kind of land you in this situation?

PAM: Right. . . . If she woulda been at home nothing woulda happened.

INTERVIEWER: Do you think that you have any responsibility in this situation? . . . Maybe a decision that you made, or . . . ?

PAM: I wish I woulda made a better decision on who I got involved with. Um . . . now I make sure that the person's old enough. I mean, I look at IDs. I-I make sure that they're over 18 because I'm not . . . gonna get stuck back in prison for another case like that ever again.

On trauma:

INTERVIEWER: I've been looking at all the tattoos on your hand. . . .

PAM: Yeah, I got a whole bunch.

INTERVIEWER: Can you tell me a little bit about them?

PAM: Um, this is, um, we had—I had an adopted sister. She got killed back in 2007. She died in my arms; it was a tragic situation—she took a bullet for me. I ended up raped in 2007 and I ended up pregnant. I lost that little girl at 6 and a half months. The person that raped me found out that I was pregnant and then he shot at me, so my sister took the bullet. And, um, I lost her, then. . . . I went to jail, and then I lost the baby.

After I lost the child, I came to prison, so it was like within 3 months I had back-to-back things happen. And it was the postpartum depression that hit me hard. I didn't wanna be messed with. I didn't want nobody talking to me. I just wanted to be left alone.

On addiction:

PAM: I'm out there doing anything that I'm not supposed to be doing. I mean, I was on Spice real bad, and I was smoking meth real bad, so those were the two drugs I was on. . . . I was basically killing myself.

INTERVIEWER: Do you have any understanding of why you were getting high so much and why you were hurting yourself like that?

PAM: To deal with the pain that I—you know—from being . . . abused as a child, and with all the depression that I had, and that was my way of coping.

INTERVIEWER: Self-medicating?

PAM: Mmm. Trying to get away from all the . . . trying to numb my pain instead of having to deal with it, even though after I get sober, it just comes back and then I get high some more.

"Susan," 58-Year-Old Caucasian Female, First-Degree Murder

Susan's presentation at the interview was both significant and notable. Her long hair was curled and her makeup was expertly applied—a feat while incarcerated. She smiled throughout and appeared to truly enjoy talking about her case.

Susan has become an expert at speaking with researchers and media alike, as her case has appeared on true crime TV shows and in various news articles and books. Despite the extra attention paid to her appearance, she declined to have her photo taken for this book because she stated that her image is "owned" by the network that covered her story. Susan further indicated that obtaining the rights to print a picture of her would be exorbitantly expensive—through no doing of her own. According to former FBI profiler Candice DeLong, who previously interviewed her, Susan exhibits traits consistent with narcissistic personality disorder (Mavety, 2010). Susan is a master of impression management.

On her crime:

SUSAN: My name is Susan. I'm here for murder—my husband, James. And I got a 60-year sentence after two trials. The first one was a hung jury, and the second one found me guilty.

(Susan was convicted of murder in the first-degree after her husband was found dead in the couple's upscale Midwestern home; he had been shot through the eye. Susan reportedly discovered the body, hid the gun, and then called 9-1-1.

Throughout the investigation, rumors circulated that prior to his death, James had been preparing to divorce Susan. When the couple met, Susan was a 24-year-old single mother and James was a 39-year-old attorney. He was successful and wealthy, and together, he and Susan lived the life of the social elite. Susan categorically denies rumors of marital discord and continues to maintain her innocence, characterizing her conviction as an egregious miscarriage of justice.)

On being a woman incarcerated:

SUSAN: When I first entered prison, it was a whole different world then. . . . I think that the—the saddest thing . . . and it still saddens me—is that we didn't have any rights as mothers to our children. For instance . . . my in-laws who agreed to take my children and raise them, the style in which they were accustomed to . . . promised me that they would never keep my children from me. They would always keep me updated on them. And I wasn't really asking for a visit every weekend or anything, just occasionally. Like every month or so, let them come and see me. Let us keep that mother and child bond—and they refused . . . so I had to suffer through that loss. In the beginning, it was also difficult because . . . the men [inmates] had all these vocational programs that were available to them, which we did not have. . . . I'm not being productive at all.

INTERVIEWER: Do you feel that your sentence was fair?

SUSAN: Um, no. Yes and no. I would say yes because it was my husband.

INTERVIEWER: Okay.

SUSAN: And I'm gonna say no because, uh, I didn't commit the crime.

INTERVIEWER: Okay.

SUSAN: . . . So now that I've been inside and I've seen how people have to live and . . . how they endure in prison, no, because at the very worst, most people who commit a murder, especially women—so let me just speak on a woman's point of view. Knowing all the women that I have that have committed murder, if they indeed did commit murder, most of 'em, it's a one-time, heat-of-the-moment thing or something that they have within their marriage that drove them to this.

INTERVIEWER: Mmhmm.

SUSAN: So what they need are more skills on how to deal in a relationship so that . . . if something is so bad there is a way out. We need more options for women, especially those with children, so they can get out of a bad relationship. . . . As long as I've been locked up, I've never seen anyone return to prison who has committed murder—admittedly committed murder. . . . Once they have done their time and gotten out . . . they have never returned.

On what she believes *really* happened to her husband:

INTERVIEWER: Can you tell me a little bit about what you think did happen to your husband? You said you didn't do it, so what do you think . . .

SUSAN: Oh.

INTERVIEWER: Yeah, I mean he was shot, right? He was shot to death?

SUSAN: I mean well, we don't know. There were two options available and they never tested him to see if he did it himself. Could he have committed suicide? Absolutely. That is a possibility that they never completely convinced us couldn't have happened. They just said, one—one expert—well he was on their side anyway, just trying to make it look like he did it—said, no, the way that the bullet entered in, it couldn't have, but it could have, they now say. So that's a possibility.

INTERVIEWER: So that is a possibility.

SUSAN: That is a possibility. Um, the only other option—I would never want to unjustly accuse anybody because I've been in that seat. . . . I just know that after almost over 4 months, they tested me for gunpowder residue; it came out negative. I took three polygraph tests and passed.

(During the course of the investigation, the lead detective asked Susan to submit to a polygraph examination, but she refused. Other persons of interest cooperated and were polygraphed [Clarkson, 1996/2014].)

SUSAN: [At the time of the murder] I was with my children clear across town, which suddenly they've got me Speedy Gonzales and Annie Oakley, shooting the gun better than anybody's ever shot in their entire life. . . . I've never shot a gun before. So that's—I don't know. I don't know.

INTERVIEWER: I had read that you had said that you were having an affair with your stepson?

SUSAN: I was. I did.

INTERVIEWER: And that he shot your husband?

SUSAN: Uh, it was his gun. It was his gun.

INTERVIEWER: And you did have an affair with him.

SUSAN: I did have an affair with him. I hate that word affair!

INTERVIEWER: Relationship.

SUSAN: I hate that word relationship!

INTERVIEWER: Okay.

SUSAN: [laughs] I had sexual intercourse with his son; yes, I did.

INTERVIEWER: Can you tell me how that came about?

SUSAN: I was not attracted to him like, though—I have to say that. But uh, when my husband would go out of town, his son and I, we just went out. We went to a bar. I love to dance. I don't drink; I've never drank, and I did that night because he ordered the drinks. We were out dancing. When I went back, I went to take a drink, um and I'm normally the designated driver.

INTERVIEWER: Okay.

SUSAN: Okay. Anyway, we had been drinking that night, so when we got home, he took advantage of the situation. I didn't resist that much either, so I'm not even gonna say that I did. And that's how that started. Then it became, "If you don't, I'll tell." So . . . that's how he got his motorcycle. I started buying him things, not because I was in love with my stepson, but because he was gonna tell. So I eventually told on myself. I eventually went to my husband and told.

INTERVIEWER: And what did he say?

SUSAN: When you're throwing yourself on the mercy of the court, you don't even look up. When you're begging for your whole marriage, your whole life, you take whatever they're gonna give you, and that man was amazing. He said, "We'll never talk about this again and I will handle everything." And I trusted and believed that that's what he would do. So uh, we had started seeing a marriage counselor. I was setting us up so that I could tell on myself and have us prepared because whatever he was gonna do, I was gonna take, because I did that. That's a horrible thing to have to tell your husband that you did. Horrible. . . . I don't know anything else that happened past that point.

INTERVIEWER: Okay. When you said that your stepson had taken advantage of the situation, but you said, "but I didn't really resist that much," what does that mean?

SUSAN: I had been drinking.

INTERVIEWER: Okay.

SUSAN: So when something's happening to you, you're just like in that state and I don't drink! I've never—I don't drink. It's just surreal, like it's not really happening. And I am—I don't know what you term them nowadays—a sexaholic. That's all there is to it. Yeah, very much.

On hiding the gun and being turned in by her own sister:

INTERVIEWER: I had also read that your own sister . . .

SUSAN: Yes, she did.

INTERVIEWER: . . . told police that you had confessed to her.

SUSAN: Yes, she did!

INTERVIEWER: Can you tell me about your relationship with your sister and how that came about?

SUSAN: That's really hard right now—really, really hard because my whole family alienated my sister. . . .

INTERVIEWER: They didn't believe her?

SUSAN: Oh, no! And it's really funny because my brother, who I just adore, who has stood beside me through all of this, said, ". . . you're family, and if you did it, there had to be something so wrong for you to do that. But regardless, we don't turn on each other like that."

SUSAN: I hid the gun. OK. That's a fact that you have to know because when I walk in and I have two small children, I did not know he had been shot. There was no blood; there was nothing to indicate to me that he had been shot. So, he's laying on a sofa . . . unresponsive, his hands out, and the gun is right there. I had no idea what a gun was doing because we do not own a gun. . . . So when I pick up the phone to call for 9-1-1, I hide the gun. It wasn't even any deep, dark secret place or anything. I put it in my sewing box; that's it. So once I had hid the gun, then I couldn't unhide it. . . . I just thought, I just want them to focus. 'Cause I'm thinking . . . Did he finally decide that what I had told him was too much? Did he just decide to take his life? Or—I didn't know.

INTERVIEWER: So you thought that he might have killed himself because you had had sex with his son?

SUSAN: And that's horrible. . . . I had no answers, so I just hid it . . . if it's sitting there and they come in, I've got to start explaining things that I don't know what I'm explaining.

(According to Susan, both her sister and her mother were complicit in hiding the murder weapon. She alleged that they helped to secure the gun in a copper kettle that was then filled with cement before her mother removed it from Susan's home to shield her from suspicion. However, collateral sources indicate that upon finding the heirloom kettle packed with cement, Susan's mother turned it over to authorities. Susan further reported that it was her sister and not she who had taken the lead with regard to making decisions about how to hide the gun.)

INTERVIEWER: So you had said that you and your sister never had the best relationship, but it seems like if she is directing what to do with the gun—it seems like she was trying to protect you.

SUSAN: She's older.

INTERVIEWER: Okay, so it was an older sister–younger sister kind of thing?

SUSAN: Yes.

INTERVIEWER: So then what would have prompted her to go to the police and say, "She told me she did it"? Why would she do that?

SUSAN: She claims—and this has all come together after some years—but she claims that they [the police] came to her because at this point they're following me. . . .

INTERVIEWER: So you were a suspect at this point.

SUSAN: Yes, yes, yes . . . but they have nothing. They claim they're following everybody because they really think we're in cahoots together. . . . So they said, "This is the way it's going down. We're gonna wire you up. You're gonna go visit her and you're gonna get a confession out of her."

INTERVIEWER: But she didn't get one, right?

SUSAN: No! Because there was none. I'm like, "What the hell are you talking about? You are insane!" That is absolutely nothing about what I said. So nothing at all.

INTERVIEWER: When she started asking you questions that were clearly meant to . . .

SUSAN: She told me she was wired. I already knew.

INTERVIEWER: You knew she was wired?

SUSAN: I knew. She mouthed it to us: "I'm wired." . . . I couldn't understand. Why are they wiring her? The worst is, they wanna know where the gun is. But that's not what she said. She didn't say, "Where's the gun?" which was the question I thought was coming. She said, ". . . remember on the drive . . . you confessed to me that you killed Jim?" I said, "What the hell are you saying? Absolutely not."

"Amy B.," 53-Year-Old Caucasian Female, Multiple Charges

Amy presented as childlike and saccharine as she discussed her offense, which has been sensationalized in the media; it has been referred to as one of the most heinous murders in the Midwest. At the age of 23, Amy was convicted of the arson-related murders of her three children, all of whom were under the age of 5.

AMY B.: My name is Amy, and I am in prison for three counts of murder and one count of sexual misconduct with a minor, and, um, I've been incarcerated now for 18 and a half years. I was 23 years old when I decided to get out of um, my marriage with my husband of 5 and a half years. I was an alcoholic and I, um, was a pot smoker and I started experimenting with pills . . . I got into a sexual affair with a 16-year-old boy who lived across the street from me. And . . . due to my addiction and my sexual affair . . . it distanced myself from my husband, from his family and my family, and my addiction changed my relationship with my children. And because of that . . . my self-esteem became very low. My expectations of myself were not reached. My husband's expectations of me and his family's expectations of me and my family's expectations of me were crumbled. And due to my addiction, being a wife and a mother was ruined. And that's how I came to be in prison . . . because of my addiction.

INTERVIEWER: Can you tell me a little bit about your relationship with your husband?

AMY B.: My relationship with my husband . . . it was kind of on and off again while we were living here. . . . When we lived in Florida, me and my husband had a wonderful relationship. Um, I think that me and my husband would have continued to have made a go of our marriage, and I believe I would not have become addicted had we stayed in Florida. And we moved to

Florida because he had gotten into a little bit of trouble up here
. . . and so we kind of cut out on bail—on his bail. And uh, we
moved to Florida because that's where my mother is at, and I
had never really had a good relationship with my mother, so
this was a chance for me to have a relationship with her. And
his family did not approve of me, and my family up here did
not approve of him. So it was a way out for both of us . . . to
kind of start over and have a new fresh outlook without a lot
of family influence. . . .

(Amy explained that she and her husband soon grew homesick
and moved back to the Midwest.)

AMY B.: Our relationship started to go sour . . . and that's when
I started drinking a lot and smoking pot, and my husband—he
didn't do any of that. He didn't smoke. He didn't drink. He
didn't do any kind of drugs; he didn't even smoke cigarettes.
He was completely drug-free and alcohol free. Nothing. It
was all me. It was me.

INTERVIEWER: At what point did you decide to become involved
with the teenage boy?

AMY B.: I decided to become involved with the teenage boy
because I had started smoking pot with his older sister. . . .
When money started getting low, my husband started making
sure that I didn't have the money for alcohol, that I didn't have
the money for pills or for pot, and so the boy across the street
decided to start hooking me up. So I had kicked my husband
out of the house and he had to move in with his family, and
I started um, portraying a relationship and a sexual affair
with the boy across the street just so I could get hooked up.
Because I did not have a job and I was out of money.

INTERVIEWER: So you were paying him in effect—he was giving
you drugs and you were giving him sex. Is that . . . ?

AMY B.: Yeah. But I portrayed it as if I cared for him. As if I had, you know—that I had feelings for him and stuff when, um, I did not. It was . . .

INTERVIEWER: Okay. You had said that you're also here on three counts of murder.

AMY B.: Yes.

INTERVIEWER: Can you tell me what that's about?

AMY B.: Um, I was accused of killing my children. The detectives and stuff convinced the prosecutor that I was the only one who could have possibly set my house on fire with the intentions of killing my children, and a jury found me guilty on it.

INTERVIEWER: How old were your kids?

AMY B.: My children were 4 and a half years old, a month and 11 days from being 3 years old, and 20 and a half months old.

INTERVIEWER: Mmm. And all three of them perished?

AMY B.: All three of them perished in a house fire.

INTERVIEWER: Were you home?

AMY B.: I was home in bed, asleep at the time and the 16-year-old boy was also in the bed with me. . . . I had woke up in the middle of the night—still unsure of how I woke up—but I know that when I woke up there was already smoke rolling out of the kitchen into my bedroom and um, the 16-year-old boy was still laying next to me in the bed. . . . The back door to my house was nothing but 3 to 5 feet from my bed. That was the only reason why we got out alive.

INTERVIEWER: The reports had said that your children's' bedroom door was locked.

AMY B.: It was in a closed position.

INTERVIEWER: So they couldn't physically open it to get out? I guess you had very young children, right?

AMY B.: Yes, but they can open up doors just fine. I don't know if the door was locked or not, but I know the reports say that the door appeared to be in a closed position.

INTERVIEWER: And the report had also said that the investigators found flammable liquid, that it looked like someone had set the fire. Is that something they had talked to you about? Or no?

AMY B.: Yeah, they talked to me about a pour pattern, and they said that because of a pour pattern, which can also be a high traffic area, that the pour pattern made it appear as if a flammable liquid had been used.

INTERVIEWER: Okay, so basically they were saying that you had poured something flammable and set the house on fire to purposely kill your children?

AMY B.: That's what they say. That's what they say, yes.

INTERVIEWER: How does being accused of that make you feel?

AMY B.: Being accused of something so heinous. At first I was just in shock because I don't see how any mother could possibly harm their child in any way, and then to be accused of doing it and then to be found guilty of doing that . . . is horrible. It's the worst thing in the world. To know that you survived something you should've died in, and then to be accused of killing your own children. Because in my mind, I don't care what a woman goes through, how bad her low self-esteem is, who she's fucking, who—whatever is going on—I don't see or understand how any mother or woman could harm a child. That's not what a mother or a woman is—is ingrained to do.

(According to the opinion handed down in Amy B.'s appeal, the investigation indicated that she had put her children to bed before pouring flammable liquid on the closet floor of their bedroom. She then locked them in their room by securing a belt to the door handle and attaching it to a hook on the wall outside the room; it was common practice for her to use a weighted belt contraption to latch the door when they slept or played. Amy B. then proceeded to pour more flammable liquid along a common wall of the children's room and an adjacent room before igniting the blaze. Four independent arson investigators examined the crime scene and identified two separate origins of the fire.)

"Elonna," 49-Year-Old African American Female, Drug-Related Charges

On addiction:

ELONNA: My charge is distribution, possession, [and] intent to distribute. My house was raided. . . . I was selling cocaine and heroin; I was using it. I've been using drugs mostly all my life—in one form or another—with a natural progression of the disease of addiction, which I believe most of my criminal activity stems from. . . . One thing I've learned is that for myself, [is] having a character that is capable of doing the wrong thing or having a misconstrued perception of life, entitlement, the lifestyle of fast money, fast love, risky behaviors, made me a prime candidate, even from a young age, to be in a life of crime and drug dealing.

On trauma and sexuality:

ELONNA: A turning point in shaping my personality and character and behaviors was the molestation by my stepfather at 14. . . . At that point, when that happened, is when I decided the world's against me; I can do what I wanna do—I'm only gonna care about me. I'm only gonna satisfy my needs, and it made me a little aggressive, a little detached with intimate, sexual relationships with spouses and mates. The sexual component of being able to be comfortable with yourself is one extreme or the other—risky or inhibited. And a few years ago, when I first started trying to find recovery, the first step was forgiving him.

On reintegration:

ELONNA: I'm in a halfway house now, integrating back into society. I was just refused parole. . . . It just is so hard to change your street mentality into a calm, not dangerous, not impulsive, not compulsive member of society. So I'm always monitoring myself, always self-aware, always careful of how I'm speaking, how I'm acting, how I'm feeling because I could go either direction at any given moment. I don't think it ever will go away. It's just a lot of—self-awareness is the only word I can say, a desire to wanna do better and being tired of being incarcerated.

"Tyleaka," 42-Year-Old African American Female, Drug Charges/Robbery

On addiction, violence, and social prejudice:

TYLEAKA: My name is Tyleaka. . . . I'm a 42-year-old African American female who was just released by the Department of Corrections. I did 20 years. The things that led up to my incarceration are common—which is sad—in my neighborhood and in our culture: drugs, abuse, sexual abuse, violence of any sort, and those things led up to drugs, which led up to my crimes. When I'm not doing drugs, I don't commit crimes.

On "the system":

TYLEAKA: My family was non-taxpayers. They were drug addicts, pimps, pushers, and whores, so I feel as though that that's why I was mistreated. . . . You're sentenced on probability. You're rarely ever sentenced for the crime. . . . I'm not saying that people who break the law shouldn't go to jail.

Absolutely they should. However, there are a lot of—there are more nonviolent criminals that are locked up than there are violent. Everybody got drug charges. . . . My bail was so astronomical that I didn't have a fighting chance to get out of jail. My bail was so much money that you would think that I had killed the president and his kids and maybe his dog. . . . That was set so high because they knew I couldn't afford it.

On feeling unable to get mental health treatment in prison:

TYLEAKA: The prison system has a way of dealing with unmanageable inmates. . . . That's what I was, an unmanageable inmate, or aka problem child. When they can't control you, they dope you; they give you psych medications. They put you in mental health groups, and I had some mental health issues, I won't lie, but my mental health issues did not need medication. I had some abuse issues. I had some rape issues that I needed to talk through. Here's the thing, though . . . with mental health in prison, you cannot actually tell them what you really think. You can't tell them the truth, so you're lying and you are not getting the help that you should get.

INTERVIEWER: Why can't you tell them the truth?

TYLEAKA: Because . . . they put you on suicide watch.

On the crime, remorse, and incarceration:

INTERVIEWER: Do you think that you deserved to do time?

TYLEAKA: I deserved to do time, not as much as I done.

INTERVIEWER: How much time did you get?

TYLEAKA: I got 20 years.

(Tyleaka served her full custodial sentence and was not released early.)

INTERVIEWER: And can you tell me about the actual crime itself?

TYLEAKA: Yes, I needed to get high. So I robbed somebody and I robbed this person repeatedly. I regret the crime, only because it gave me a lot of time. My remorse for the victim is genuine remorse. It's genuine remorse, but I have more remorse for myself 'cause I suffered more than the victim suffered. Where does our justice system balance that? It's not balanced because they don't just lock you up. You're locked up, cool. That's no problem, but then you're violated. You're violated in so many ways that it's not even funny. Thank God that I'm not an attractive woman because if I was, I could have been raped because that's how it goes. Thank God I was a violent inmate because if I wasn't, I could have been raped.

INTERVIEWER: So it's kind of a survival thing to be violent in there?

TYLEAKA: Yeah, you have to be. You have to be a loose cannon. For me, I had to be a loose cannon. I had to be an inmate that couldn't be trusted, so that way I wouldn't be preyed upon.

On interacting with other inmates:

Tyleaka was sent to Ad Seg (Administrative Segregation, also known as "the hole" or solitary confinement) following an altercation with a fellow inmate, during which she burned the other woman with scalding water from a microwave after the other inmate reportedly spit on her.

INTERVIEWER: What precipitated that? Did she just spit on you out of the blue?

TYLEAKA: No, she thought I wanted her girlfriend and I didn't. And that's another thing in there, you know. Women fight over women as if they're fighting over men.

INTERVIEWER: Straight women?

TYLEAKA: You're only straight when your visitor comes. You're not straight when you go in there. *Orange is the New Black* has it dead on—they are dead on . . . it goes down like that, you know? I spent a lot of time in administrative segregation because I like the quiet. I like the solitude and I just, I have an interaction problem. I can't interact with too many different people at the same time. Twenty-four hours a day, 7 days a week, 365 days a year. It's just really too much. . . . I just find that I will never go to prison again. I will be dead before I go to prison again.

On institutionalization:

TYLEAKA: I am not the same person I was when I went to jail. I'm not. I don't even have a boyfriend because I'm socially awkward on a personal level. I can interact. I can work, but on a personal level, I cannot communicate properly because prison teaches you in so many ways—you can't hug anyone; you get a sex charge. You can't be friends with anyone; you might be dykes. It's always, "This is no, no, no, no, no, no." So when you're out in society, you're afraid.

"Serena," 34-Year-Old African American Female, Drug Trafficking

INTERVIEWER: Tell me a little bit about how you got here [prison] today.

SERENA: Drug charges. I guess, being around the wrong people. I had drug charges and money laundering charges and that's how I ended up here.

INTERVIEWER: I had seen a newspaper article about your case, and it said there was kind of a drug ring going on—drugs moving around. So at what point did you get involved in that?

SERENA: Basically, from the beginning, but I didn't know it was that deep because I wasn't distributing all that stuff. But yeah.

INTERVIEWER: But you still got charged with it?

SERENA: Mmm.

(Serena was arrested in conjunction with an interstate drug ring that used the U.S. mail and other parcel delivery services to traffic cocaine and other narcotics around the country for mass distribution. The leader of the ring was a Jamaica-based recording artist.)

INTERVIEWER: So at the time that you were arrested for this, what was going on in your life?

SERENA: I had two kids and I was working, and when I got arrested, it was just like a surprise because I didn't know that we were under investigation, like me and my codefendants. ... So they just practically come to my house and pick me up, so I didn't really know what was going on. ... I didn't know a lot of stuff until the case was being tried.

INTERVIEWER: So when you did get involved in it [the drug ring] ... what was your purpose or what was your goal ... ?

SERENA: I didn't have a goal when I got involved. Basically, it was just around me. Like I knew the people that was affiliated with it and I just got involved. ...

INTERVIEWER: How long are you in [prison] for?

SERENA: A 15 with a 6, so the least is 6 years.

INTERVIEWER: Why do you think that there are more men locked up across the United States than there are women?

SERENA: I guess because men get—men more get involved in crime than women. . . . I guess they're . . . braver and they take risks that women wouldn't take, and I guess they always get caught. Women is least likely to get caught probably. Both men and women do stuff that's illegal and stuff that we're not supposed to do, but I guess the men always just get caught more than the female.

INTERVIEWER: So do you think that they're more brazen about what they're willing to do?

SERENA: Mmm. They will more go like the extra mile than, I guess, what we would do. Like we would have boundaries and fear, but they—they are more brave.

INTERVIEWER: Like in your case where you said you weren't distributing because you kind of had those boundaries?

SERENA: Yeah.

INTERVIEWER: You said to yourself, "I don't want to get caught?"

SERENA: Yeah, I don't want to get involved in certain stuff so. . . .

INTERVIEWER: That makes sense. You said that us women, we have fear. Fear of what, specifically?

SERENA: Like, most women got kids. . . . We don't want to leave our children. Men . . . think . . . the child more needs their mom

A Poem by Donielle (as provided to the interviewer)

I rather be beaten
I rather have broken bones
I rather have bruises
Because they heal
But words scar you all the way
   down to your deepest soul

than their dad. . . . Not every man, but some men maybe feel like they—they don't really have to play the role of a dad. While the female, we have to play the role of the mom, and if we have to play the role of both the mom and the dad, we're going to play the role of both mom and the dad. For instance, if you're home and you got kids and they're supposed to go to school and they need lunch money, you're gonna find it. You got to get it. Like if they call the dad and he's like, "I don't have it," then . . . that's it. But the mom, we have to get it. Wherever we're going to get it, we're going to find it.

"Donielle," 32-Year-Old Caucasian Female, Conspiracy to Commit Murder

DONIELLE: My name is Donielle. I am here for conspiracy to commit murder. I have been incarcerated since March 13th of 2007. I have four other codefendants in this situation: one female, three males. Two of 'em were sentenced to 65 years and the other three, ranging with me, anywhere from 30 to 35 years. Two of us are about to be released. . . . What happened, it was a very emotional situation. My daughter was 2 years old and a friend of ours, who is also a codefendant, told us that our friend/live-in babysitter was molesting our daughter. Within a matter of an hour, it was, she was gone. . . . Two of us picked her up, dropped her off, and after we left, she was murdered.

INTERVIEWER: So did you know that you were effectively driving her to her death?

DONIELLE: Yeah. It was like I-I-I don't think my codefendant really understood it. Then I look back at it and I-I'm dealing with mixed emotions about my situation because one of my codefendants is very manipulative, and I don't know if she said this because me and my ex-husband are both victims of sexual abuse as children and that was one of our—and it wasn't as if I—it was as if I was angry for my child, but I was also angry for the child in me because my predator did not get in trouble. You know? . . . I felt like she knew what button to push to get a reaction to see how far things would go.

INTERVIEWER: Do you have any understanding of what her reason would have been for targeting this particular person?

DONIELLE: We used to be friends. We were friends. We were, and I felt like maybe it was jealousy or . . . I can't quite comprehend it because . . . Prior to this situation happening, my ex-husband was incarcerated . . . He was just released the August before this happened. . . . Something happened to me while he was incarcerated and me and her had this promise not to tell him. I was raped . . . and I didn't want him to know because even though he was violent towards me . . . nobody could be violent towards me, only he could.

(Donielle went on to describe various situations in the days immediately prior to the murder in which she believes that her codefendant triggered or encouraged her husband to act out aggressively and/or violently, thus priming him for murder. While Donielle was unable to definitively articulate her codefendant's motivation, she now seriously doubts the veracity of the accusation made against her murder victim. Therefore, she surmises that her codefendant used the sexual abuse allegation to set in motion a chain of events that would lead to what was, for her codefendant, a thrill kill of sorts, used to mollify the need for excitement.)

DONIELLE: I can't even use the excuse I was on drugs, 'cause I wasn't. I was completely sober. I was running off of emotions, pure emotions. But to have an understanding of everything, to have the big picture, like I have now. . . . I don't think anything like this woulda happened.

INTERVIEWER: How do you feel about your involvement in this?

DONIELLE: I beat myself up on a daily basis. I wake up every morning knowing the fact that this person died. I go to bed every night knowing that I'm in prison . . . that my actions could not be strong enough to prevent a death of a person. I, for the longest time, I wouldn't even talk to people. I wouldn't do nothing. I would walk with my head down. I-I was ashamed.

On learning that she was in a prison program with her victim's relative:

DONIELLE: I was gonna quit. I was gonna leave. I was not gonna put that on her family. I was not gonna do that to her family . . . but that person said, "No, you need to stay. I need you to stay," and that there was my turning point. It was okay. I can never get this out. This will be a part of my life until the day I die, but it's gonna be depending on how I am gonna honor it. I can either hold my head in shame or I can speak on behalf of other women that are . . . a victim of a domestic violence. I can, you know, because on the other hand of my ex-husband, I feared him, you know, but I can do something in the honor of [the victim] because if it wasn't—as sad as it is to say this—if it wasn't for her death, I probably would have been dead. So I have to live my life in honor of her . . . I can't even tell you when I was told I was gonna be worthless, I was stupid, I was fat, I was ugly, I was gonna be all these things, but now I have a college education, something that I would have never had if I didn't go to prison. I have the ability to speak for myself, whereas before, I couldn't even tell you my favorite food, my favorite nothing because I based it off of my husband. I couldn't do none of that stuff . . . but now I'm a person. I'm an individual with a mind. . . . My whole goal is to work with people that think, or that they've been told that they are ugly or stupid, or they will never amount to nothing because I'm proof right here that you can amount to something, no matter what. But I wouldn't have got that if . . . I never came to prison.

References

Abadinsky, H. (2003). *Organized crime* (7th ed.). Thomson/Wadsworth Learning.

ABC15. (2016). *Jodi Arias planning a dream wedding? Rumors swirl about the infamous killer.* [Video file].

ABC News. (2004). Barbara Walters' exclusive interview with Mary Kay Letourneau. *20/20.* abcnews.go.com/2020/video/Barbara-walters-eclusive-interview-mary-kay-letoureanu

Achenbach, T. M. (1991). *Manual for the child behavior checklist.* Burlington: University of Vermont, Department of Psychiatry.

Adler, F. (1975). *Sisters in crime: The rise of the new female criminal.* McGraw-Hill.

Agnew, R., & Scheuerman, H. (2015). *Strain theories.* http://www.oxfordbibliographies.com/view/document/obo-9780195396607/obo-9780195396607–0005. xml. doi:10.1093/OBO/9780195396607–0005

Ahern, A. (2001). *A biography of Aileen Wuornos.* http://www.courttv.com/onair/shows/mugshots/indepth/wuornos.html

Albrecht, S. (2012, August 10). Female teachers as sexual predators: The double standard remains [blog post]. *Act of Violence.* https://www.psychologytoday.com/blog/the-act-violence/201208/female-teachers-sexual-predators

Al-Sha'arawi, H. (Creator). (2009, July 3). Nassur and the children of Reem Riyashi [TV series episode]. In *Tomorrow's Pioneers.* Palestine: Al-Aqsa Television.

American Association of University Women. (2001). *Hostile hallways.* AAUW Educational Foundation.

American Psychiatric Association. (2000). *Diagnostic and statistical manual of mental disorders* (4th ed.).

American Psychiatric Association. (2013). *Diagnostic and statistical manual of mental disorders* (5th ed.). American Psychiatric Publishing.

Anderson, P. (2015, June 30). Mormon sex in chains case: Beauty queen Joyce McKinney insists manacled missionary consented. *Herald Sun.* http://www.heraldsun.com.au/news/law-order/true-crime-scene/

Anthes, E. (2015, May 9). Lady killers. *New Yorker.* https://www.newyorker.com/tech/elements/female-serial-killers

Archer, D. (2013a). Does Jodi Arias have borderline personality disorder? *Psychology Today.* https://www.psychologytoday.com/blog/reading-between-the-headlines/201303/does-jodi-arias-have-borderline-personality-disorder

Archer, D. (2013b). Is Jodi Arias a battered woman? *Psychology Today.* https://www.psychologytoday.com/blog/reading-between-the-headlines/201304/is-jodi-arias-battered-woman

Arrigo, B. A., & Griffin, A. (2004). Serial murder and the case of Aileen Wuornos: Attachment theory, psychopathy, and predatory aggression. *Behavioral Sciences and the Law, 22*(3), 375–393.

Artingstall, K. (1999). *Practical aspects of Munchausen by proxy and Munchausen syndrome investigation.* CRC Press.

Asher, R. (1951). Munchausen's syndrome. *The Lancet, 257*(6650), 339–341.

Associated Press. (2013, April 5). Parents of Jodi Arias said in police interview that their "daughter had mental problems and would freak out" as ousted juror turns up to watch murder trial. *Daily Mail.* http://www.dailymail.co.uk/news/article-2304338/Jodi-Arias-trial-Her-parents-say-daughter-mental-problems-tried-murder-Arizona.html

Atran, S. (2003, March 7). Genesis of suicide terrorism. *Science, 299*(5612), 1534–1539.

Bachman, R., & Saltzman, L. E. (1995). Violence against women: Estimates form the redesigned survey. *National Crime Victimization Survey.* U.S. Department of Justice.

Bailey, J. E., Kellermann, A. L., Somes, G. W., Banton, J. G., Rivara, F. P., & Rushforth, N. P. (1997). Risk factors for violent death of women in the home. *Archives of Internal Medicine, 157*(7), 777–782.

Bandura, A. (1978). The self-system in reciprocal determinism. *American Psychologist, 33*(4), 344–358.

Baron, S. W. (2004). General strain, street youth and crime. *Criminology, 42*(2), 457–483.

Barrett, D., Headly, K., Stovall, B., & Witte, J. (2006). Teachers' perceptions of the frequency and seriousness of violations of ethical standards. *Journal of Psychology, 140*(5), 421–433.

Bartol, C., & Bartol, A. (2008) *Criminal behavior: A psychosocial approach.* (8th ed.). Pearson Education.

Baum, P. (n.d.). Interview with Leila Khaled. *Aviation Security International.* http://www.avsec.com/editorial/leilakhaled.htm

Beaber, D., Gomez, M., & Barber, L. (n.d.). *Betty Lou Beets: "Texas Black Widow."* http://maamodt.asp.radford.edu/Psyc%20405/serial%20killers/Beets,%20Betty%20Lou%20_spring%202007_.pdf

Beare, M. (2010). *Women and organized crime,* Report no. 013. Research and National Coordination Organized Crime Division, Law Enforcement and Policy Branch. Public Safety Canada.

Becker, J. V., Hall, S. R., & Stinson, J. D. (2001). Female sexual offenders. *Journal of Forensic Psychology in Practice, 1*(3), 31–53.

Beine, K. H. (2003). Homicides of patients in hospitals and nursing homes: A comparative analysis of case series. *International Journal of Law and Psychiatry, 26*(4), 373–386.

Belknap, J. (2015). *The invisible woman: Gender, crime and justice* (4th ed.). Cengage.

Belknap, J. & Holzinger, K. (1998). An overview of delinquent girls. In R. T. Zaplin (Ed.), *Female offenders: Critical perspectives and effective interventions* (pp. 31–64). Aspen Publishers.

Bennett, J. (2002, February 11). Arab press glorifies bomber as heroine. *New York Times,* p. 8. https://www.nytimes.com/2002/02/11/world/arab-press-glorifies-bomber-as-heroine.html

Bindel, J. (2013, April 22). Women sex trafficking other women: The problem is getting worse. *The Guardian.* https://www.theguardian.com/lifeandstyle/2013/apr/22/women-sex-trafficking-women-problem

Biography.com (n.d.). *Jodi Arias biography.* http://www.biography.com/people/jodi-arias-21221959

Biography.com (2017). *Griselda Blanco biography.* https://www.biography.com/people/griselda-blanco-20965407

Bockler, N., Seeger, T., Sitzer, P., & Heitmeyer W. (2012). *School shootings: International research, case studies, and concepts for prevention.* Springer.

Bonn, S. A. (2015, January 12). Why some women kill again and again. *Psychology Today.* https://www.psychologytoday.com/blog/wicked-deeds/201501/why-some-women-kill-again-and-again

Bonn, S. A. (2017, February 26). Wicked deeds. *Psychology Today.* https://www.psychologytoday.com/blog/wicked-deeds/201702/psychopathic-killers-hide-in-plain-sight

Boros, S. J., Ophoven, J. P., Andersen, R., & Brubaker, L. C. (1995). Munchausen syndrome by proxy: A profile for medical child abuse. *Australian Family Physician, 24*(5), 768–773.

Bourget, D., & Bradford, J. M. W. (1990). Homicidal parents. *Canadian Journal of Psychiatry, 35*(3), 233–238.

Bourget, D., Grace, J., & Whitehurst, L. (2006). A review of maternal and paternal filicide. *Journal of the American Academy of Psychiatry and the Law, 35*(1), 74–82.

Bovsun, M. (2014, November 30). Belle Gunness, queen of black widows, murdered dozens and planted victims around farm. *Daily News.* http://www.nydailynews.com/news/crime/queen-black-widows-murdered-dozens-farm-article-1.2028012

Bowering, G., & Crone, P. (Eds.). (2013). Jihad. *Princeton Encyclopedia of Islamic Political Thought.* Princeton University Press.

Bowlby, J. (1973). *Attachment and loss.* Basic Books.

Broidy, L. (2001). A test of general strain theory. *Criminology, 39*(1), 9–36.

Broomfield, N., & Churchill, J. (Directors). (2003). *Aileen: Life and death of a serial killer* [Documentary film]. Lafayette Films.

Burke, L. K., & Follingstad, D. R. (1999). Violence in lesbian and gay relationships: Theory, prevalence, and correlational factors. *Clinical Psychology Review, 19*(5), 487–512.

Bursten, B. (1965). On Munchausen's syndrome. *Archives of General Psychiatry, 13*(3), 261–268.

Cairns, A., & Fenlon, B. (2005, June 1). Ex-pal: Karla psychopath—wants her jailed for life. *Toronto Sun.* http://canadiancrc.com/Newspaper_Articles/Toronto_Sun_Ex-pal_Karla_jailed_for_life_01JUN05.aspx

Calderon, F. (2015, September 8). Drug trafficking and organized crime: Connected but different. *Harvard International Review.* http://hir.harvard.edu/article/?a=11786

Campbell, H. (2008). Female drug smugglers on the U.S.–Mexico border: Gender, crime, and empowerment. *Anthropological Quarterly, 81*(1), 233–267.

Carroll, A. (2009). Brand communications in fashion categories using celebrity endorsement. *Journal of Brand Management, 17*(2), 145–158.

Carroll, J. S., Nelson, D. A., Yorgason, J. B., Harper, J. M., Ashton, R. H., & Jensen, A. C. (2010). Relational aggression in marriage. *Aggressive Behavior, 36*(5), 315–329.

Cauffman, E. (2008). Understanding the female offender. *The Future of Children, 18*(2), 119–142.

CBS News. (2000, February 24). *Texas executes Betty Lou Beets.* http://www.cbsnews.com/news/texas-executes-betty-lou-beets/

Center for Sex Offender Management (CSOM). (2007). *Female sex offenders.* Office of Justice Programs, USDOJ.

Centers for Disease Control and Prevention. (2006). *Rates of homicide, suicide, and fire-arm related death among children—26 industrialized countries.* https://www.cdc.gov/MMWR/preview/mmwrhtml/00046149.htm

Centers for Disease Control and Prevention. (2009). *Chronic disease prevention and health promotion.* http://www.cdc.gov/chronicdisease/resources/publications/aag/chronic.htm

Centers for Disease Control and Prevention. (2011). *The National Intimate Partner and Sexual Violence Survey: 2010 summary report.* National Center for Injury Prevention and Control.

Chesney-Lind, M. (1997). Women and crime: The female offender. *Sign*, *12*(1), 78–96.

Chesney-Lind, M., & Shelden, R. G. (2014). *Girls, delinquency, and juvenile justice.* (4th ed.). Wiley-Blackwell.

Christian Broadcasting Network (CBN). (2003). www.cbn.com.

City News Service. (2016, May 14). Alleged prostitute pleads not guilty in connection with trafficking case involving rape of 15-year-old. *Orange County Register.* https://www.ocregister.com/2016/03/14/alleged-prostitute-pleads-not-guilty-in-connection-with-trafficking-case-involving-rape-of-15-year-old/

Clark County Prosecuting Attorney. (n.d.). *Betty Lou Beets.* http://www.clarkprosecutor.org/html/death/US/beets616.htm

Clarkson, W. (1996/2014). *Deadly seduction.* Macmillan, St. Martin's Press.

CNN Library. (2017, December 12). *ISIS fast facts.* https://www.cnn.com/2014/08/08/world/isis-fast-facts/index.html

Cohn, P. (2015, May 19). Mary Kay Letourneau and Vili Fualauu: A timeline of their forbidden relationship. *Biography.com.* https://www.biography.com/news/mary-kay-letourneau-vili-fualaau-wedding-anniversary-scandal

Coid, J. W. (1993). An affective syndrome in psychopaths with borderline personality disorder? *British Journal of Psychiatry, 162*(5), 641–650.

Contreras, J. (2007, October 9). Mexico's suspected drug queenpin. *Newsweek.* http://www.newsweek.com/mexicos-suspected-drug-queenpin-103459.

Cook, S. (2017, February, 20). Child killer Tinning denied parole for sixth time. *The Daily Gazette* (Schenectady, NY). https://dailygazette.com/article/2017/02/20/tinning-denied-parole-for-6th-time

Cooke, D. J., & Michie, C. (2001). Refining the construct of psychopathy: Toward a hierarchical model. *Psychological Assessment, 13*(2), 171–188.

Copeland, L. (2002, April 27). Female suicide bombers: The new factor in Mideast's deadly equation. *Washington Post,* p. C1. https://www.washingtonpost.com/archive/lifestyle/2002/04/27/female-suicide-bombers-the-new-factor-in-mideasts-deadly-equation/52b4e38e-0798-4746-929c-5664d7f49004/?utm_term=.5b6dd95e83e4

Council on Hemispheric Affairs (COHA). (2011, October 28). *The rise of femicide and women in drug trafficking*. http://www .coha.org/the-rise-of-femicide-and-women-in-drug-trafficking/

Court Services and Offender Supervision Agency (CSOSA) for the District of Columbia. (2014, January). Statistics on women in the justice system. https://www.csosa.gov/newsmedia/factsheets/statistics-on-women-of-fenders-2014.pdf

Cressey, D. R. (1964). *Delinquency, crime and differential association*. Springer.

Crick, N. R. (1995). Relational aggression: The role of intent, attributions, feelings of distress, and provocation type. *Developmental Psychopathology, 7*(2), 313–322.

Crick, N. R., & Grotpeter, J. J. (1996). Children's treatment by peers: Victims of relational and covert aggression. *Development and Psychopathology, 8*(2), 367–380.

Crimmins, S., Langley, S., Brownstein, H. H., & Spunt, B. J. (1997). Convicted women who have killed children: A self-psychology perspective. *Journal of Interpersonal Violence, 12*(1), 49–69.

Cronk, T. M. (2015). *Iraq progresses in ISIL fight, key extremist confirmed dead*. www.defense.gov

D'Emilio, F. (2009, August 29). The godmothers calling the shots in the Naples mafia. *The Independent*. https://www .independent.co.uk/news/world/europe/the-godmothers-calling-the-shots-in-the-naples-mafia-1779395.html

d'Orban, P. T. (1979). Women who kill their children. *British Journal of Psychiatry, 134*(6), 560–571.

Dalton, M., Varela, T., & Laundauro, I. (2015, November 14). Paris attacks were an "act of war" by Islamic State, French president Francois Hollande says. *Wall Street Journal*. https://www.wsj.com/articles/ paris-attacks-were-an-act-of-war-by-islamic-state-french-president-francois-hollande-says-1447498080

Daly, K., & Chesney-Lind, M. (1988). Feminism and criminology. *Justice Quarterly, 5*(4), 497–538.

Daly, M. (2014, May 30). The first modern school shooter feels responsible for the rest. *Daily Beast*. http://www.thedailybeast .com/the-first-modern-school-shooter-feels-responsible-for-the-rest

Daly, M., & Wilson, M. (1988). *Homicide.* Hawthorne.

Datesman, S., & Scarpitti, F. (1980). *Women, crime and justice.* Oxford University Press.

Davies, N. (1993). *Murder on ward four.* Chatto and Windus.

Davis, K., Winsler, A., & Middleton, M. (2006). Students' perception of rewards for academic performance by parents and teachers: Relations with achievement and motivation in college. *Journal Genetic Psychology, 167*(2), 211–220.

Day, L. (2017). Chamari Liyanage, doctor who killed abusive husband, talks about domestic violence trap: "I thought he would change." *ABC News.* http://www.abc.net.au/news/2017–03–06/doctor-chimara-liyanage-speaks-about-killing-abusive-husband/8327370

DeAngelis, T. (2009, November). Understanding terrorism. *Monitor on Psychology, 40*(10), 60.

Death Penalty Information Center. (2017). *Facts about the death penalty.* www.deathpenaltyinfo.org

Del Giudice, M. (2009). Sex, attachment and the development of reproductive strategies. *Behavioral Brain Science, 32*(1), 1–21.

Denisova, T. A. (2001). Trafficking in women and children for purposes of sexual exploitation: The criminological aspect. *Trends in Organized Crime, 6*(3), 30–36.

Denov, M. (2004). *Perspectives on female sex offending: A culture of denial.* Ashgate.

Denove, M. (2001). A culture of denial: Exploring professional perspectives on female sex offending. *Canadian Journal of Criminology, 43*(3), 313–329.

Dickey, C., & Kovach, G. C. (2002, January 14). Married to Jihad. *Newsweek,* p. 48.

Dixon v. U.S., No. 05–7053 (2006).

Dodge, K. A., & Pettit, G. S. (2003). A biopsychological model of the development of chronic conduct problems in adolescence. *Developmental Psychology, 39*(2), 349–371.

Dolan, M., & Vollm, B. (2009). Antisocial personality disorder and psychopathy in women: A literature review on the reliability of assessment instruments. *International Journal of Law and Psychiatry, 32*(1), 2–9.

Dore, L. K. (1995). Downward adjustment and the slippery slope: The use of duress in defense of battered offenders. *Ohio State Law Journal*, *56*(3), 665–773.

Dower, J. (2006). *I don't like Mondays* [TV movie]. London, UK: Channel 4 Television Corporation.

Draznin, H., Candiotti, S., & Welch, C. (2014, February 18). Woman accused in Craigslist slaying tells newspaper: I've killed lots of others. *CNN*. http://www.cnn.com/2014/02/16/justice/craigslist-thrill-killing-confession/index.html

Dryden-Edwards, R., & Shiel, W. C. (2016). *Munchausen syndrome by proxy (MSBP)*. https://www.medicinenet.com/munchausen_syndrome_by_proxy/article.htm

Duerson, M. H. (2012, May 28). Women rise to power in Mexico drug cartels: Report. *New York Daily News*. http://www.nydailynews.com/news/world/women-rise-power-mexico-drug-cartels-report-article-1.1085610

Edgely, M., & Marchetti, E. (2011). Women who kill their abusers: How Queensland's new abusive domestic relationships defence continues to ignore reality. *Flinders Law Journal*, *13*(2), 125–178.

Elliot, M., Browne, K., & Kilcoyne, J. (1995). Child sexual abuse prevention: What offenders tell us. *Child Abuse & Neglect*, *19*(5), 579–594.

Esposito, J. L. (Ed.). (2014). Jihad. *Oxford Dictionary of Islam*. Oxford University Press.

Eysenck, H. J. (1967). *The biological basis of personality*. Charles C. Thomas.

Eysenck, H. J. (1973). *The inequality of man*. EDITS Publishers.

Eysenck, H. J. (1977). *Crime and personality* (2nd ed.). Routledge & Kegan Paul.

Eysenck, H. J. (1996). Personality and crime: Where do we stand? *Psychology, Crime & Law*, *2*(3), 143–152.

Eysenck, H. J., & Gudjonsson, G. H. (1989). *The causes and cures of criminality*. Plenum.

Eysenck, S. B. G., & Eysenck, H. J. (1970). Crime and personality: An empirical study of the three-factor theory. *British Journal of Criminology*, *10*(3), 225–239.

Fabj, V. (1998). Intolerance, forgiveness, and promise in the rhetoric of conversion: Italian women defy the Mafia. *Quarterly Journal of Speech*, *84*(2), 190–208.

Fairchild, G., Goozen, S., Calder, A. J., & Goodyer, I. M. (2013). Research review: Evaluating and reformulating the developmental taxonomic theory of antisocial behavior. *Journal of Child Psychology and Psychiatry*, *54*(9), 924–940.

Faith, K. (1993). *Unruly women*. Press Gang Publishers.

Farrell, A. L., Keppel, R., & Titterington, V. B. (2013). Testing existing classifications of serial murder considering gender: An exploratory analysis of solo female serial murderers. *Journal of Investigative Psychology and Offender Profiling*, *10*(3), 268–252.

Farrington, D. P. (1993). Motivations for conduct disorder and delinquency. *Development and Psychopathology*, *5*(1–2), 225–241.

Farrington, D. P. (2003). Developmental and life-course criminology: Key theoretical and empirical issues–the 2002 Sutherland Address. *Criminology*, *41*(2), 221–255.

Fearson, R. P, Bakermans-Kranenburg, M. J., Ijzendoorn, M. H., Lapsley A. M., & Roisman, G. I. (2010). The significance of insecure attachment and disorganization in the development of children's externalizing behavior: A meta-analytic study. *Child Development*, *81*(2), 435–456.

Federal Bureau of Investigation (FBI). (n.d.-a). *Terrorism*. https://www.fbi.gov/investigate/terrorism

Federal Bureau of Investigation (FBI). (n.d.-b). *Transnational organized crime*. https://www.fbi.gov/investigate/organized-crime

Federal Bureau of Investigation (FBI). (2005). *Serial murder: Multidisciplinary perspectives for investigators*. Behavioral Analysis Unit, National Center for the Analysis of Violent Crime.

Federal Bureau of Investigation (FBI). (2006). *Crime in the United States, 2005*. Uniform Crime Reports. U.S. Department of Justice, Federal Bureau of Investigation.

Fiandaca, G. (2007). *Women and the mafia: Female roles in organized crime structures*. Springer.

Fisher, J. (2016). Marybeth Tinning: America's worst Munchausen syndrome by proxy case. *Jim Fisher True Crime Blog*. http://

jimfishertruecrime.blogspot.com/2013/07/marybeth-tinning-worst-munchausen.html

Foa, E. B., Keane, T. M., & Friedman, M. J. (2000). *Effective treatments for PTSD*. Guilford Press.

Franklin, J. (2016, May 16). Queen of cartels: Most famous female leader of Mexico's underworld speaks out. *The Guardian*. https://www.theguardian.com/society/2016/may/16/mexico-drug-cartels-famous-female-leader-sandra-avila

Frei, A., Vollm, B., Graf, M., & Dittmann, V. (2006). Female serial killing: Review and case report. *Criminal Behaviour and Mental Health, 16*(3), 167–176.

Freud, S. (1933). *New introductory lectures on psychoanalysis*. Hogarth Press and Institute of Psychoanalysis.

Friedman, S. H., Horwitz, S. M., & Resnick, P. J. (2005). A critical analysis of the current state of knowledge and a research agenda. *American Journal of Psychiatry, 162*(9), 1578–1587.

Friedman, S. H., Hrouda, D. R., Holden, C. E., Noffsinger, S. G., & Resnick, P. J. (2005). Child murder committed by severely mentally ill mothers: An examination of mothers found not guilty by reason of insanity. *Journal of Forensic Science, 50*(6), 1466–1471.

Fromuth, M., & Holt, A. (2008). Perception of teacher sexual misconduct by age of student. *Journal of Child Sexual Abuse, 17*(2), 163–179.

Fromuth, M., Holt, A., & Parker, A. (2001). Factors affecting college students' perceptions of sexual relationships between high school students and teachers. *Journal of Child Sexual Abuse, 10*(3), 59–73.

Fulgham v. State of Alabama (1871).

Gabrielli, W. F., & Mednick, S. A. (1983). Genetic correlates of criminal behavior. *American Behavioral Scientist, 27*(1), 59–74.

Gadher, D. (2014, September 7). Sally Jones: My son and I love life with the beheaders. *Sunday Times*. https://www.thetimes.co.uk/article/sally-jones-my-son-and-i-love-life-with-the-beheaders-wtvzx0xwqjb

Gadher, D. (2015, August 15). Jihadist Sally lived on church aid. *Sunday Times*. https://www.thetimes.co.uk/article/jihadist-sally-lived-on-church-aid-wbxmj0rv9qz

Gadher, D. (2017, May 7). "Mrs Terror" the Kent jihadist Sally Jones, shoots up US kill list. *Sunday Times*. https://www.thetimes.co.uk/article/mrs-terror-the-kent-jihadist-shoots-up-us-kill-list-xckcx73b2

Gage, N. (1971). *The mafia is not an equal opportunity employer*. McGraw-Hill.

Galvin, D. M. (1983). The female terrorist: A socio-psychological perspective. *Behavioral Sciences and the Law, 1*(2), 19–32.

Gillespie, C. K. (1989). *Justifiable homicide: battered woman, self-defense, and the law*. Ohio State University Press.

Glaze, L., & Bonczar, T. (2006). *Probation and parole in the United States, 2005*. U.S. Department of Justice, Office of Justice Programs, Bureau of Justice Statistics.

Goffman, E. (1979). *Gender advertisement*. Harvard University Press.

Gottfredson, M. R., & Hirschi, T. (1990). *A general theory of crime*. Stanford University Press.

Grayston, A. D., & DeLuca, R. V. (1999). Female perpetrators of child sexual abuse: A review of the clinical and empirical literature. *Aggression and Violent Behavior, 4*(1), 93–106.

Green, A. H., & Kaplan, M. S. (1994). Psychiatric impairment and childhood victimization experiences in female child molesters. *Journal of the American Academy of Child and Adolescent Psychiatry, 33*(7), 954–961.

Greenberg, J. (2002, April 5). 2 girls, divided by war, joined in carnage. *New York Times*, p. A1.

Gunaratna, R. (2002). *Inside Al Qaeda: Global network of terror*. Columbia University Press.

Hagan, J., Gillis, A. R., & Simpson, J. H. (1985). The class structure of gender and delinquency. *American Journal of Sociology, 90*(6), 1151–1178.

Hagan, J., Simpson, J. H., & Gillis, A. R. (1987). Class in the household: A power-control theory of gender and delinquency. *American Journal of Sociology, 92*(4), 788–816.

Hanlon, R. E., Brook, M., Demery, J. A., & Cunningham, M. D. (2016). Domestic homicide: Neuropsychological profiles of murderers who kill family members and intimate partners. *Journal of Forensic Sciences, 61*(S1), S163–S170.

Hanna, J. (2017, September 15). The London train explosion is the latest of 5 terror incidents in 2017 in the UK. *CNN.* https://www.cnn.com/2017/09/15/world/uk-terror-events-2017/index.html

Hare, R. D. (1985). The Psychopathy Checklist [Unpublished manuscript]. University of British Columbia.

Hare, R. D. (1991). *Manual for the revised Psychopathy Checklist.* Multi-Health Systems.

Hare, R. D. (1994). This charming psychopath: How to spot social predators before they attack. *Psychology Today.* https://www.psychologytoday.com/articles/199401/charming-psychopath

Hare, R. D. (2003). *Manual for the Hare Psychopathy Checklist–Revised.* (2nd ed.). Multi-Health System.

Hare, R. D. (2006). A clinical construct whose time has come. In C. R. Bartol & A. M. Bartol (Eds.), *Current perspectives in forensic psychology and criminal justice* (pp. 107–118). SAGE.

Hare, R. D., Harpur, T. J., Hakstian, A. R., Forth, A. E., Hart, S. D., & Newman, J. P. (1990). The revised Psychopathy Checklist: Reliability and factor structure. *Psychological Assessment: A Journal of Consulting and Clinical Psychology, 2*(3), 338–341.

Hare, R. D., Hart, S. D., & Harpur, T. L. (1991). Psychopathy and the DSM-IV criteria for antisocial personality disorder. *Journal of Abnormal Psychology, 100*(3), 391–398.

Hare, R. D., & Neumann, C. S. (2008). Psychopathy as a clinical and empirical construct. *Annual Review of Clinical Psychology, 4,* 217–246.

Harenski, C. L., Edwards, B. G., Harenski, K. A., & Kiehl, K. A. (2014). Neural correlates of moral and non-moral emotion in female psychopathy. *Frontiers in Human Neuroscience, 8,* 741. doi:10.3389/fnhum.2014.00741

Harpur, T. J., Hare, R. D., & Hakstian, A. R. (1989). Two-factor conceptualization of psychopathy: Construct validity and assessment implications. *Psychological Assessment: A Journal of Consulting and Clinical Psychology, 1*(1), 6–7.

Harrison, M. A., Murphy, E. A., Ho, L. Y., Bowers, T. G., & Flaherty, C. V. (2015). Female serial killers in the United States: Means, motives, and makings. *Journal of Forensic Psychiatry & Psychology, 26*(3), 383–406.

Harrison, P. M., & Beck, A. J. (2005). *Prison and jail inmates at midyear 2004*. U.S. Department of Justice, Office of Justice Programs, Bureau of Justice Statistics.

Hart, S. D., & Dempster, R. J. (1997). Impulsivity and psychopathy. In C. D. Webster & M. S. Jackson (Eds.), *Impulsivity: Theory, assessment and treatment* (pp. 212–232). Guilford.

Hatton, E., & Trautner, M. N. (2011). Equal opportunity objectification? The sexualization of men and women on the cover of Rolling Stone. *Sexuality & Culture, 15*(3), 256–278.

Hay, C. (2003). Family strain, gender, and delinquency. *Sociological Perspectives, 46*(1), 107–135.

Hay, D. (2007). The gradual emergence of sex differences in aggression: Alternative hypotheses. *Psychological Medicine, 37*(11), 1527–1537.

Hazelwood, R. R., & Douglas, J. E. (1980). Lust murder. *FBI Law Enforcement Bulletin, 49*(4), 18–22.

Hendriks, J., & Bijleveld, C. C. J. H. (2006). Female adolescent sex offenders: An exploratory study. *Journal of Sexual Aggression, 12*(1), 31–41.

Hickey, E. (1991). *Serial murderers and their victims*. Thomson/Wadsworth.

Hickey, E. (2006). *Sex crimes and pedophilia*. Pearson.

Hickey, E. (2010). *Serial murderers and their victims* (5th ed.). Thomson/Wadsworth.

Hicks, B. M., Vaidyana-than, U., & Patrick C. J. (2010). Validating female psychopathy subtypes: Differences in personality, antisocial and violent behavior, substance abuse, trauma, and mental health. *Personality Disorders: Theory, Research, and Treatment, 1*(1), 38–57.

Hirschberger, G., Florian, V. Mikulincer, M., Goldenberg, J. L., & Pyszczynski, T. (2010). Gender differences in the willingness to engage in risky behavior: A terror management perspective. *Journal of Death Studies, 26*(2), 117–141.

Hirschi, T. (1969). *Cases of delinquency*. University of California Press.

Hislop, J. (2001). *Female sex offenders: What therapists, law enforcement and child protective services need to know*. Issues Press/Idyll Arbor.

Hoffman-Bustamante, D. (1973). The nature of female criminality. *Issues in Criminology, 8*(2), 117–136.

Hofmann, P. (1977, August). Women active among radicals in Western Europe. *New York Times*, p. 7.

Holmes, R., & DeBurger, J. (1985). Profiles in terror: The serial murderer. *Federal Probation, 53*(4), 53–59.

Holmes, R. M., & Holmes, S. T. (1998). *Serial murder* (2nd ed.). SAGE.

Holmes, S. T., Hickey, E., & Holmes, R. M. (1991). Female serial murderesses: Constructing differentiating typologies. *Journal of Contemporary Criminal Justice, 7*(4), 245–256.

Horgan, J. (2008). From profiles to pathways and roots to routes: Perspectives from psychology on radicalization into terrorism. *Annals of the American Academy of Political and Social Science, 618*(1), 80–94.

Hornberger, F. (2002). *Mistresses of mayhem: The book of women criminals*. Alpha Books.

Hubbard, D. J., & Pratt, T. J. (2002). A meta-analysis of the predictors of delinquency among girls. *Journal of Offender Rehabilitation, 34*(3), 1–13.

Hull, C. L. (1943). *Principles of behavior*. Appleton-Century-Crofts.

Hull, C. L. (1951). *Essentials of behavior*. Yale University Press.

Hume, L. (2016). *The National Union of Women's Suffrage Societies 1897–1914*. Routledge.

Humphries, W. (2017, October 13). Sally Jones profile: How online love affair turned single mother into fanatic. *Sunday Times*. https://www.thetimes.co.uk/article/sally-jones-life-history-who-profile-how-online-love-affair-turned-single-mother-into-a-fanatic-dqz0nkrks

Hutchings, B., & Mednick, S. A. (1975). Registered criminality in the adoptive and biological parents of registered male criminal adoptees. In R. R. Fieve, D. Rosenthal, & H. Brill (Eds.), *Genetic research in psychiatry*. Johns Hopkins University Press.

Iaccino, L. (2016, October 16). Is the targeting of ISIS member Sally Jones legally justified? *The Guardian*. http://www.ibtimes.co.uk/was-sally-joness-12-year-old-son-legitimate-target-us-drone-strike-isis-white-widow-questioned-1642991

Iannelli, J. (2018, January 20). Who was Griselda Blanco, the Miami drug queen profiled in Lifetime's *Cocaine Godmother? Miami New Times*. http://www.miaminewtimes.com/news/the-true-story-behind-cocaine-godmother-griselda-blanco-10010116

Indiana Coalition Against Domestic Violence. (2009). *History of battered women's movement.* www.icadvinc.org

Intelligence and Terrorism Information Center at the Center for Special Studies. (2004, January). *Special Bulletin.*

International Labour Office. (2011). *Global employment trends 2011: The challenge of a jobs recovery.*

In Touch Weekly. (2016, August 10). *Jodi Arias' letter from prison reveals plans to marry another woman's man (exclusive).* www .intouchweekly.com

Investigation Discovery Editors. (n.d.). *Five famous black widows.* https:// www.investigationdiscovery.com

Ishikawa, S. S., & Raine, A. (2004). Prefrontal deficits and antisocial behavior: A causal model. In B. B. Lahey, T. E. Moffitt, & A. Caspi (Eds.), *Causes of conduct disorder and juvenile delinquency* (pp. 277–304). Guilford.

Islam, M. J., Banarjee, S., & Khatun, N. (2014). Theories of female criminality: A criminological analysis. *International Journal of Criminology and Sociological Theory, 7*(1), 1–8.

Islamic Supreme Council of America. (n.d.). *Jihad: A misunderstood concept from Islam—What Jihad is, and is not.* http:// islamicsupremecouncil.org/understanding-islam/legal-rulings/ 5-jihad-a-misunderstood-concept-from-islam.html?start=9

Jacinto, L. (2017, June 20). Italian mafia sees rise of girl power. *ABC News.* http://abcnews.go.com/International/story? id=80900&page=1

Jackson, R. (2014). *What is Islamic philosophy?* Routledge.

Jacques, K., & Taylor, P. J. (2008). Male and female suicide bombers: Different sexes, different reasons? *Studies in Conflict and Terrorism, 31*(4), 304–326.

Jacques, K., & Taylor, P. J. (2013). Myths and realities of female-perpetrated terrorism. *Law and Human Behavior, 37*(1), 35–44.

Jamieson, A. (1999). *The antimafia: Italy's fight against organized crime.* Palgrave Macmillan.

Jeltsen, M. (2016a, May 25). Should domestic violence victims go to prison for killing their abusers? *The Huffington Post.* http:// www.huffingtonpost.com/entry/domestic-violence-prison- legislation_us_573deaa3e4b0aee7b8e94236

Jeltsen, M. (2016b, August 17). Women in jail are the fastest growing segment of America's incarcerated population. *Huffington Post.* http://www.huffingtonpost.com/entry/women-jail_us_57b1e69de4b007c36e4f692f? section=

Johnston, J. E. (2012a). Black widows on the web: Female serial killers who kill for profit. *Psychology Today.* https://www.psychologytoday.com

Johnston, J. E. (2012b). Fatal attraction: The chemistry between serial killer couples [blog post]. *Human Equation.* https://www.psychologytoday.com/blog/the-human-equation/201210/fatal-attraction

Johnston, J. E. (2012c). Female psychopaths: Are there more than we think? *Psychology Today.* https://www.psychologytoday.com/blog/the-human-equation/201205/female-psychopaths

Johnston, J. E. (2012d). A psychological profile of a poisoner: Serial murder by subterfuge [blog post]. *Human Equation.* https://www.psychologytoday.com/us/blog/the-human-equation/201207/psychological-profile-poisoner

Johnston, J. E. (2012e). Serial killer couples: Understanding the wife [blog post]. *Human Equation.* https://www.psychologytoday.com/blog/the-human-equation/201209/serial-killer-couples

Johnston, J. E. (2014). Partners in crime: Peer pressure, dysfunctional relationships, and murder [blog post]. *Human Equation.* https://www.psychologytoday.com/blog/the-human-equation/201401/partners-in-crime

Jones, A. (2009). *Women who kill.* Feminist Press.

Joseph, J., Stangeland, B., Putrino, L., & Effron, L. (2015, August 15). Mary Kay Letourneau Fualaau, Vili Fualaau detail their path from teacher–student sex scandal to raising teenagers. *ABC News.* http://abcnews.go.com/US/mary-kay-letourneau-fualaau-vili-fualaau-detail-path/story?id=30160737

Kaplan, M. S., & Green, A. (1995). Incarcerated female sexual offenders: A comparison of sexual histories with eleven female nonsexual offenders. *Sexual Abuse: A Journal of Research and Treatment, 7*(4), 287–300.

Kaufman, J. M. (2009). Gendered responses to serious strain. *Justice Quarterly, 26*(3), 410–444.

Keeney, B. T., & Heide, K. M. (1994). Gender differences in serial murderers: A preliminary analysis. *Journal of Interpersonal Violence, 9*(3), 383–398.

Kelleher, M. D., & Kelleher, C. L. (1998). *Murder most rare: The female serial killer.* Dell.

Kessler, R. C., Chiu, W. T., Demler, O., & Walters, E. E. (2005). Prevalence, severity, and comorbidity of 12-month DSM-IV disorders in the National Comorbidity Survey Replication. *Archives of General Psychiatry, 62*(6), 617–627.

Khoury-Kassabri, M. (2006). Student victimization by educational staff in Israel. *Child Abuse & Neglect, 30*(6), 691–707.

Kiehl, K. A. (2015). *The psychopath whisperer: The science of those without conscience.* Broadway Books.

Kiehl, K. A., Bates, A. T., Laurens, K. R., Hare, R. D., & Liddle, P. F. (2006). Brain potentials implicate temporal lobe abnormalities in criminal psychopaths. *Journal of Abnormal Psychology, 115*(3), 443–453.

Kienast, J., Lakner, M., Neulet, A. (2014). *The role of female offending in sex trafficking organizations.* Regional Academy on the United Nations.

Kilty, J. M., & Frigon, S. (2016). *The enigma of a violent woman: A critical examination of the case of Karla Homolka.* Routledge.

Klemesrud, J. (1979, January 9). A criminologist's view of women terrorists. *New York Times*, p. A24.

Knepper, P. (2001). *Theories and symptoms in criminology.* Carolina Academic Press.

Knoll, J. (2010). Teacher sexual misconduct: Grooming patterns and female offenders. *Journal of Child Sexual Abuse, 19*(4), 371–386.

Kohlberg, L. (1984). *The psychology of moral development: The nature and validity of moral stages* (18th ed.). Harper & Row.

Kraemer, G. W., Lord, W. D., & Heilbrun, K. (2004). Comparing single and serial homicide offenses. *Behavioral Sciences and the Law, 22*(3), 325–343.

Kratzer, L., & Hodgins, S. (1999). A typology of offenders: A test of Moffitt's theory among males and females from childhood to age 30. *Criminal Behaviour and Mental Health, 9*(1), 57–73.

Kreisman, J. J. (2013). Borderline personality and violence: Is Jodi Arias a "fatal attraction?" *Psychology Today.* https://www.

psychologytoday.com/blog/i-hate-you-dont-leave-me/201305/borderline-peronality-and-violence

Krolokke, C., & Sorensen, A. S. (2005). From suffragettes to grrls. In *Gender communication theory and analyses: From silence to performance* (pp. 1–24). SAGE.

Krueger, A., & Maleckova, J. (2003). Education, poverty and terrorism: Is there a causal connection? *Journal of Economic Perspectives, 17*(4), 119–144.

Laidler, K. J., & Hunt, G. (2001). Accomplishing femininity among the girls in the gang. *British Journal of Criminology, 41*(4), 656–678.

Lake, E. S. (1993). An exploration of the violent victim experiences of female offenders. *Violence and Victims, 8*(1), 41–51.

Langton, L., & Piquero, N. L. (2007). Can general strain theory explain white-collar crime? A preliminary investigation of the relationship between strain and select white-collar offenses. *Journal of Criminal Justice, 35*(1), 1–15.

Larimer, S., & Zauzmer, J. (2016, December 29). She said she killed her husband after years of abuse. Now Francoise Hollande has set her free. *Washington Post.* https://www.washingtonpost.com/news/worldviews/wp/2016/12/29/she-said-she-killed-her-husband-after-years-of-abuse-now-francois-hollande-has-set-her-free/?utm_term=.7054e0abc951

Latham, N. (2000, June 8). Queens now rule where kingpins once reigned: Women are running drug rings after fall of Colombian cartels. *New York Post.* https://nypost.com/2000/06/08/queens-now-rule-where-kingpins-once-reigned-women-are-running-drug-rings-after-fall-of-colombian-cartels/

Laub, J. H., & Sampson, R. J. (1993). Turning points in the life course: Why change matters to the study of crime. *Criminology, 31*(3), 301–325.

Lauritsen, J. L. (1993). Sibling resemblance in juvenile delinquency. *Criminology, 31*(3), 387–410.

Lawson, L. (2003). Isolation, gratification, justification: Offenders' explanations of child molesting. *Issues of Mental Health Nursing, 24*(607), 695–705.

Lenzenweger, M. F., Lane, M. C., Loranger, A. W., & Kessler, R. C. (2007). DSM-IV personality disorders in the National Comorbidity Survey Replication. *Biological Psychiatry, 62*(6), 553–564.

Lesaca, T. G. (1995). At mother's mercy: The nightmare of Munchausen syndrome by proxy. *West Virginia Medical Journal, 91*(7), 318–319.

Lewis, C. F., & Stanley, C. R. (2000). Women accused of sexual offences. *Behavioural Sciences and the Law, 18*(1), 73–81.

Li, S. D. (1999). Social control, delinquency, and youth status achievement. *Sociological Perspectives, 42*(2), 305–324.

Lindner, K. (2004). Images of women in general interest and fashion magazine advertisements from 1955 to 2002. *Sex Roles, 51*(7–8), 409–421.

Loeber, R. (1996). Developmental continuity, change, and pathways in male juvenile problem behavior. In J. D. Hawkins (Ed.), *Delinquency and crime* (pp. 1–27). Cambridge University Press.

Loeber, R., & Stouthamer-Loeber, M. (1986). Family factors as correlates and predictors of juvenile conduct problems and delinquency. In M. H. Tonry & N. Morris (Eds.). *Crime and justice: An annual review of research* (pp. 29–149). University of Chicago Press.

Long, J. G., & Wilsey, D. D. (2006). Understanding battered woman syndrome and its application to the duress defense. *The Prosecutor, 4*(2).

Longrigg, C. (1998). *Mafia women*. Vintage.

Lysiak, M. (2014, April 28). Exclusive: Craigslist Killer Miranda Barbour tells how and why she killed. *Newsweek*. http://www.newsweek.com/2014/05/09/exclusive-craigslist-killer-miranda-barbour-tells-how-and-why-she-killed-248670. html

MacKinnon, I. (2004, January 15). "It was my wish to turn my body into deadly shrapnel against the Zionists": Suicide-bomb mother fakes disability to kill four as Hamas launches fresh front. *The Times*. https://www.thetimes.co.uk/article/it-was-my-wish-to-turn-my-body-into-deadly-shrapnel-against-the-zionists-3q29wgpsqmh

Mahari, A. J. (2009). *Borderline personality and abuse*. http://mental-health-matters.com/borderline-personality-and-abuse/

Mariano, T., Chan, H. C., & Myers, W. C. (2014). Toward a more holistic understanding of filicide: A multidisciplinary analysis of 32 years of U.S. arrest data. *Forensic Science International, 236*, 46–53.

Mathews, R., Matthews, J., & Speltz, K. (1989). *Female sexual offenders: An exploratory study*. Safer Society Press.

Matthews, J. (1998). An 11-year perspective of working with female sexual offenders. In W. L. Marshall, T. Ward, & S. M. Hudson (Eds.), *Sourcebook of treatment programs for sexual offenders* (pp. 259–272). Plenum Press.

Matthews, J. K., Mathews, R., & Speltz, K. (1991). Female sexual offenders: A typology. In M. Q. Patton (Ed.), *Family sexual abuse: Frontline research and evaluation* (pp. 199–219). SAGE.

Mavety, J. (2010). For love of oneself. In Deutsch, P. *Facing evil with Candice DeLong*. Investigation Discovery.

Mayo Clinic Staff. (2017). *Diseases and conditions: Factitious disorder*. http://www.mayoclinic.org/diseases-conditions/factitious-disorder/basics/definition/con-20031319

Mazerolle, P. (2008). The poverty of a gender neutral criminology: Introduction to the special issue on current approaches to understanding female offending. *Australian and New Zealand Journal of Criminology, 41*(1), 1–8.

McCray, R. (2015). *When battered women are punished with prison*. http://www.takepart.com/article/2015/09/24/battered-women-prison

McGreal, C. (2004, January 14). Human-bomb mother kills four Israelis at Gaza checkpoint. *The Guardian*. https://www.theguardian.com/world/2004/jan/15/Israel

McLaughlin, E., & Muncie, J. (2013). *Criminological perspectives: Essential readings*. SAGE.

McLellan, F. (2006). Mental health and justice: The case of Andrea Yates. *The Lancet, 368*(9551), 1951–1954.

Meadow, R. (1993). Non-accidental salt poisoning. *Archives of Disease in Childhood, 68*(4), 448–452.

Mednick, S. A., Gabrielli, W. F., & Hutchings, B. (1984). Genetic influences in criminal convictions: Evidence from an adoption cohort. *Science, 234*, 891–894.

Mednick, S. A., Gabrielli, W. F., & Hutchings, B. (1987). Genetic factors in the etiology of criminal behavior. In S. A. Mednick, T. E. Moffitt, & S. A. Stack (Eds.). *The causes of crime: New biological approaches* (pp. 74–91). Cambridge University Press.

Meloy, R. J. (1992). *The psychopathic mind: Origins, dynamics, and treatment.* Rowman & Littlefield.

Merton, R. K. (1938). Social structure and anomie. *American Sociological Review, 3*(5), 672–682.

Meyer, C., & Oberman, M. (2001). *Mothers who kill their children: Inside the minds of moms from Susan Smith to the "Prom Mom."* New York University Press.

Meyers, S. (2015, August 10). Your field guide to the female psychopath: And why we rarely see her coming. *Psychology Today.* https://www.psychologytoday.com/blog/insight-is-2020/201508/your-field-guide-the-female-psychopath

Middle East Media Research Institute (MEMRI). (2004, January 27). *Conflicting Arab press reactions to the Gaza suicide bombing.* https://www.memri.org/reports/conflicting-arab-press-reactions-gaza-suicide-bombing

Miller, W. (1978). Lower class culture as a generating milieu of gang delinquency. *Journal of Social Issues, 14*(3), 5–19.

Millet, K. (1970). *Sexual policies.* Doubleday.

Mize, K. D., & Shackelford, T. K. (2008). Intimate partner homicide methods in heterosexual, gay, and lesbian relationships. *Violence and Victims, 23*(1), 98–114.

Moffitt, T. E. (1993). Adolescence-limited and life-course-persistent antisocial behavior: A developmental taxonomy. *Psychological Review, 100*(4), 674–701.

Morton, R.J., & Hilts, M.A. (Eds.). (2008). *Serial murder: Multidisciplinary perspectives for investigators.* Federal Bureau of Investigation.

Mulder, R. T., Wells, J. E., Joyce, P. R., & Bushnell, J. A. (1994). Antisocial women. *Journal of Personality Disorders, 8*(4), 279–287.

Mullins, S. (2009). Parallels between crime and terrorism: A social psychological perspective. *Studies in Conflict and Terrorism, 32*(9), 811–830.

Murphy, D. (2014, March 30). 'Craigslist Killer' Miranda Barbour claims two men survived death trap. *Daily News.* http://www.nydailynews.com/news/national/craigslist-killer-miranda-barbour-claims-men-survived-death-trap-article-1.1739570

Muskens, M., Bogaerts, S., van Casteren, M., & Labrijn, S. (2011). Adult female sexual offending: A comparison between co-offenders and solo offenders in a Dutch sample. *Journal of Sexual Aggression, 17*(1), 46–60.

Myers, W. C., Gooch, E., & Meloy, J. R. (2005). The role of psychopathy and sexuality in a female serial killer. *Journal of Forensic Science, 50*(3), 652–657.

Nacos, B. L. (2005). The portrayal of female terrorists in the media; Similar framing patterns in the news coverage of women in politics and in terrorism. *Studies in Conflict and Terrorism, 28*(5), 435–451.

Nathan, P., & Ward, T. (2002). Female sex offenders: Clinical and demographic features. *Journal of Sexual Aggression, 8*(1), 5–21.

National Alliance on Mental Illness (NAMI). (2017). *Borderline personality disorder.* http://www.nami.org/Learn-More/Mental-Health-Conditions/Borderline-Personality-Disorder

National Coalition Against Domestic Violence. (n.d.). www.ncadv.org

National Coalition of Anti-Violence Programs. (1999). *Lesbian, gay, transgender and bisexual domestic violence in 1998.* NCAVP.

National Coalition of Anti-Violence Programs. (2014). *Lesbian, gay, bisexual, transgender, queer, and HIV-affected intimate partner violence in 2013.* http://avp.org/wp-content/uploads/2017/04/ncavp2013ipvreport_webfinal.pdf

National Human Trafficking Resource Center. (2007). *What is human trafficking?* https://traffickingresourcecenter.org/

Neumann, C. S., Hare, R.D., & Newman, J. P. (2007). The super-ordinate nature of the Psychopathy Checklist-revised. *Journal of Personality Disorders, 21*(2), 102–117.

Newton, M. (2006). *Hunting humans: An encyclopedia of modern serial killers* (2nd ed.). Facts on File.

Newton, M. (2008). *Criminal investigations: Serial killers.* Chelsea House.

New York State Office for the Prevention of Domestic Violence. (2016). www.opdv.ny.gov

Ngo, F. T., & Paternoster, R. (2013). Stalking strain, concurrent negative emotions, and legitimate coping strategies: A preliminary test of gendered strain theory. *American Journal of Criminal Justice, 38*(3), 369–391.

Nicaise, V., Bois, J., Fairclough, S., Amorose, A., & Cogerino, G (2007). Girls' and boys' perceptions of physical education teachers' feedback: Effects on performance and psychological responses. *Journal of Sports Science, 25*(8), 915–926.

Nicholson, L., McCann, C., & Seung-Kyung, K. (Eds.). (2010). *Feminism in "waves": Useful metaphor not?* (3rd ed.). Routledge.

Nock, M. K., Kazdin, A. E., Hiripi, E., & Kessler, R. C. (2006). Prevalence, subtypes, and correlates of DSM-IV conduct disorder in the National Comorbidity Survey Replication. *Psychological Medicine, 36*(5), 699–710.

Nock, M. K., & Marzuk, P. M. (1999). Murder-suicide: Phenomenology and clinical implications. In D. G. Jacobs (Ed.), *Harvard Medical School guide to suicide and assessment and intervention* (pp. 188–209). Jossey-Bass.

Nye, F. I. (1958). *Family relationships and delinquent behavior.* Wiley.

O'Brien, S. A. (2015, April 14). *78 cents on the dollar: The facts about the gender wage gap.* CNN Money.

Odgers, C. L., Moffitt, T. E., Broadbent, J. M., Dickson, N., Hancox, R. J., Harrington, H., Poulton, R., Sears, M. R., Thomson, W. M., & Caspi, A. (2008). Female and male antisocial trajectories: From childhood origins to adult outcomes. *Developmental Psychopathology, 20*(2), 673–716.

O'Donnell, C. (2016). *New arrest made in human trafficking ring* [video]. https://www.youtube.com/watch?v=veQRwHHgrwA

Office of Public Affairs. (2016). Houston sex trafficking ring leader gets life in federal prison. *Justice News.* Department of Justice.

Office on Violence Against Women. (2015). *Domestic violence.* U.S. Department of Justice.

Ostrosky-Solis, F., Velez-Garcia, A., Santana-Vargas, D., Perez, M., & Ardila, A. (2008). A middle-aged female serial killer. *Journal of Forensic Sciences, 53*(5), 1223–1230.

Ostrowsky, M. K., & Messner, S. F. (2005). Explaining crime for a young adult population: An application of general strain theory. *Journal of Criminal Justice, 33*(5), 463–476.

Overpeck, M. D., Brenner, R. A., Trumble, A. C., Trigiletti, M. A., & Heinz, W. (1998). Risk factors for infant homicide in the United States. *The New England Journal of Medicine, 339*(17), 1211–1216.

Owens, R. (2013, January 3). Jodi Arias trial: Jurors shown photos of victim's dead body in shower. *ABC News.* http://abcnews .go.com/US/jodi-arias-trial-defense-claims-victim-sexual-deviant/ story? id=18119972

Paoli, L. (2003). *Mafia brotherhoods: Organized crime, Italian style.* Oxford University Press.

Pape, R. A. (2003, September 23). Dying to kill us. *New York Times,* sec. 1A, p. 19.

Pape, R. (2005). *Dying to win: The strategic logic of suicide terrorism.* Random House.

Parry, H. (2016). Notorious murderer Jodi Arias 'finds love behind bars and is even planning a prison wedding' as she serves life for brutal killing of her boyfriend. *Daily Mail.* http://www .dailymail.co.uk/news/article-3575280/Notorious-murderer-Jodi-Aria-finds-love-bars-planning-prison-wedding-serves-life-brutal-killing-boyfriend.html

Pearson, P. (1997). *When she was bad.* Viking.

Pearson, P. (1998). *When she was bad: How and why women get away with murder.* Random House.

Pellegrini-Bettoli, G. (2017). *Women in ISIS: Prison study reveals face of female jihadists.* https://www.worldcrunch.com/world-affairs/ women-in-isis-prison-study-reveals-face-of-female-jihadists

Pennell, H., & Behm-Morawitz, E. (2015). The empowering (super) heroine? The effects of sexualized female characters in superhero films on women. *Sex Roles, 72*(5/6), 211–220.

Perri, F. S., & Lichtenwald, T. G. (2008). Exposing fraud-detection homicide. *Forensic Examiner.* http://www.all-about-psychology.com/support-files/exposing_fraud_detection_homicide .pdf

Perri, F. S., & Lichtenwald, T. G. (2010). The last frontier: Myths and the female psychopathic killer. *Forensic Examiner.* http://www.all-about-fo-rensic-psychology.com/support-files/female-psychopathic-killers.pdf

Peters, R., & Cook, D. (2014). Jihad. *Oxford Encyclopedia of Islam and Politics*. Oxford University Press.

Pietrangelo, A., & Krucik, G. (2016). *Munchausen syndrome by proxy*. http://www.healthline.com/health/munchausen-syndrome-by-proxy#Overview1

Pincus, A. (2002, Fall). The psychodynamics of gender and gender role [Review of the book by R. F. Bornstein & J. M. Masling]. *APA Psychoanalysis Division*, 46–51.

Proops, R., & Seibert, J. (Eds.). (2009). *Fabricated or induced illness by carers: A practical guide for paediatricians*. Royal College of Paedatrics and Child Health.

Pyszczynski, T., Solomon, S., & Greenberg, J. (2003). *In the wake of 9/11: The psychology of terror*. American Psychological Association.

Quay, H. C. (1965). Psychopathic personality: Pathological stimulation-seeking. *American Journal of Psychiatry, 122*(2), 180–183.

Raine, A., Brennan, P., & Mednick, S. A. (1997). Interaction between birth complications and early maternal rejection in predisposing individuals to adult violence: Specificity to serious, early-onset violence. *American Journal of Psychiatry, 154*(9), 1265–1271.

Ramsland, K. (2014). Interview with the psychopath whisperer: A neuropsychologist explains why psychopaths don't fully grasp morality. *Psychology Today*. https://www.psychologytoday.com/blog/shadow-boxing/201404/interview-the-psychopath-whisperer

Rand, D. C., & Feldman, D. M. (2001/2002). An exploratory model for Munchausen by proxy abuse. *International Journal of Psychiatry in Medicine, 31*(2), 113–126.

Renzetti, C. M. (2009, December 14). *Feminist theories*. http://www.oxfordbibliographies.com/view/document/obo-9780195396607/obo-9780195396607-0013.xml

Renzetti, C. M., Goodstein, L., & Miller, S. L. (Eds.). (2006). *Rethinking gender, crime, and justice: Feminist readings*. Roxbury.

Resnick, P. J. (1969). Child murder by parents: A psychiatric review of filicide. *American Journal of Psychiatry, 126*(3), 325–334.

Resnick, P. J. (1970). Murder of the newborn: A psychiatric review of neonaticide. *American Journal of Psychiatry, 126*(10), 1414–20.

Ressler, R., Burgess, A., & Douglas, J. (1988). *Sexual homicide*. Lexington Books.

Rhee, S. H., & Waldman, I. D. (2002). Genetic and environmental influences on antisocial behavior: A meta-analysis of twin and adoption studies. *Psychological Bulletin, 128*(3), 490–529.

Richie, B. (1996). *Compelled to crime: The gender entrapment of battered black women*. Routledge.

Riser, S. (2011). Munchausen's syndrome: Towards a psychodynamic understanding. *Jefferson Journal of Psychiatry, 3*(1). doi:10.29046/JJP.003.1.001

Robins, L. N. (1966). *Deviant children grown up: A sociological and psychiatric study of sociopathic personality*. Williams and Wilkins.

Robins, S. L. (2000). *Protecting our students*. Ministry of the Attorney General.

Rodenburg, M. (1971). Child murder by depressed parents. *Canadian Psychiatric Association Journal, 16*(1), 41.

Rogstad, J. E. & Rogers, R. (2008). Gender differences in contributions of emotions to psychopathy and antisocial personality disorder. *Clinical Psychology Review, 28*(8), 1472–1484.

Rothbaum, R., & Weisz, J. R. (1994). Parental caregiving and child externalizing behavior in nonclinical samples: A meta-analysis. *Psychological Bulletin, 116*(1), 55–74.

Rothman, E., Hathaway, J., Stidsen, A., & de Vries, H. (2007). How employment helps female victims of intimate partner abuse: A qualitative study. *Journal of Occupational Health Psychology, 12*(2), 136–143.

Rouge-Maillart, C., Jousset, N., Gaudin, A., Bouju, B., & Penneau, M. (2005). Women who kill their children. *American Journal of Forensic Medicine and Pathology, 26*(4), 320–326.

Russell, S. (1992). *Damsel of death*. BCA.

Saad, G. (2010). Munchausen by proxy: The dark side of parental investment theory. *Medical Hypotheses, 75*(6), 479–481.

Salekin, R. T., Rogers, R., & Sewell, K. W. (1997). Construct validity of psychopathy in a female offender sample: A multitrait-multimethod evaluation. *Journal of Abnormal Psychology, 106*(4), 576–585.

Salinger, T. (2016, January 21). Brothel madam "Tencha" gets life sentence for international sex trafficking ring at Houston cantina. *Daily News*.

http://www.nydailynews.com/news/crime/brothel-madam-life-sentence-sex-ring-houston-bar-article-1.2504953

Sammons, A. (n.d.). Psychodynamic theories of offending. *Criminological psychology.* http://www.psychlotron.org.uk/newResources/criminological/A2_AQB_crim_psychodynamic-Theories.pdf

Sansone, R. A., & Sansone, L. A. (2012). Borderline personality and externalized aggression. *Innovations in Clinical Neuroscience, 9*(3), 23–26.

Saradjian, J., & Hanks, H. (1996). *Women who sexually abuse children: From research to clinical practice.* Wiley.

Sari, A. (2017, October 18). Was the drone strike on IS recruiter Sally Jones lawful? *The Conversation.* https://theconversation.com/was-the-drone-strike-on-is-recruiter-sally-jones-lawful-85781

Schaeffer, C. M., Petras, H., Ialongo, N., Masyn, K. E., Hubbard, S., Poduska, J., & Kellam, S. (2006). A comparison of girls' and boys' aggressive-disruptive behavior trajectories across elementary school: Prediction to young adult antisocial outcomes. *Journal of Consulting and Clinical Psychology, 74*(3), 500–510.

Schreier, H. A., & Libow, J. A. (1994). Munchausen by proxy syndrome: A modern pediatric challenge. *Journal of Pediatrics, 125*(6 Pt 2), S110–S115.

Schurman-Kauflin, D. (2000). *The new predator: Women who kill.* Algora.

Schweitzer, Y. (2006). Female suicide bombers: Dying for equality? *Tel Aviv University, Jaffee Center for Strategic Studies (JCSS), Memorandum No. 84.* http://www.inss.org.il/publication/female-suicide-bombers-dying-for-equality/

Scott-Snyder, S. (2016). *Introduction for forensic psychology: Essentials for law enforcement.* CRC Press/Taylor and Francis.

Selzer, A. (2016). *Mysterious Chicago: History at its coolest.* Skyhorse.

Sentencing Project. (2015). *Fact sheet: Incarcerated women and girls.* http://www.sentencingproject.org/wp-content/uploads/2016/02/Incarcerated-Women-and-Girls.pdf

Seto, M. C., & Barbaree, H. E. (1999). Psychopathy, treatment behavior, and sex offender recidivism. *Journal of Interpersonal Violence, 14*(12), 1235–1248.

Shakeshaft, C. (2003, Spring). Educator sexual abuse. *Hofstra Horizons,* 10–13.

Shakeshaft, C. (2004). *Educator sexual misconduct: A synthesis of existing literature.* U.S. Department of Education Document No. 2004-09. U.S. Department of Education.

Shelley, L. (2008). Youth, crime and terrorism. In M. D. Ulusoy (Ed.). *Political violence, organized crimes, terrorism and youth* (pp. 133–141). IOS Press.

Shemin, S. (2002, June 18). Wrongheadedness of female suicide bombers. *Chicago Tribune,* p. 23.

Shpancer, N. (2011). *Male and female: The overlapping curves.* https://www.psychologytoday.com/blog/insight-therapy/201108/ male-and-female-the-overlapping-curves

Siebert, R. (1996). *Secrets of life and death, women and the mafia.* Verso.

Siegel, D. (2005). *Russiche bizniz.* Meulenhoff.

Siegel, D. (2014). Women in transnational organized crime. *Trends in Organized Crime, 17*(1–2), 52–65.

Siegel, D., & de Blank, S. (2010). Women who traffic women: The role of women in human trafficking networks—Dutch cases. *Journal of Global Crime, 11*(4), 436–447.

Silverthorn, P., & Frick, P. J. (1999). Developmental pathways to antisocial behavior: The delayed-onset pathway in girls. *Development and Psychopathology, 11*(1), 101–126.

Silverthorn, P., Frick, P. J., & Reynolds, R. (2001). Timing of onset and correlates of severe conduct problems in adjudicated girls and boys. *Journal of Psychopathology and Behavioral Assessment, 23*(3), 171–181.

Simon, R. J. (1975). *Women and crime.* Lexington Books.

Skolnik, J. (1966). *Justice without trial: Law enforcement in democratic society.* Wiley.

Small, K. (2000). Female crime in the United States 1963–1998: An update. *Gender Issues, 18*(3), 75–90.

Spears, L. (2012, September 18). *Garnett's journey: Healing takes courage, and we all have courage, even if we have to dig a little to find it.* garnettsjourney.blogspot.com

Speckhard, A. (2008). The emergence of female suicide terrorists. *Studies in Conflict and Terrorism, 31*(11), 995–1023.

Spiro, H. (1968). Chronic factitious illness, Munchausen's syndrome. *Archives of General Psychiatry, 18*(5), 569–579.

Sprague, J., Javdani, S., Sadeh, N., Newman, J.P., & Verona, E. (2012). Borderline personality disorder as a female phenotypic expression of psychopathy? *Personality Disorders, 3*(2), 127–139.

Sroufe, L. A., Carlson, E. A., Levy, A. K., & Egeland, B. (1999). Implications of attachment theory for developmental psychopathology. *Development and Psychopathy, 11*(1), 1–13.

Starr, S. (2012). Estimating gender disparities in federal criminal cases. *Law & Economics Working Papers, 57.* http://repository.law.umich.edu/law_econ_current/57

Steffensmeier, D., & Allan, E. (1996). Gender and crime: Toward a gendered theory of female offending. *Annual Review of Sociology, 22*(1), 459–487.

Stein, T. (2016, August 11). Narcissist or sociopath? Similarities, differences and signs. *Psychology Today.* https://www.psychologytoday.com/blog/the-integrationist/201608/narcissist-or-sociopath-similarities-differences-and- signs

St. Estephe (2016, September 20). *Beverly Allitt, serial killer nurse—England, 1991.* http://unknownmisandry.blogspot.com/2016/09/beverly-allitt- serial-killer-nurse.html

Stirling, J. (2007). Beyond Munchausen syndrome by proxy: Identification and treatment of child abuse in a medical setting. *Pediatrics, 119*(5), 1026–1030.

Stone, M. H., Steinmeyer, E., Dreher, J., & Krischer, M. (2005). Infanticide in female forensic patients: The view from the evolutionary standpoint. *Journal of Psychiatric Practice, 11*(1), 35–45.

Sutton, L. (2004, December). Preventing educator sexual misconduct. *School Business Affairs,* 9–10.

Swavola, E., Riley, K., & Subramanian, R. (2016). *Overlooked: Women and jails in an era of reform.* Vera Institute of Justice. www.vera.org

Swisher, K., & Wekesser, C. (Eds.). (1994). *Violence against women*. Greenhaven Press.

Syed, F., & Williams, S. (1996). *Case studies of female sexual offenders in the correctional service of Canada*. Correctional Service of Canada.

Tangney, J. P., & Dearing, R. L. (2002). Gender differences in morality. In Bornstein, R. F., & Masling, J. M. (Eds.), *The psychodynamics of gender and gender role*. American Psychological Association.

Taylor, C. (2001). The relationship between social and self-control. *Theoretical Criminology, 5*(3), 369–388.

Taylor, D. M., & Lewis, W. (2004). Terrorism and the quest for identity. In F. M. Moghaddam & A. J. Marsella (Eds.). *Understanding terrorism: Psychosocial roots, consequences, and interventions* (pp. 169–185). American Psychological Association.

Tewksbury, R. (2004). Experiences and attitudes of registered female sex offenders. *Federal Probation, 68*(3), 30–33.

Thornton, D., & Blud, L. (2007). The influence of psychopathic traits on response to treatment. In H. Herve & J. C. Yuille (Eds.), *The psychopath: Theory, research and practice* (pp. 505–539). Lawrence Erlbaum.

Turner, K., Miller, H. A., & Henderson, C. E. (2008). Latent profile analyses of offence and personality characteristics in a sample of incarcerated female sexual offenders. *Criminal Justice and Behaviour, 35*(7), 879–894.

Tyan, E. (2012). Djihad. In P. Bearman, T. Bianquis, C. E. Bosworth, E. van Donzel, & W. P. Heinrichs (Eds.), *Encyclopaedia of Islam* (2nd ed). Brill.

United Nations Office on Drugs and Crime. (2009). *Global report on trafficking in persons*. United Nations Global Initiative to Fight Human Trafficking.

U.S. Commission on Civil Rights. (1982, January). *Under the rule of thumb: Battered women and the administration of justice*. Office of Justice Programs.

Vandiver, D. M. (2006). Female sex offenders: A comparison of solo offenders and co-offenders. *Violence & Victims, 21*(3), 339–354.

Vandiver, D. M., & Kercher, G. (2004). Offender and victim characteristics of registered female sex offenders in Texas: A proposed typology of female sexual offenders. *Sexual Abuse: A Journal of Research and Treatment, 16*(2), 121–137.

Vaughn, M. G., Litschge, C., DeLisi, M., Beaver, K. M., & McMillen, C. J. (2008). Psychopathic personality features and risks for criminal justice system involvement among emancipating foster youth. *Children and Youth Services Review, 30*(10), 1101–1110.

Verona, E., & Vitale, J. (2006). Psychopathy in women: Assessment, manifestations and etiology. In C. J. Patrick (Ed.), *Handbook of psychopathy* (pp. 415–436). Guilford.

Viner, K. (2001, January). Palestinian liberation fighter Leila Khaled. *The Guardian*.

Vronsky, P. (2004). *Serial killers: The method and madness of monsters.* Berkley.

Vronsky, P. (2007). *Female serial killers: How and why women become monsters.* Penguin Group.

Walker, J. S., & Bright, J. A. (2009). False inflated self-esteem and violence: A systematic review and cognitive model. *Journal of Forensic Psychiatry & Psychology, 20*(1), 1–32.

Walker, L. (1979). *The battered woman.* Harper & Row.

Walters, B. (2015, April 10). American scandal: Mary Kay Letoureanu Fualaau, Vili Fualaau open up. *20/20.* ABC News.

Walters, G. D. (2003). Predicting institutional adjustment and recidivism with the Psychopathy Checklist factor scores: A meta-analysis. *Law and Human Behavior, 27,* 541–558.

Ward, B. W., Dahlham, J. M., Galinsky, A. M., & Joestl, S. S. (2014). Sexual orientation and health among U.S. adults: National Health Interview Survey, 2013. *National Health Statistics Reports.* U.S. Department of Health and Human Services, Centers for Disease Control and Prevention, and National Center for Health Statistics.

Warren, J. I., Burnette, M. L., South, S. C., Chauhan, P., Bale, R., Friend, R., & Van Patten, I. (2003). Psychopathy in women: Structural modeling and comorbidity. *International Journal of Law and Psychiatry, 26*(3), 223–242.

Weaver, M. (2017, October 12). Sally Jones: UK punk singer who became leading ISIS recruiter. *The Guardian*. https://www.theguardian.com/world/2017/oct/12/sally-jones-the-uk-punk-singer-who-became-isiss-white-widow

Weizmann-Henelius, G., Viemero, V., & Eronen, M. (2004). Psychopathy in violent female offenders in Finland. *Psychopathology, 37*(5), 213–221.

West, S. G. (2007). An overview of filicide. *Psychiatry, 4*(2), 48–57.

White, J., & Lester, D. (2012). A study of female serial killers. *American Journal of Forensic Psychology, 30*(1), 25–29.

White, N. A., & Piquero, A. R. (2004). A preliminary empirical test of Silverthorn and Frick's delayed-onset pathway in girls using an urban, African American, U.S.-based sample. *Criminal Behaviour and Mental Health, 14*(4), 291–309.

Whitehead, T. (2015, September 15). Widow of British jihadist 'proud' he was killed by US. *The Telegraph.* http://www.telegraph.co.uk/news/worldnews/islamic-state/11866046/Widow-of-British-jihadist-proud-he-was-killed-by-US.html

Widom, C. S. (1998). Child victims: Searching for opportunities to break the cycle of violence. *Applied and Preventive Psychology, 7,* 225–234.

Wilsey, D. D. (2006). Battered woman's syndrome: A defense to child abuse? *American Prosecutors Research Institute.* http://www.ndaa.org/pdf/update_vol_19_number_3_2006. pdf

Wilson, W., & Hilton, T. (1998). Modus operandi of female serial killers. *Psychological Reports, 82*(2), 495–498.

Wimberly, M. H. (2007). Defending victims of domestic violence who kill their batterers: Using the trial expert to change social norms. *ABA Commission on Domestic Violence.* http://www.americanbar.org/content/dam/aba/migrated/domviol/priorwinners/Wimberly2. authcheckdam.pdf

WomenSafe. (2002). *Same sex domestic violence.* http://www.womensafe.net/dv/dvsamesex.html

WomenSafe. (2011). *Overview of historical laws that supported domestic violence.* http://www.womensafe.net/home/index.php/domesticviolence/29-overview-of-historical-laws-that-supported-domestic-violence

Worcester, N. (2001). Women who use force in heterosexual domestic violence: Putting the context (back in) the picture. *Educational Journal, 20*(1), 2–5, 16–17.

World Health Organization. (2012). *Prevalence of alcohol use disorders (%), adult males and females, 2004*. http://gamapserver. who.int/gho/interactive_charts/substance_abuse/bod_alcohol_ prevalence/atlas.html

Wrightson, K. (1971). Infanticide in earlier seventeenth century England. *Local Population Study, 15,* 10–22.

Wynn, R., Hoiseth, M. H., & Petersen, G. (2012). Psychopathy in women: Theoretical and clinical perspectives. *International Journal of Women's Health, 4,* 257–263.

Yardley, E., & Wilson, D. (2015). *Female serial killers in social context: Criminological institutionalism and the case of Mary Ann Cotton.* Policy Press.

Yorker, B. C. (1996). *Hospital epidemics of factitious disorder by proxy: The spectrum of factitious disorders.* American Psychiatric Press.

Yorker, B. C., Kizer, K. W., Lampe, P., Forrest, A. R. W., Lannan, J. M., & Russell, D. A. (2006). Serial murder by healthcare professionals. *Journal of Forensic Science, 51*(6), 1362–1371.

Zaparniuk, J., & Paris, F. (1995, April). *Female psychopaths: Violence and recidivism.* Paper presented at conference on Mental Disorder and Criminal Justice: Changes, Challenges, and Solutions. Vancouver, British Columbia, Canada.

Zedalis, D. (2004). Female suicide bombers. *Strategic Studies Institute.* https://ssi.armywarcollege.edu/pdffiles/PUB408.pdf

Zheng, C. (2017, March 18). Women in ISIS: The rise of female Jihadists. *Harvard Political Review.* http://harvardpolitics.com/world/ women-isis-rise-female-jihadists/

Index

poverty, 208
Power Control Theory (PCT),
26
power syndicate, 210
predatory women, 48
prediction, 40–42
problematic sexual behavior,
53
profit-motivated
black widow, 47
female serial killers
(FSKs), 45
profit or crime killer, 47
prostitution-related offenses,
16
psychodynamic approach, 15
psychological abuse, 259
psychological theories, 15
behavioral approach, 17–18
psychodynamic approach,
15–17
psychopathic personality, 177
psychopathology, 19
psychopathy, 187, 189–193
and narcissists, 197
and serial homicide,
201–205
behavioral indicators, 195
brain dysfunction, 194
causes, 193–194
differentiating, 196–198
gender-based expression,
195
gender differences in
development and
expression, 194–198

measuring, 191–193
physical violence, 195
prevalence of, 190–191
social predators, 190
Psychopathy Checklist–Revised
(PCL-R), 191
psychopathic features as
measured by, 192
psychosis, 62, 129
psychotic episode, 126
Puente, Dorothea, 6

Q
Queen of Cocaine, 223

R
racism, 257
rape, 205
recurrent self-mutilation, 106
respiratory infection, 89
revenge, 48
revenge killer, 47
right to vote, 60
Riyashi, Reem, 229
romantic relationships, 101

S
saccharine presentation, 157
Sach, Amelia, 180–181
Sacra Corona Unita, 214
sadism, 147, 173, 227
same–sex couples, 111, 178
same-sex domestic violence
(SSDV), 114
satanic killing, 168
school shootings, 199

CPSIA information can be obtained
at www.ICGtesting.com
Printed in the USA
BVHW051045080821
613940BV00011B/715

9 781516 515158